John Wesley in the Reformation Tradition

THE ROMNEY PORTRAIT OF WESLEY

John Wesley
in the Reformation Tradition

The Protestant and Puritan Nature of Methodism Rediscovered

Roland Burrows

'Where the Spirit of the Lord is there is Liberty'
(2 Cor. 3:17)

Tentmaker Publications
121 Hartshill Road
Stoke-on-Trent
Staffs.
ST4 7LU
Tel: 01782 746879
www.tentmaker.org.uk (UK)
www.tentmakerpublications.com (US)

ISBN: 978-1-901670-88-2

First printing, 2009
Second printing, 2009
Third printing, 2010

DEDICATION

To my wife and family—
Anne, Elizabeth and Wesley.

APPRECIATION

With appreciation to my wife Anne, for her help and advice in regard to the use of the computer. Also to the staff of Dudley Public Library; especially Mrs Patricia Turner for her help in locating and making available out of print books and articles. To Mrs Barbara Davies, Mrs Janet Grosvenor and Mr Martin Wells M.A.(Oxon) for their many hours spent in proof reading, and to Mr Phil Roberts of Tentmaker Publications for his invaluable help and advice.

PREFACE

Several reasons have motivated me to prepare this work. The first is that I have Methodism in my blood and that in order to understand myself I must understand the powerful influence of Methodism which had such a formative effect upon my own early years and upon the lives of many of my forebears. Secondly I have carried about these thoughts for a long time now, and I feel that it is high time that I set them down in writing. The third reason is a certain sense of irritation long felt, that John Wesley and essential Methodism has been sadly misrepresented by so-called friends and foes alike for something in the region of the last hundred years. Fourthly, I believe that the Church today, and not least the Reformed Churches of which I myself am a member, have a great deal to learn from John Wesley and those who truly followed in his steps.

I was born in 1949 into a Methodist family of several generations, the year being significant in that it was 100 years after the disruptions in Methodism which caused the formation of the United Methodist Free Church, with which my family were associated. In our own family folk-lore it is well remembered that our great-grandmother carried the water to mix the mortar, when in 1859, the congregation of Ellesmere St. United Methodist Free Church, Chapel, Runcorn, Cheshire, decided that they would themselves build their Sunday school premises. This was the chapel in which I grew up. I imbibed its culture, its atmosphere, and it's ethos from my earliest years and later after my conversion and discovery of the great Reformation and Puritan writers and preachers realised that so many of the principles on which I had been brought up coincided with their attitudes and their teachings. To understand this and to see why this was so has been part of the burden of this study. Also being born at that time meant that I caught a glimpse of the way that Methodism since Victorian times had exerted such a strong moral and social influence upon the great manufacturing towns of the North and the Midlands. I also witnessed its rapid and devastating collapse in the 1960's. Some elements of this study I hope will throw light on some of the reasons why that collapse took place. Another thing I have witnessed in my lifetime has been the way that Methodism has changed over these years, almost unrecognisably and I believe, not for the better. I have often heard Wesley and Methodism criticised and have wanted to say, 'But wait, you haven't seen the real thing.' To show something of the 'real thing' has also been the aim of this work.

One of the main areas of misunderstanding in regard to John Wesley that I have tried to correct is that he was not a true Protestant or child of the Reformation. I have sought to show that he was a true Protestant and an evangelical and that he was manifestly not in the Laudian High Church tradition as some would argue.

I note that Samuel Taylor Coleridge said that when he felt a spirit of languor and weariness come over him, he would read the life of Wesley. Wesley's close walk with God, his focus on the great work of preaching the Gospel, his urgency, his reality, his zeal, his courage, his undauntedness in the face of difficulty and his utter confidence in God is a tremendous tonic for weary and discouraged ministers and downcast and languishing Christians of all ages. I have often felt that when that most powerful hymn of Charles Wesley's, 'And can it be', often called the Methodist national anthem, is sung by a large congregation just before the preaching of the Gospel, one's spirit is lifted. Certainly in my own case I can testify that a great desire seems to be created to set before the congregation something of the unsearchable riches of Christ.

Wesley was a man altogether free from cant and hypocrisy. He was not a mere talker, or armchair theologian, but rather was a doer of the Word of God. He believed in living his faith. His religion was not a quiet corner affair; rather it embraced the whole of life, and went out to touch the whole of life. In its day Methodism changed the whole character of the nation. We need this kind of ministry today.

It was once said that, 'The Methodists were the best organised and most effective religious body in England.' It is time to look at it again in its essential nature and learn from what we see.

CONTENTS

9

FOREWORD

Great men of God have often been misunderstood and misquoted. John Wesley was no exception. To this day there is much confusion as to some of the doctrines he believed and taught. The book takes many of these cloudy issues and brings them out into the sunlight. There is a fascinating tracing of the Wesley ancestry which, in itself, is a most interesting study. God greatly favoured him with a powerful Puritan influence that came down from his illustrious forebears. Perhaps the strongest line of argument is our being shown that Wesley was a genuine friend of the reformation tradition and that he was a thoroughgoing Protestant. Many attempts have been made to show him otherwise, but the evidence from his own writings, liberally scattered throughout the book, make such a case impossible to uphold.

The part played by the Moravians in Wesley's conversion is well known. But the way the book opens up the history of these good people, showing their rich heritage and Reformation theology, and then how it came to bear on Wesley's spiritual pilgrimage, is extremely helpful. The Moravians, in the genuine Protestant tradition, suffered greatly, but pressed on not only to influence the future founder of Methodism, but many others who were to walk in the same Christ-like way.

An excellent case is made for Wesley's deviation from the false Calvinism of his day. This hyper-Calvinism was widespread, unbiblical and anti-evangelistic. His views on the necessity of a sovereign work of God in a man before he could be converted are made clear by many helpful quotations from Wesley's own writings. On the other hand a good case is made in showing that his Arminianism was a far cry from much of the Arminianism of his day, and certainly from that of our day.

The many present day Arminians who see John Wesley as their champion, will do well to give this book a fair reading. It will dispel many of the popular beliefs that have long surrounded the good man, and will surely cause many to think again. Those who hold that Wesley's Arminianism led him a thousand miles from the doctrines of the Reformers and the Puritans, will be surprised to learn that his own words to describe his position were that he was 'within a hair's breadth of Calvinism'.

For those Methodists who have lost sight of their roots, here is a clear and precise account of true Methodism which they would do well to read. For those Methodists who have remained true to the faith of their forebears, this will help to strengthen their resolve whilst they wait and work and pray for a recovery of these old gospel truths. All Christians cannot but profit from this account, which deals so clearly with the efforts of one man to strive for the glory of God in preaching the gospel of saving grace, and, at the same time, doing all he could to maintain those truths that set that gospel in its true biblical setting.

Alun McNabb
Great Bridgeford
Staffordshire

CHAPTER ONE

WESLEY'S PURITAN PEDIGREE

Ancestry has its effect on personality, and we cannot easily set aside Wesley's family tree. This preparation for the work of evangelism, to which God had destined him, began long before he came into the world. Like the prophet Jeremiah, he was aware that the divine purpose stretched back to influence his antecedents. 'Before I formed thee in the belly I knew thee; and before thou came forth out of the womb I sanctified thee, and I ordained thee to be a prophet unto the nations' (Jeremiah 1:5).[1]

For more than 50 years Methodism was dominated by the personality of its founder, the Rev. John Wesley A.M., sometime fellow of Lincoln College, Oxford. It has been observed that the substance of the Epistles of Paul consists of the outworking and fruition of the Apostle's Damascus Road experience, so Methodism, we may argue, was the outworking and fruition of John Wesley's Aldersgate Street experience. In the same way as the Apostle Paul was prepared by his previous experience, parentage and background for his great life's work, so also was John Wesley, to such an extent that we cannot understand the man or Methodism without a thorough tracing out of these influences. Wesley himself was very much aware of this, remarking on one occasion to Adam Clarke, the great Bible commentator, *'If I were to write my own life I should begin it before I was born.'* It is also, I believe, true to say, and this is part of the thesis of this study, that these same background influences, which can be traced out in the character of this complex man, also find their fruition and are partly an explanation for the various divisions that occurred within Methodism in the 19th century.

Referring to Wesley's untiring ministry throughout the land, Dr Maldwyn Edwards asks,

What thrust him out upon these ceaseless journeyings?—In a strict sense one could say, it was in his blood.

Wesley's pedigree is a fascinating one from a spiritual viewpoint. He himself had no interest in his genealogy for the usual reasons, since he was singularly free from any pride of class or descent. But after his evangelical conversion and when he had embarked on the mission God had given to him, he realised how providentially he had been prepared for it by his family background. For, as Canon Leatham reminds us, 'If we were to trace the goodly heritage of Wesley's ancestry it would be to discover Puritanism at its intellectual, cultural and religious best.[2]

Wesley's parents, Samuel and Susanna Wesley, were high church Anglicans and here clearly was the source of one side of his nature. Wesley was by nature an aristocrat, a lover of order and a conservative. At the same time however we need to keep in view the fact that Wesley's grandfather and great-grandfather were staunchly committed to the Puritan position. Wesley's paternal grandfather, Bartholomew Westley[3], was a Puritan and Rector of the Parish of Allington near Bridport and it was from this living that he was ejected in 1662. After his ejection he identified with the persecuted Non-conformists and preached in their assemblies. Martin Schmidt gives the following account of him:

> Bartholomew Westley, who was born about 1600, although whether in Bridport, where he spent his youth, we do not know. Bartholomew's father, Sir Henry Westley, belonged to the lesser nobility, and his mother, Elisabeth de Wellesley, was Irish. Bartholomew studied medicine and theology concurrently, probably at Oxford.[4]

Bartholomew Westley's son John was described by Nehemiah Curnock as "the brave, witty, scholarly, simple-minded itinerant evangelist".[5] Schmidt says that "in many respects he was prophetic of his famous grandson".[6]

Though of course they never met, Wesley's grandfather clearly had a most striking influence upon him. A. Skevington-Wood brings this out most clearly:

> A portrait of him which has survived reveals his character. Although he wears clerical dress, he looks more like a soldier than

a minister: not because he appears aggressive, but by reason of a certain unyielding determination in his aspect and bearing. He was a protégé of John Owen, the Puritan divine who was Vice Chancellor of Oxford University. Calamy recorded that Owen had 'great kindness' towards John Westley when he was at New Inn Hall, where he studied oriental languages as well as theology. Amongst his contemporaries were Thomas Goodwin, Steven Charnock, John Howe, Philip Henry and Joseph Alleine—all to become shining lights in the Puritan galaxy.[7]

On leaving the University he was associated for a time with John Janeway's 'Particular Church' at Melcome Regis, whilst preaching in the district and acting as port chaplain. He became an itinerant evangelist and saw many conversions. In 1658 he was approved by Cromwell's Triers as minister at Winterbourne Whitchurch, although he was not episcopally ordained. He married the daughter of John White, one of the two assessors at the Westminster Assembly, and who earlier had been a thorn in the flesh to Archbishop Laud because of his protest against Arminian doctrine and undue ceremonialism.

In 1661 charges were brought against him on the ground of his refusal to use the liturgy of the Prayer Book. As a result he was put into prison and in the following year removed from his cure. Calamy recorded an interview which John Westley had with Gilbert Ironside, Bishop of Bristol. It was copied from Westley's own diary, which unfortunately has been lost. John Wesley came across it in 1765, and felt it to be of such importance that he transcribed it in full in his *Journal*. It so remarkably anticipated the position of the eighteenth century evangelist that we must examine it with some care.

Not unnaturally, the first question put by the bishop concerns the authenticity of Westley's ordination, if indeed he claimed to be ordained. This was neatly turned as Westley simply replied that he had been sent to preach the Gospel.

'By whom were you sent?' pressed the Bishop. 'By a church of Jesus Christ,' was the answer. 'What church is that?' 'The church of Christ at Melcome' (this was Janeway's congregation). The bishop dismissed it as 'fractious and heretical'. But Westley stoutly resisted the imputation. 'In what manner did the church you speak of send you to preach? At this rate everybody might preach' the

Bishop continued. 'Not everyone,' responded Westley. 'Everybody has not preaching gifts and preaching graces. Besides, that is not all I have to offer to your Lordship to justify my preaching.'

The Bishop replied that if Westley preached he must be ordained into the Church of England ministry. His reply again was typical of John Wesley's response 100 years later. (W. and B. are abbreviations for Westley and the Bishop in the quotation.)

B. 'If you preach, it must be according to order: the order of the Church of England upon ordination.' W. 'What does your Lordship mean by ordination?' B. 'Do you not know what I mean?' W. 'If you mean that sending spoken of in Romans 10, I had it.' B. 'I mean that. What mission had you?' W. 'I had a mission from God and man.' B. 'You must have it according to law, and the order of the Church of England...' W. 'I am not satisfied in conscience as touching the ordination you speak of.' B. 'What reason have you that you will not be thus ordained?' W. 'I am not called to office, and therefore cannot be ordained.' B. 'Why have you preached then all this while?' W. 'I was called to the work of the ministry, though not the office. There is, as we may believe, *vocatio ad opus, et ad munus* [a call to the work, and a call to the office].' B. 'Why may you not have the office of the ministry?' W. 'May it please your Lordship, because they are not a people who are fit subjects for me to exercise office work amongst them.' B. 'You mean a gathered church: but we must have no gathered churches in England, and you will see it so; for there must be a unity without divisions among us, and there can be no unity without uniformity.' W. 'It pleased God to seal my labour with success, in the apparent conversion of many souls.' B. 'Yea, that is, it may be, to your way.' W. 'Yea, to the power of godliness, from ignorance and profaneness. If it please your Lordship to lay down any evidence of godliness agreeing with Scripture, and that are not found in those persons intended, I am content to be discharged from the ministry. I will stand or fall on the issue thereof.' B. 'You talk of the power of godliness, such as you fancy.' W. 'Yea, to the reality of religion. Let us appeal to any common-place book for evidence of graces, and they are found in and upon them.' B. 'How many are there of them?' W. 'I number not the people.' B. 'Where are they?' W. 'Wherever I have been called to preach: at Radpole, Melcombe, Turnwood, Whitchurch, and at sea. I shall add another ingredient of my mission: When the church saw the presence of God going along with me, they did, by fasting and prayer, in a day set apart for that end, seek an abundant blessing on my endeavours.' B. 'A particular church?' W. 'Yes, my lord. I am not ashamed to own myself a member of one.' B. 'Why, you may mistake the apostles' intent. They went about to convert heathens; you have no warrant for your particular churches.' W. 'We have a plain, full, and sufficient rule for gospel worship, in the New Testament, recorded in the Acts of the Apostles, and in the Epistles.' This, however, the Bishop flatly denied. He was ready to accept the precepts of the Apostles as binding, but not their practice. Westley accepted both.

The interview closed cordially. It was clear that though Dr Ironside, as an Episcopalian, could hardly have been expected to have agreed with John Westley's Puritan arguments, he nevertheless respected the integrity and also the intellectual acumen of this strange young evangelist. This is how the conversation wound up: B. 'Well, then, you will justify your preaching, will you, without ordination according to law?' W. 'All these things laid together, are satisfactory to me, for my procedure therein.' B. 'They are not enough.' W. 'There has been more written in proof of preaching of gifted men, with such approbation, than has been answered yet by anyone.' B. 'Have you anything more to say to me, Mr Westley?' W. 'Nothing; your lordship sent for me.' B. 'I am glad to hear this from your mouth; you will stand to your principles, you say?' W. 'I intend it, through the grace of God; and to be faithful to the King's Majesty, however you deal with me.' B. 'I will not meddle with you.' W. 'Farewell to you, sir.' B. 'Farewell, good Mr Westley.'[8]

We see that Westley's strongest defence of his ministry lay in the fact that it was owned by God and very fruitful. This was to be the exact line taken by his illustrious grandson in the century following.

It is obvious that all this had a tremendous bearing on the way that John Wesley faced the dilemma of Church order and the necessity of exercising an itinerant ministry that involved the unauthorised intrusion into other men's parishes.

The proud consciousness of having been sent, which yet unreservedly subjects personal activity to the judgment of the

Bible, the determination to conform to primitive Christianity, the stress on visible results as the fruit and conversion as a definite aim... all this comes out in his grandson.[9]

John Westley's wife was the niece of the celebrated church historian Thomas Fuller and only surviving daughter of John White, *The Patriarch of Dorchester*. White was minister in Dorchester for 42 years. He had been a member of the Westminster Assembly of Divines. He was behind the departure from Dorchester of those who helped to found the Puritan state of Massachusetts in New England. Along with others he had started a fishing company there, intending at the same time to gather together the fishermen into a Christian congregation.

Samuel Wesley, John Wesley's father, was born in the fateful year 1662 not long after the ejection of his father, although the birth took place in the vicarage at Winterborne Whitchurch. Southey comments:

> The Wesleys had a large family but only two seem to have grown up—Matthew and Samuel. Samuel the younger was only eight or nine years old at the time of his father's death. The former was bred to the medical profession; the latter received the first part of his education at the Free School of Dorchester, under Mr. Henry Dolling, till he was almost fit for university, and was then, without any solicitation on his mother's part, taken notice of by some Dissenters, and sent by them to London.[10]

Some say this academy was actually at Nettlebed in Oxfordshire. The significant point however lies in the fact that his tutor was the Hyper-Calvinist, Richard Davis. Davis was a fiery Welshman with very decided views. Later he took up the pastorate in Rothwell, Northants, and antagonised many within his own Independent denomination and beyond. John King of the Congregational Church in Wellingborough issued a written condemnation of him accusing him of divisiveness, unsoundness and antinomianism.[11]

It seems that this was one of the influences that made the Wesleys so guarded in their reaction to Hyper-Calvinism. What is clear is that it was this kind of hard and contentious spirit which precipitated Samuel Wesley's departure into Anglicanism. It was at this point that

JOHN WESTLEY, ejected from Winterbourne, Whitchurch, and imprisoned for Nonconformity, 1662. John Wesley's grandfather.

DR. S. ANNESLEY, father of Susanna Wesley, ejected from Cripplegate Vicarage, 1662.

SUSANNA WESLEY, 1669–1742. 'The Mother of Methodism.'

SAMUEL WESLEY, 1662–1735, Rector of Epworth. Father of John and Charles Wesley.

SAMUEL WESLEY, Junr., 1689–1739. Elder Brother of John and Charles Wesley.

WESLEY'S ANCESTORS

SUSANNA WESLEY

the unexpected happened. Samuel Wesley was given the task of refuting an Anglican polemic against the Dissenters, but in the course of working on this came to the conclusion that its attacks were valid. Ever impetuous, the twenty-one year old young man broke with the rich tradition of his family. As wholeheartedly as he had been on the side of the Dissenters, so he now went over to the Anglican Church.

Early one morning in August 1683 he set out for Oxford, in his pocket a carefully saved forty-shillings, which was just sufficient for his entrance and caution money. He first became a sizar at Exeter College, earning money by private tuition and by preparing exercises for wealthy students who were too lazy to do so for themselves. By his indefatigable industry he acquired in this way a second solid education which, unlike the one he received from the Dissenters, was centred mainly upon the classics and the historical and archaeological learning of the Enlightenment. The usual course his life had taken explains the two features which subsequently characterized his outlook. On the one hand he always owed a great deal to the Puritan emphasis upon the importance of repentance, conversion and rebirth; on the other hand he had the historical interest of the Enlightenment. Although he severely pilloried conditions in the Dissenting Academies in an ungrateful satire which he wrote, he consciously retained the interest in the biblical instruction he had received in them. In London he devoted his spare time to pastoral visitation in the prison, obviously under the influence of the social activity which characterized the movement for renewal within the Church of his time, that of the religious societies.

Certainly he was a dedicated Anglican, a 'high church' man, as the term was then used. He desired the end of Dissent, but repudiated the use of forceful means. He knew that he was truly at home in the Established Church of his country, but was conscious of being in the succession of Bishop Lancelot Andrews and not that of William Laud. This is to say that he regarded as most important catholic continuity with the early Church and the whole Church on earth rather than the system of the hierarchy and the canon law.

For these reasons he felt attracted to the free and broad spirit of the Established Church. In 1710 he came out strongly in support of the High Church sermon preached by Dr Henry Sacheverell in 1709, in St Paul's Cathedral, which had demanded unconditional obedience to the King/Queen and made violent attacks on Dissenters. When Sacheverell was arraigned before Parliament Samuel Wesley drew up his defence.[12]

These comments on Samuel Wesley throw a great deal of light on the subsequent character and actions of his illustrious son. John Wesley's view of Calvinism seems to have been strongly influenced by his father's experience under the tutelage of Richard Davis. Here is evidence of the low watermark of Dissent at the close of the 17th century embroiled as it was in Hyper-Calvinistic squabbles over the free offer of the Gospel and the icy winds of Unitarianism that were already beginning to blow through the Churches, long wearied with doctrinal controversy. Here is the root of John Wesley's love of the early Church, his catholic spirit and later lack of patience with the restrictive rules of Anglican Canon Law. 'The world is my parish.' Here, in this glimpse of his paternal ancestry, we see the tension between Puritan Dissenter and Anglican High Churchman that made up his complex character. Here is the conservative and the innovative, the lover of order and the zealous evangelist.

Similar insights are gained as we now turn to Wesley's maternal ancestry. John Wesley's maternal grandfather was amongst the most notable of the Puritan nonconformists in the 17th Century. Curnock described him as their primate.[13] This was Dr. Samuel Annesley, minister of St. Giles, Cripplegate, and ejected from that church in 1662. It was this same church in which Oliver Cromwell married his young bride Elizabeth Bourchier, and by whose son Richard he had been presented with the living. He published a volume of sermons, which Schmidt observes, "occupy an important place in the literature of the Puritan theology of conscience and the conscience-guided life."[14] John Wesley was later to use one of these for his own sermon on *Conscience*.

Dr. Annesley was ejected from his living in 1662 but later founded a meeting house in Little St Helen's, Bishopsgate Street, which became one of the centres of Nonconformity in the Capital. For more than thirty years, Schmidt reminds us, he ruled as the patriarch of Dissent in the Capital. He dared to undertake the first public ordination of Nonconformist ministers after the Great Ejection.

While he never swerved from his principles as a Nonconformist, he never offensively obtruded them as matters of noisy contention. When the ablest of Presbyterians, Independents, and Prelatists gathered up their strength and girded on their armour to champion the church principles of their respective denominations; when Baxter, Bates, and even the 'seraphic Howe', left the higher themes of celestial contemplation to mingle in the wordy strife, not one controversial pamphlet issued from Annesley's pen.

He was a man of marked prominence among his sect; a very prince in the tribe to which he belonged. He possessed an intellect capable of grasping the leading points of the discussions going on around him. His judgment was apparently clear and serene. The weight of his moral character was beyond all price to his party. He could not be indifferent to his principles, for he had sacrificed seven hundred-a-year rather than abjure them. How was it, then, that he stood aloof from the all-absorbing strife? There were other themes more congenial to his thoughts, and in the contemplation and enforcement of which he probably believed he could more glorify God, and better serve the spiritual interests of his community.

He could walk about Zion, telling the towers thereof, marking well her bulwarks, and considering her palaces; but he felt that his calling was not to labour upon these outer-works of the City of God. The temple and the altar were the place of his ministry. Catching the Holy light streaming from the Heavenly Shechinah, keeping the fire of a living love ever burning upon the altar, he bade the worshipping throngs 'draw nigh unto God,' while he offered 'incense and a pure offering.' 'How we may attain to love God with all our hearts:' how 'we may give Christ a satisfactory account why we attend upon the ministry of the Word:' how to 'understand the Covenant of Grace:' and how we may enjoy 'communion with God,'—these were the sacred casuistries which he was most anxious to discuss and settle for himself and his people. His preaching, consisting largely in what was then called 'the solution of cases,' was lively, simple, and attractive.'[15]

His liberality was only bounded by the extent of his means. He consecrated a tenth of all his own substance to the Lord, and was a faithful almoner of many.

The sick, the widows, the orphans were innumerable whom he relieved and settled. The poor looked up to him as a common father. He spent much in the relief of needy ministers, in the education of candidates for holy orders, and in the circulation of Bibles, Catechisms, and profitable books. 'O, how many places had sat in darkness,' exclaims Williams in his funeral sermon; 'how many ministers had been starved, if Dr Annesley had died thirty-four years since! The Gospel he even forced into several ignorant places, and was the chief instrument in the education as well as subsistence of several ministers.'

'Every day he prayed twice in his family,—and domestic worship was a more extensive service in those days, than now,—and three or four times in his closet. Every extraordinary occurrence in his household was celebrated by a religious fast. Every affliction, 'before he would speak of it, or pitch upon any means to redress it,' was spread before God in prayer.

His supplications 'were mighty,' and the returns were remarkable and frequent. Though a sensitive and most affectionate husband, grace enabled him calmly to bear the tidings of his wife's death. 'The Lord gave, and the Lord hath taken way; blessed be the name of the Lord,' was his saintly utterance. Consecrated to God in infancy, he declared he 'never knew the time when he was not converted.' Need we wonder that the ministry of such a man was greatly honoured of God?

Living in the unclouded light of the Divine countenance, and holding unbroken communion with Heaven, his doctrine dropped as the rain, his speech distilled as the dew; 'as the small rain upon the tender herb, and as the showers upon the grass.' He had great success. Many called him father, as the instrument of their conversion; and many called him comforter.'[16]

I have given this description in full as it so perfectly illustrates not only John Wesley's impeccable Puritan pedigree but also how, both in precept and practice, it guided and influenced his own ministry. The old Puritan insistence on *down-right godliness* clearly re-emerged in John Wesley.

When we hear Annesley pleading for 'a humble, serious, constant course of godliness', we are reminded of Wesley's persistent quest for holiness of heart and life, and of his passion for Christianity in earnest.

This likeness is most strikingly seen in a remarkable passage from one of Dr Annesley's sermons, which might well have been written by John Wesley, who did in fact reprint it in his *Christian Library*. As we hear Annesley's words, it might almost be Wesley expounding this master text that for him embraced the whole dimension of Christian living, *Faith working by love*. The passage runs:

> Remember these two words, though you forget all the rest of the sermon, viz., 'Christ and Holiness, Holiness and Christ': interweave these all manner of ways, in your whole conversation... It is serious Christianity that I press, as the only way to better every condition: it is Christianity, downright Christianity, that alone can do it: it is not morality without faith; that is but refined heathenism: it is not faith without morality: that is but downright hypocrisy: it must be a divine faith, wrought by the Holy Ghost, where God and man concur in the operation; such a faith as works by love, both to God and man; a holy faith, full of good works.[17]

Dr Annesley married the daughter of another John White, a Puritan lawyer who sat in the Long Parliament as member for Southwark and distinguished himself as Chairman of the Committee for Religion. In 1643 White published an account of the first hundred clergymen whom Parliament deprived of their livings for immorality or neglect of duty. The book was entitled *The First Century of Scandalous Malignant Priests*, and earned him the nickname of *Century White*.[18]

One of the most famous portraits of John Wesley is that by the academician, John Michael Williams.

> When Dr. Alexander Maclaren stood before it, he exclaimed, 'Now I have seen the man who moved England.' 'No one can look at the Williams' painting,' claimed Dr. Simon, 'without seeing Wesley's Puritan ancestors looking out from the canvas.' The bibliographer, Richard Green, was correct in describing Wesley's face in this portrait as being 'of the Miltonic type'. Indeed, unnamed engravings of Wesley and Milton have sometimes been confused. Dean Hutton rightly referred to Wesley's hereditary determination, and even 'conscientious obstinacy', which made him run rather against than with the current. Some would conclude, he added, that Wesley 'had non-conformity in his blood'.[19]

As, however, we cannot understand John Wesley without taking into account his Puritan ancestry, neither can we ignore the fact that both his parents were devout Anglicans. Indeed it is in this combination of influences that we begin to understand the make-up of the man.

> Anglican and Puritan were fused, as Cadman put it, the order and dignity of the one, the fearless initiative and asceticism of the other.[20]

The reason for the change of heart in Wesley's father has already been alluded to, though we do not have as much information coming down to us as we would have desired. We might have had some most helpful information regarding this in the case of Susanna Wesley, but for the original papers in which she described her reasons being lost in the Epworth fire of 1709. John A. Newton makes the following observations:

> Susanna wrote down a carefully considered account of her reasons for becoming an Anglican, and was about to send it to her son, Samuel, when the rectory fire of 1709 destroyed all her papers. As she explained to Samuel, 'Because I was educated among the Dissenters, and there was somewhat remarkable in my leaving them at so early an age, not being full thirteen, I had drawn up an account of the whole transaction, under which head I had included the main (points) of the Controversy between them and the Established Church, as far as they had come to my knowledge; and then followed the reasons that determined my judgment to the preference of the Church of England.
>
> 'I had fairly transcribed a great part of it, but you writing to me for some directions about receiving the Sacrament, I begun a short discourse on that head, intending to send all together; but before I could finish my design, the flames consumed that with all the rest of my writings.'
>
> This document would have been of supreme interest for an understanding of Susanna Wesley's religious development, and it is tantalizing to have to guess at its contents.[21]

Newton comments:

> Why did she become an Anglican? Was it through disenchantment with Nonconformity, or because her mind was gripped by the

attractiveness of the Anglican synthesis—its carefully ordered worship, its sense of Christian continuity, its studied moderation? It may well have been both. Certainly, she must have been familiar from girlhood with the main issues which divided Dissent from the Church of England, for her father's home and meeting house were the scene of frequent discussions among his Nonconformist colleagues. [See reference to Latin disputations taking place in Dr. Annesley's vestry.—J. Stoughton, *Religion in England*, Vol. 5. p.287.]

When she decided to join the Church in 1683, the Great Ejection of 1662 was more than twenty years away, and must have seemed to this intelligent child rather a matter of old, unhappy, far-off things, and battles of long ago. At any rate, it had all happened before she was born, and she could view it fairly dispassionately. She must have heard the rights and wrongs of conformity debated *ad nauseam*.

She would hear, too, equally bitter debates which centred on the internal divisions of Nonconformity, ranged as it was under its Presbyterian, Baptist, and Independent banners. Did the obsession with 1662 and the interminable wrangles which marked the dissidence of Dissent, incline her to give a long, thoughtful, sympathetic look at the alternative presented by the Established Church?[22]

We might also add that this was the period of the emergence of the Hyper-Calvinistic controversies largely provoked by the re-publication of the works of Tobias Crisp, 1600-1643. These writings had been condemned by the Westminster Assembly because they contained doctrinal antinomianism.[23]

The controversy was further compounded by the publication of Daniel Williams's *Gospel Truth Vindicated*, in which he sought to counter what he saw as Crisp's errors with the doctrines of Neonomianism. Isaac Chauncy then sought to counter both errors, and defend orthodox Calvinism in his *Neonomianism Unmasked or the Ancient Gospel Preached against another called New Law* in 1692. These controversies produced a weariness of controversy amongst the general populace as summed up in the words of the philosopher John Locke:

I have talked with some of their teachers, who confess themselves not to understand the difference in debate between them; and yet the points they stand on are reckoned of so great weight, so

material, so fundamental in religion that they divide communion
and separate upon them.[24]

It may have been this same weariness with controversy that enabled
Richard Baxter to sit under the ministry of the Latitudinarian
William Tillotson. (Tillotson favoured of course toleration of
Nonconformists within the Established Church, a subject dear to
Richard Baxter.) We might note that the principles of John Locke
were not unknown in the home of John Wesley's childhood.

> Susanna Wesley was influenced by the educational methods of
> John Locke. Charles Wesley, in dealing with the upbringing of
> his own first child, John, suggests a link between Susanna's
> determination to 'conquer the will' and Locke's similar ideas.
>   Writing to his wife, Sally, Charles urges her confidently, 'the
> most important of all Locke's rules you will not forget: it is that
> in which the whole secret of education consists—make it your
> invariable rule to cross his will, in some one instance at least, every
> day of your life. The Lord give you wisdom and resolution to do so.'[25]

As we have noted above, Samuel Annesley was a Presbyterian
and held fast to his principles through very difficult times but he
was not a controversialist. In the same way Susanna Wesley, though
a witty and spirited young woman, did not have a likeness for
denominational or unprofitable doctrinal controversy. She was
clearly attracted by what she saw in the Anglican synthesis: ordered
worship, moderation and a sense of ancient continuity. Essentially,
the devoted daughter is very much following her father's principles;
had he not taught her to be utterly loyal to a conscience illuminated
by the Word of God? Further, we may note that Susanna Wesley
was not departing from her father's beliefs as far as we may at
first sight believe. Newton reminds us:

> It is indeed a serious mistake to see 1662 as creating a complete
> rupture between the non-conforming Puritans. Richard Baxter
> could write, some years after the Great Ejection— 'I still profess,
> that in all my experience those called Nonconformists, did
> heartily love, honour, praise and hear a Bishop or Conformist
> that preached and lived seriously, spiritually, and in Christian
> love, such as through God's mercy we have had many...'[26]

Ralph Thoresby describes an impressive funeral of a leading Puritan divine, at which he saw more ministers together than on any previous occasion of his life. They followed the coffin two by two, a conformist and a nonconformist together, as a demonstration of their solidarity in mourning their brother. The Puritans of 1662 did not all make the same choice, but among the moderates of both sides there was no final breach of fellowship, and the same was true of Susanna and her father when they were found on opposite sides of the Anglican-Nonconformist division after 1682. Susanna's continuing fellowship with her father, and the retention of her Puritan heritage, were to be vital factors in influencing her own household when she began to bring up her children in the faith of their fathers. The Annesley tradition was not lost upon the little Wesleys, and in one parsonage at least it was to prove true that if one scratched an Anglican, one would find a Puritan.[27]

Undoubtedly also there was in some areas of Nonconformity during this period, the latter part of the 17th Century, a decline from the warmth and vigour of earlier years. Oliver Heywood wrote in 1682,

What deadness, what decay, the old Puritan spirit is gone.[28]

Susanna Wesley herself wrote:

I have been acquainted with predestinarians. They consist of two types, the first serious and desirous to enter the Kingdom of God and yet always seeking the marks of grace and almost desponding. Others are so sure of their election that they become over-confident, such is their carnal security, that they do not see their sin at all.[29]

These were the days of the antinomian controversies, and the period when Hyper-Calvinism and 'no free offer' teaching began to enter the Dissenting denominations through the teaching of Hussey, Skepp and others. At all events Susanna must have heard the arguments for Calvinism versus Hyper-Calvinism, Presbyterianism and Independency constantly debated, all of which may well have caused her to look long and hard at the alternative presented by the Established Church.

Several other aspects in relation to Susanna Wesley's change from Dissent to Conformity are notable. One is that she was only

13 years old when she decided to do so. Also remarkable is that Dr Annesley did not try to dissuade her. He rather respected her decision even though he had suffered much through the actions of Anglicans. He was ejected in 1662 and also suffered a further attack upon his home twenty years later.

> On Saturday November 18th 1682, Dr. Annesley suffered a disturbance when his house was raided and his goods seized to pay fines incurred by conducting Nonconformist worship. The Declaration of Indulgence (1672) had been revoked the following year, and sporadic persecution of Dissenters began again.
>
> A contemporary chronicle of events recorded laconically that, 'Dr. Annesley's house was broken into by the informers on Saturday and his goods distrained upon for several latent convictions.' Such a raid was a vicious affair, in which the constables, incited by the informers, ransacked a man's house and plundered his goods far beyond the limits of the legal fine. Not that the fines were negligible. One London minister in the same year was fined £840 for holding meetings, and even Dr Annesley's private means cannot have stood such losses for long.[30]

His reaction shows extraordinary charity and understanding. Susanna remained his favourite daughter to his life's end and to her he bequeathed all his manuscripts and sermons. We might note that we see more than a touch of the 'catholic spirit' of John Wesley in his grandfather's life and character.

This hereditary Puritan influence was transmitted to John Wesley through his Anglican parents. Dr. A.W. Harrison does not give detailed evidence for his statement that the Epworth Rectory was *essentially a Puritan home*, but we can readily concur with his claim when we see that her whole devotional life was shaped by the Puritan tradition in which she was reared.

> Among her favourite authors was Richard Baxter, one of the most prolific and powerful of Puritan authors and an acquaintance of her father. Her carefully ordered timetable, her regular times set apart for meditation and self-examination before God, her keeping of a spiritual journal or day-book, her observation of the strict Puritan Sabbath—these were all part of her 'method' of

life, to use the Puritan key-word which was current long before
John Wesley began his work.[31]

We may note in regard to Samuel Wesley that, though designated
a High Churchman, he was not so in the modern sense. It is vitally
important to distinguish between the 17th and 18th century meaning
of the term 'High Church' and its later usage. Skevington-Wood
comments:

> Although the designation Low Church and High Church had
> already appeared, they had not yet acquired the connotation with
> which we are today familiar. We must beware of interpreting
> early latitudinarianism in terms of 19th-century Tractarian
> predilections, or even of developing theories in the later 18th
> century. Samuel Wesley's High Churchmanship was more
> political and ecclesiastical than doctrinal and sacerdotal. He was
> vigorously opposed to Dissent (so strong was his reaction against
> his upbringing) and warmly upheld the crown, although he found
> no difficulty in transferring his allegiance to the house of Orange.
>
> But in his theological convictions he remained 'a true friend to
> the Protestant cause,' as Moore put it, and he did not jettison the
> Reformed principles which he had imbibed in his youth. His abiding
> interest in Biblical Exegesis was derived from his Puritan training.
>
> In a letter to 'John Smith' in 1748, John Wesley referred to his
> father's views. He was acquainted 'with the faith of the Gospel, of
> the primitive Christians, and of our first Reformers; the same which,
> by the grace of God, I preach, which is just as new as Christianity.'
>
> It is significant that John Wesley included his father in the
> line of those in the family before him who preached the genuine
> Gospel. On his deathbed, Samuel confided to John: 'The inward
> witness, son, the inward witness; that is the proof, the strongest
> proof of Christianity.' These words harked back to a typical Puritan
> emphasis, and also looked forward to John Wesley's teaching on
> assurance.[32]

To a greater extent this was true of Susanna Wesley, especially
as regards her spiritual ideals, the habits of reflection, and the
distinctive Methodism of her son John. Cripplegate Church, from
which her father was ejected in 1662, the house in Spital Square
in which she was born when he was minister of the meeting house

in Little St Helen's, and a part of St Leonard's, Shoreditch where he was buried in 1696, remain as the London memorials of the dignified and liberal-minded Nonconformist Divine. He had graduated with honours at Queen's College, Oxford, and that doughty Royalist, Anthony A. Wood, marvelled how this could be done without copious libations of college ale, and adds:

> He seldom drank any beer, only water, nevertheless he was rarely sick, and his sight was so strong he could read the smallest print in his seventy-seventh year. He 'charmed with godliness', and passed away exclaiming, 'I will die praising Thee... I shall be satisfied when I awake with Thy likeness... satisfied! Satisfied!' His daughter Susanna commended to her sons his abstemious wholesome habits of life and his contempt for Royalist roistering and unmanly 'delicacy'.[33]

So we conclude this section seeing that Wesley, both on his paternal and maternal sides, had a most notable Puritan ancestry. Many of these Puritan traits and characteristics were to appear in his life and ministry, notably his rejection of Hyper Calvinism, his lack of patience with restrictive ecclesiastical laws, his insistence on 'down-right godliness', the pursuit of holiness, the need to be personally submissive to the rule of Scripture, a strong sense of being sent by God and of being ultimately answerable to God, not men. Though, as mentioned above, Wesley in his early life seems largely uninterested in his family relationship with the Puritans and Nonconformists, as time goes on, the awareness and interest increases and his admiration of them finds expression in his *Journal*, in his beliefs and practices and in the compiling of *The Christian Library*. I will seek to examine the very significant extent of this influence in the following chapters.

CHAPTER TWO

THE NATURE OF ARMINIANISM IN THE ANGLICAN CHURCH PRIOR TO AND AT THE TIME OF WESLEY

The purpose of this chapter is to see that the Arminianism of Archbishop Laud and his successors was distinctly different from the 'Arminianism' of John Wesley.

In order properly to assess this complex subject, it is perhaps appropriate first of all to give some consideration to the nature of the theological formularies, generally known as *The Thirty Nine Articles of The Church of England*. In 1538 Archbishop Thomas Cranmer, accompanied by his advisors, visited Germany for consultation with his Lutheran counterparts. The fundamentals of the Christian faith were discussed based on the formularies of the Augsburg Confession of 1530.

Upon his return Cranmer drew up his own articles of faith, and after referring them to other bishops for their approval and comment, produced what came to be called *The Forty Two Articles*. These articles represented the first thoroughly Protestant articles of the modern English church. There is clearly a link between the English Articles and those of the German Lutherans. W. I. Haugaard describes these articles as *leaning heavily in the direction of the Melancthonian type of Lutherans.*[1] After various revisions these articles emerged as *The Thirty Nine Articles* in 1571 and have remained as the official formularies of the Established Church to this day.

It was in 1553 that an article on predestination appeared for the first time as official Church of England dogma. Article XVII of *The Forty Two Articles* was entitled, *Of Predestination and Election*, and the first of its four paragraphs defined predestination:

> Predestination to life, is the everlasting purpose of God, whereby (before the foundations of the world were laid) he has constantly

decreed by His own judgment, secret to us, to deliver from curse, and damnation those whom He has chosen out of mankind, and to bring them to everlasting salvation by Christ, as vessels made unto honour.

We may note the 1571 revision of the words, 'those whom He has chosen in Christ out of mankind'. The wording of this Article was careful and definite. It spoke only of 'predestination to life', and nothing was said about a decree of reprobation. Nor was it explicit on the cause of predestination. There was no reference to an arbitrary divine decree that operates irrespective of what is in the predestined, nor did it postulate predestination based on God's foreknowledge of all men, good and bad.

The assertion [made is] that God 'hath constantly decreed by His own judgment secret to us, to deliver ...those whom He has chosen in Christ'.... The fourth paragraph of this Article, as drafted in 1553, reads: 'Furthermore, although the Decrees of predestination are unknown to us...' In the 1571 revision the words 'although the decrees of predestination are unknown to us' were omitted altogether. Article XVII showed evidence of being worded in such a way that neither Theodore Beza nor Jacobus Arminius would have been entirely happy with it. And that probably was the intention.[2]

Or as Patrick Collinson puts it:

The Church of England was putting down its anchors in the outer roads of the broad harbour of Calvinist or (better) Reformed Tradition.[3]

Clearly the 17th Article owes more to Genevan influence than that of Augsberg and is an evidence of the growing strength of Calvinistic conviction within the Church of England. However, we might concede that Philip Schaff's observation is correct when he concludes that the article can only be understood in a moderately Calvinistic sense. The *Thirty Nine Articles* indicate that from the beginning there were shades of opinion within the Established Church on the subject of Predestination and Election. These tensions were later to manifest themselves in the Calvinist-Arminian controversies of the next century.

Harrison in his *Arminianism in England* dates the origin of Arminianism proper in England to the visit of Hugo Grotius to London in 1613.[4] William Knight [5] takes the same view, commenting,

He was openly on a political mission, but secretly, to the knowledge of all men of affairs, carrying on a mission on behalf of the Dutch Arminians.

Grotius discovered in England, men who were already thinking on the same lines and ready to concur with him. We may note Patrick Collinson's point that there was a residuum of Lutheranism in England ready to challenge Predestinarian teaching.[6]

In England as in the Netherlands and elsewhere, the worm in the apple was presently identified as 'Arminianism': belief in the potential universality of divine redemption and in the capacity of man's free will to appropriate God's grace or to spurn it. This doctrine was not so much the 'spawn of a papist', as an English critic put it, as a residuum of Lutheran teaching on these matters. In mid-Elizabethan England, a reviving preference for the optimistic evangelicalism of the Lutheran tradition was revealed in the popularity in some quarters of the writings of the Danish syncretist, Niel Hemmingsen. Aspects of the Calvinistic scheme of strictly predestinate grace came under fire in England some years before the views of Arminius of Leiden became notorious. There was a capacity within the Church of England to set up a more fundamental and broadly-based reaction against Calvinism than was implied in the Arminian onslaught on the predestinarians. For the English liturgy implied in its undertones and ethos as much as in any explicitly dogmatic statement the universal availability of grace through the sacraments and the use of petitionary prayer.

Lancelot Andrews, Bishop of Ely, along with Baro, the Lady Margaret Professor of Divinity at Cambridge, had already openly criticised the *Lambeth Articles* of 1595 and had proposed that they should not be integrated with the *Thirty Nine Articles*, in order to more thoroughly establish the Church of England on Calvinistic lines. Bishop Overall, in 1604 had effectively prevented the acceptance of the *Lambeth Articles* as being on a par with the *Thirty Nine Articles*, and thereby dealt a blow against the perpetuation of High Calvinistic views in the *Book of Common Prayer*. However, it cannot be disputed that the Church of England of the Elizabethan and early Jacobean period was broadly Calvinistic in doctrine.

Patrick Collinson, in *England and International Calvinism 1551-1715,* states:

> The time has come to acknowledge that there was a... broadly-based reception of Calvinism in the Elizabethan and Jacobean Church of England. It has often been said that the Church of England is not a Confessional Church. Nevertheless, the account of salvation, faith, grace, and predestination rendered by the Articles was broadly consistent with the Reformed consensus on these matters.[7]

It is to be noted, that from its first appearance in England, Arminianism was identified as tending towards Popery. In 1595 a certain William Barratt, fellow of Caius College Cambridge, in a Latin sermon preached for the degree of Bachelor of Divinity, attacked the Calvinistic doctrine of assurance and the indefectibility of faith.[8] A great outcry went up and Barratt was forced to recant his popish sermon.

This same identification of Arminianism with Popery gained further credence with the rising prominence of Archbishop Laud. Laud is a complex character and one of the most illuminating accounts of his strengths and weaknesses is to be found in Mandell Creighton's *Historical Essays.*[9] Laud differed from the Puritan teaching on the continuity of the Church, tracing its continuity through Rome in an Episcopal line, rather than through the Waldensians and the spiritual line, as held by the Puritans. Under Laud, the term Arminian took on the meaning of anti-Puritan and, although opposed to the claims of the papacy, yet in effect turned the face of the Church of England back to Roman rites and dogmas. Under Laud, the term Arminian also took on political connotations, so much so that Laud's Arminianism became one of the factors leading to the Civil War.

> Throughout most of the reign of Charles I, Archbishop Laud's influence grew immeasurably, and his open Arminianism, coupled with his sacramentalism, and what might be called his 'high churchmanship', made him and his supporters the target of Puritan wrath.
>
> Laud's love of ceremonialism and sacramentalism, use of candles and crosses in worship, and his precise regulations about the position of a railed-in communion table, smacked of 'Popery' to

ardent Puritans. The widening rift between King and Parliament came to a head in 1629, and in the last session, before an angry Charles I dissolved it, the chief grievance was Arminianism.

Frances Rous led the attack: 'I desire that we may consider the increase of Arminianism... that we may look into the belly and bowels of this Trojan horse, to see if there be not men in it ready to open the gates to Romish tyranny and Spanish monarchy. For an Arminian is the spawn of a Papist... a Papist a Jesuit, a Jesuit gives one hand to the Pope and another to the King of Spain.' [10]

It is not without significance that the only references to Laud in Wesley's works are negative. It is, however, possible to identify a less strident and non-politically motivated form of Arminianism both within Anglicanism and Dissent emerging at this period. One significant Anglican Arminian was John Plaifere, a Suffolk rector, who in 1651 wrote his *Appeal for the True Doctrine of Divine Predestination*. In this he attempted to prove that Arminian teachings were in harmony with the teachings of the Church Fathers prior to Augustine. He sought to identify five opinions on predestination. The first, the supralapsarian High Calvinistic view of Beza and Perkins, which the English delegates to the Synod of Dort had rejected. Secondly, there was the sublapsarian/ infralapsarian view, first advanced by Augustine and defended at Dort. Thirdly, there was the view held by the English scholars John Overall and Richard Thompson, which said that in addition to common grace given to all men, God decreed to 'add a special grace more effectual and abundant to whosoever he pleased.' (Was this the source of Wesley's doctrine of prevenient grace?) A fourth opinion was that advocated by Melanchthon, some other Lutherans, and the Remonstrants, which understood a general and conditional decree to elect to eternal life those whom God foresaw would believe and persevere. The fifth opinion, which according to Plaifere was that held by Arminius himself and as he also maintained was that taught by the 17th Article of the Church of England.

He (God) predestined to life those particular men, to whom out of his own good pleasure, he decreed to give those happy means, which being given unto them, he foreknew they would, thereby, become vessels fit for honour; he rejected those, letting them perish, to whom he decreed to give no other means than such, under which he foreknew that, through their own ingratitude, they would be fit for wrath.[11]

John Wesley was clearly conversant with the writings of Plaifere and published extracts from them in the *Arminian Magazine* of 1778 and 1779. We also find in Plaifere a doctrine of prevenient grace to explain how fallen men were able to respond to the invitation of the Gospel.

> I maintain that the grace which restoreth freedom to the will, to will the good of the gospel, cometh with the gospel, which preventeth man's will, and prepareth it by infusing into it the power to will, the spiritual good things required by the gospel.[12]

In the same year, 1651, the Puritan Arminian, John Goodwin, published his *Apolutosis Apolutroses* or *Redemption Redeemed*. Goodwin, 1594-1665, was fellow of Queen's College, Cambridge, a rector in Norfolk and then in London, finally becoming minister of an Independent congregation also in London. Goodwin is an example of evangelical Arminianism, strongly emphasizing the grace of God in salvation, siding with the Puritans in their ecclesiastical struggle, and totally opposed to Roman Catholicism and Anglo Catholicism. He showed no sympathy with the teaching of Archbishop Laud or those who followed him, castigating them as 'tyrannical prelates'.

> Goodwin claimed he found his creed in Scripture and the Church Fathers. His purpose was not to defend Dutch Remonstrant theology, but to set out the richness of Christ's grace for all men, a richness he believed compromised by Calvinistic predestination. Goodwin followed his Redemption Redeemed two years later with his Exposition of the Ninth chapter of Romans.
>
> In his opening pages, 'To the reader,' he asserted that he had purposely not read Arminius' treatment of Romans 9 until his own work was finished. Neither had he borrowed from what the Remonstrant Scholars, Episcopius and Grotius, had written on this chapter. Goodwin argued that Romans 9 is not concerned with individual election or reprobation, rather Paul is defending God's plan for the redemption of Gentiles, and showing unbelief to be the cause of Israel's rejection.[13]

Goodwin remains largely unknown today; an enigmatic figure as Wesley was, a Puritan yet not really at home amongst Congregationalist or Presbyterian; one who played his part in the fight for English liberty yet was clearly a Republican in politics. Although he was very different from Wesley in these matters, yet Wesley clearly was aware of his writings and published an extract from his exposition in the *Arminian Magazine* of 1780. Dr Thomas Jackson, the eminent Methodist scholar, recognised this connection and produced the only 'modern in-depth' biography of him.

There are however intricacies of theological development at this point that need to be carefully noted. Goodwin was not guilty of this, but both Anglican and Non-conformist Armininians at this period in their teaching on justification, in effect if not intentionally, had changed the meaning of faith from being the means whereby we receive grace from God to being a work that merits grace from God. J I Packer comments:

> Anti-Puritan, anti-Calvinistic Anglicans such as Henry Hammond, Herbert Thorndike, and Jeremy Taylor taught justification on the basis of a personal righteousness which— God accepts, despite its shortcomings, for Jesus' sake. They spell out the nature of this righteousness in terms of repentance and effort for holiness, and their concept was canonized after the Restoration by the unhappily influential George Bull, who interpreted Paul by James and understood both as teaching Justification by works. The trick was done by defining faith moralistically, as 'virtually the whole of evangelical obedience' as 'all obedience required by the Gospel'.
>
> Teaching of this kind led inevitably to a new legalism of which the key thought was that the exerting of steady moral effort now is the way to salvation here-after. By Wesley's time, the true meaning of justification by faith had been forgotten almost everywhere in the Church of England.[14]

It is this shift of understanding of the meaning of faith, amongst 17th and 18th Century Anglican Arminians that enables us to see that Wesley was not an Arminian in the sense in which the term was understood in the early 18th Century. It also enables us to see that Wesley was not in the Laudian line. The significant point to be made is that it was the Arminians of the 18th century who rejected the doctrines of John Wesley as alien to their teaching. This point is made most strongly by George Croft Cell in his *Rediscovery of John Wesley*.

Perhaps the most universal tradition about John Wesley as preacher and pastor, superintendent of the Revival, above all, as its doctrinal guide, has been that he was the arch foe of Calvinism, root and branch. His doctrinal convictions are supposed to have been in their origin and development a radical Arminian reaction against the influences of Geneva in English Christianity.

He is therefore the true historical successor and finisher of the work of Archbishop Laud (1573 – 1645) who found the Anglican Church saturated with the doctrines and practices of Geneva and set himself to redeem the Church of England from the influence of Calvinism. He undertook to break the blood bond between the Reformation and English Christianity and to restore the Catholic tradition. Laud's anti-Calvinism passed through the Wesleys into the structure of Methodism. Wesley's influence in the Modern church has done more than anything else to discredit Calvinism.

This is in bold outline the historical account generally given of the origin and essence of Wesley's theology. It is scarcely necessary to point out that this radically anti-Calvinist view of Wesley holds undisputed sway in the secondary sources and is in most recent interpretations of Wesley almost axiomatic. What exposition of Wesley does not begin, continue, and end with his anti-Calvinism? He cannot be pictured in history as standing on the shoulders of Luther and Calvin. It is now quite the fashion to represent him as originally, i.e. from 1738 onward, the antithesis of Calvinism, as thinly affiliated with Luther, but deeply grounded, and steadfast in the catholic tradition of the Anglican Church.

This total reversal of the facts reaches then a limit in the recent attempt to represent Wesley as a reaction against genuine Protestantism and at heart a High Churchman not far from the Catholic fold. He did indeed say of himself that he had been, prior to 1738 without knowing it, a Catholic humanist; but he has also said that he found himself out and broke radically alike with the Catholic conception of the Church and with the humanist conception of faith.

Cell goes on to argue that:

> The Wesleyan Revival in its origin and earliest stages was:
>
> 1. A powerful reaction against Arminian Anglicanism in the doctrine of Christian experience and against High Church principles in the theory of Church institutions and the exercise of the pastoral office.
>
> 2. A return to the faith of the first Reformers. Moreover the Revival retained in spite of the Calvinistic controversy, in which it was involved, its original character so long as Wesley's hand was at the helm. There is in the birth of the Evangelical reaction, as summed up in Wesley, no traceable consciousness of any antagonism, much less of polemic, against the faith of Luther and Calvin. That element in the theology of Luther and Calvin which Wesley later withstood was in the Spring of 1738 entirely crowded out of his consciousness and banished from his attention by his fiery interest in that part of the Reformation faith which he then first found out and accepted.
>
> 3. There is no sign in Wesley's thinking at the point where he crossed his Religious Rubicon of the least interest or concern to correct or oppose Calvinism, either all of it or any part of it. The issues which soon after arose from that source were in the spring of 1738 simply outside his field of vision....
>
> 4. Wesley's conversion experience is then in no sense to be construed as a reaction against Calvinism. It was in its origin and principle character a reaction against the current religion of the Church of England. The facts are that Wesley, as we shall see in due course, not only rejected the Arminian divines of the Anglican Church as untrustworthy expounders of Christianity, but he arraigned them as 'betrayers of the church, sappers of the foundations of the Gospel of Christ'. He saw in their doctrines a common apostasy from the 'fundamental of all the Reformed Churches.'
>
> 5. He brought under this condemnation not only most of the living teachers of the Anglican Church but also 'the general stream of writers and preachers'. Indeed very few can we find who simply and earnestly teach and preach the faith of the first Reformers. He cited in his sermon on 'True Christianity Defended' (significant title), written June 1741, to be preached

at Oxford, the greatest Anglican divines of former times, Tillotson, Bull, as examples of this Arminian apostasy from the Reformed faith. He seems to have had this situation in mind when a little later he remonstrated against 'running away from Calvinism as far as ever we can,' when as a matter of fact 'the truth of the Gospel lies within a hair's breadth of Calvinism'.

Wesley was clearly at odds with the Arminian establishment of his day. Cell continues:

One of the leading Bishops who always spoke of Wesley with respect, never with rancour, said: 'You have gone back into the old and exploded Calvinistic expositions of the Christian faith.' He told Wesley he was rejecting the counsel and guidance of the Modern or present Anglican Church which was Arminian in spirit and understood the faith in the Arminian sense and was going back to the Church of England when it was Calvinistic in spirit and understood the faith in the Calvinistic sense. Here we come upon a fact of great, and perhaps decisive, importance.

The mass of writing and public utterance against Wesley from Anglican sources, ranging from a mild to a militant opposition, all shares the opinion that Wesley's message was a radical reaction against the Arminian sense and spirit of Anglican teaching and preaching. How can these things be? It is also quite remarkable that Wesley never refers to the Anglican Arminians in support of his own position but to Arminius himself who, as Wesley observed, very largely agreed with Calvin, taught two of his three points in terms as strong and clearly expressed as John Calvin himself, so that in respect to original sin and justification by faith both parties fully agree, that is, all evangelicals do, and 'There is not a hair's breadth difference between Mr. Wesley and Mr. Whitefield'. He also believed that the evangelicals were divided only on matters of opinion, whereas the Arminians were divided on the essentials of Christian experience. Wesley clearly appears to concur with his Anglican critics as to closer doctrinal affiliation with the Calvinists than with the Anglican Arminians. This is passing strange![15]

At this point it is necessary to identify more clearly the rationalistic strand of Arminianism that emerged during the 17th Century.

Rational Arminianism

James Packer identifies this as in effect, if not intentionally, a *revival of the semi-Pelagian reaction to Augustinianism which developed in the 5th Century by John Cassian and Faustus of Ries.*[16] The movement developed by way of a reaction to the high doctrine of predestination taught by Beza, Calvin's successor and head of the Geneva Academy. It first appeared in Holland, though similar reactions were germinating at the same time in England and Germany and *'was part of a Europe-wide encroachment on the theology of the Reformation by the rationalism of the Renaissance'*.

Jacob Arminius [17] who was the father of the movement and whose name was subsequently given to it, was a brilliant young clergyman of Amsterdam, who had studied for a year with Beza and became professor at Leyden in 1603. Arminius was asked by Beza to respond to an attack by a humanist layman, Dirk Koornhert of Delft, on the supralapsarian view of predestination, and also to a tract by two ministers who, persuaded by Koornhert's arguments, had moved to the position that came to be known as sublapsarianism. (Supralapsarianism, as held by Beza and those who followed him at the end of the 16th Century, was the view that God before the world was made had made election of some to salvation and decreed to pass by others, not on the basis of seeing man as fallen, but prior to his decree to permit the Fall. Sub or Infralapsarianism, the view that was expressed by the Synod of Dort and the majority of English Calvinists, believed that the elect were chosen out of the race of mankind seen as already fallen and ruined.)

Arminius gave a great deal of time and preparation to his reply, but his studies led him to reject the supralapsarian position and then to the position of conditional predestination and the condition of foreseen faith. Arminius died of tuberculosis in 1609. A year later a group of his followers issued a remonstrance, stating five theological positions for which they claimed toleration and protection. They were:

1. That predestination is not the cause of faith which saves or the unbelief which damns.
2. That Christ died to redeem all men, not just the elect.

3. Man's utter need of the grace of God (a disclaimer of Pelagianism).
4. That grace is resistible.[18]
5. The uncertainty of perseverance (On this point the later Arminians went further and taught the possibility of a final fall of believers from grace).

It was in reaction to these five points of Arminianism that the famous *Five Points of Calvinism* were formulated by the Synod of Dort in 1617-1619. After the Synod, the Arminians were forced into exile, but with the death of the Dutch Prince Maurice in 1625, returned and were allowed by Prince Henry to establish their own churches and set up a Theological Seminary in Amsterdam, where Simon Episcopius, Stephanus Curcellaeus and Philip von Limborch, taught in succession. What was established was, in Philip Schaff's words,[19] *an elastic, progressive, changing liberalism.* Packer notes that:

> The Continental Arminian scholars drifted into undogmatic moralism and pietism, with Arian, Socinian, Deist and Immanentist flavouring from time to time.The Remonstrant Brotherhood (Remonstantse Broedschap) still exists. Lambertus Jackbus van Holk, one of its leading theologians, described it in 1960 as 'the only basically non-conformist denomination in the Netherlands'.[20]

The divergence of Remonstrant Arminianism, from that of Reformation Protestantism is seen by comparing the following points, helpfully set out by Packer as follows:

1. Every man faces the judgment seat of God and must answer to God there for himself; nothing can shield him from this.
2. Every man is a sinner by nature and practice, a nonconformist so far as God's Law is concerned, and therefore all he can expect is God's wrath and rejection.
3. Justification is God's judicial act of pardoning a guilty sinner, accepting him as righteous, and receiving him as a son and heir.
4. The sole source of justification is God's grace, not man's effort or initiative.
5. The sole ground of justification is Christ's vicarious righteousness and blood shedding, not our own merit; nor do

supposed works of superogation, purchase of indulgences, or multiplication of masses make any contribution to it; nor do the purgatorial pains of medieval imagination have any significance, or indeed reality to it. Justification is not the prize to work for, but a gift to be received through Christ.

6. The means of justification, here and now, is faith in Christ, understood as a pacifying and energising trust that Christ's sacrificial death atoned for all one's sins.

7. The fruit of faith, the evidence of its reality and therefore the proof that a man is a Christian as he claims to be, is a manifested repentance and life of good works.

Calvin sums up the point thus:

It is entirely by the intervention of Christ's righteousness that we obtain justification before God. This is equivalent to saying that man is not righteous in himself, but that the righteousness of Christ is communicated to him by imputation, while he is strictly deserving of punishment. Thus vanishes the absurd dogma, that man is justified by faith inasmuch as faith brings him under the influence of the Spirit of God, by whom he is rendered righteous... You see that our righteousness is not in us but in Christ, that we possess it only because we are partakers in Christ.[21]

The Westminster Confession Article II states the same as follows:

Those whom God effectually calleth he also freely justifieth; not by infusing righteousness into them, but by pardoning their sins, and by accounting and accepting their persons as righteous; not for anything wrought in them, or done by them, but for Christ's sake alone, not by imputing faith itself, the act of believing, or any other evangelical obedience, to them as their righteousness; but by imputing the obedience and satisfaction of Christ unto them, they receiving and resting on Him and His righteousness by faith; which faith they have not of themselves—it is the gift of God.[22]

The Remonstrants have, together with the Roman Catholics, found the ground of justification in the believer himself. Faith for the believer is the new law and this faith is counted for righteousness. Why, asks Packer, did the Arminians take the line they did concerning the ground of justification? The answer is that they were driven to it by the inescapable logic of their basic denial that the individual's salvation is wholly God's work. The consequences of this denial are—

1. The denial that the individual's act of faith is wholly God's gift.

2. The denial that there is a correlation in God's plan between the obtaining of redemption by Christ's obedience to death and the saving application of redemption by the Holy Ghost, direct, that is in the sense that the former secures and guarantees the latter. The Arminian view was that atonement made salvation possible for all but not necessarily actual for any.

3. The third denial was that the Covenant of Grace is a relationship which God imposes unilaterally and unconditionally, by effectively calling, saying to his elect, 'I will, and you shall be.' The Arminian idea was that the Covenant of Grace is a new law, offering present pardon on condition of present faith and final salvation on condition of sustained faith.

4. The fourth denial was that faith is essentially fiducial (a matter of trustful knowledge, assured and animating of what, another has done). The Arminian alternative was that faith is essentially volitional (a matter of committing oneself to do something, i.e. live by the new law which Christ procured). Pietists from the 17th to 20th centuries have so regularly fastened onto the Arminian conception as to make it appear an evangelical axiom, but the fact remains that it marks a shift from the original Reformed teaching, and one that can quickly breed both anti-intellectualism and the idea of faith as a meritorious work.

5. The fifth denial was that the ground of justification is Christ's righteousness imputed. The Arminian notion was that faith itself is the ground of justification, being itself righteousness (obedience to the new law) and accepted by God as such. Arminius' formula was that Christ's righteousness is imputed to us not for righteousness, but as a basis on which faith may be imputed to us for righteousness. Appeal was made to the

phraseology of faith being reckoned for righteousness in Romans 4:3 and 5:9 echoing Gen 15:6 but Paul's insistence that the Christian's righteousness is God's gift (Rom 5:15-17), and his emphatic declarations that sinners, though ungodly (Rom 4:5, 5:6-8), are justified by faith through Christ's blood irrespective of their works, made this exegesis really impossible.
Packer sums up the teaching of the rational Arminians thus:

The Arminian teaching on justification is in effect, if not in intention, legalistic, turning faith from a means of receiving from God into work that merits before God. As such, it corresponds in principle with the doctrine of the Council of Trent; at this point its critics were right. But it, or perhaps we should say, the way of thinking which it represented, had a wide influence, not least in England. Anti-Puritan, and anti-Calvinist Anglicans such as Henry Hammond, Herbert Thorndike, and Jeremy Taylor taught justification on the basis of a personal righteousness which God accepts, despite its shortcomings, for Jesus' sake.
They spell out the nature of this righteousness in terms of repentance and effort for holiness, and their concept was canonized after the restoration by the (unhappily) influential Bishop George Bull, who interpreted Paul by James and understood both as teaching justification by works. (The trick was done by defining faith moralistically, as 'virtually the whole of evangelical obedience,' and, 'all the obedience required by the Gospel.' (Bull Harmonia Apostolica p I:58,57). Teaching of this kind led inevitably to a new legalism of which the key thought was that the exerting of steady moral effort now is the way to salvation hereafter. By Wesley's day the true meaning of justification by faith had been forgotten almost everywhere in the Church of England.[23]

Wesley's or Evangelical 'Arminianism'

Wesley was brought up in that form of Anglicanism which had in the main adopted the views described above. He also inherited as we have seen an aversion to High-Calvinism from his parents. Both Samuel and Susanna had moved out from Calvinistic Nonconformity into Arminian Anglicanism, and were sharply hostile to the teaching they had left behind. (The psychology of such attitudes is well known.)

A letter from Susanna to John in 1725, when he was 22, states the view of Article XVII prevailing amongst the majority of Anglicans at that time.

> The doctrine of predestination as maintained by rigid Calvinists, is very shocking—because it charges the most holy God with being the author of sin—I do firmly believe that God from all eternity hath elected some to everlasting life, but then I humbly conceive that this election is founded in His foreknowledge, according to Romans 8:29, 30. Whom in his eternal prescience God saw would make a right use of their powers, and accept of offered mercy, He did predestinate—nor can it with more reason be supposed that the prescience of God is the cause that many finally perish than our knowing the sun will rise tomorrow is the cause of its rising.[24]

We have also observed that Wesley's parents could not be described as Rational Arminians. Whatever of rational Arminianism Wesley may have imbibed during his time at Oxford it was undoubtedly John Wesley's association with the Moravians which completely overthrew and discredited it in his thinking. It is not without significance that the human instrument in his conversion was the reading of Luther's *Preface to the Epistle to the Romans*. The famous Aldersgate Street experience of May 24th 1738,

> In the evening, I went very reluctantly to a society in Aldersgate St, where one was reading Luther's Preface to the Epistle to the Romans. About a quarter before nine, while he was describing the change which God works in the heart through faith in Christ, I felt my heart strangely warmed, I felt I did trust in Christ alone for my salvation; and an assurance was given me that he had taken away my sins, even mine, and saved me from the law of sin and death.[25]

From this point on we shall see Wesley stressing conversion as essential and (unlike the decisionists of today) making clear man's utter inability and helpless dependence on God to give faith, and seeing faith as a compound of trust and assurance, the subjective expression of the Spirit's inner witness. Here Wesley's views entirely correspond to those of Calvin and the Reformers.

Faith is a sure knowledge of the divine favour towards us, founded on the truth of a free promise in Christ, and revealed to our minds, and sealed on our hearts, by the Holy Spirit.[26]

Packer rightly observes that Wesley's teaching on faith represents a return from the world of synergism and self-determination to that of monergism and sovereign grace.

> It was Wesley's Aldersgate Street experience that determined his view of faith. There, as his heart was 'strangely warmed' through the reading of Luther on Romans, he entered into what his Moravian friends had told him that real faith was: namely, assurance of pardon and acceptance through the cross. 'I felt I did trust in Christ, Christ alone, for salvation; and an assurance was given me, that He had taken away my sin even mine.' Habitually (though not in perfect verbal consistency), Wesley taught that this assurance is an integral element in the faith that God gives—the faith that saves. Repentance was to him faith's precondition, manifested by sorrow for sin and reform of manners. Sometimes, indeed as in his 1744 Conference Minutes, he would describe repentance as a 'low state of faith', or as the faith of a servant in contrast with that of a son (compare Gal 4:1-7; Rom. 8:1ff.). His basic thought, however, was that, whereas repentance is a state of seeking God, faith is a state of finding God, or rather of being found by Him. A person seeking God can do no more than wait on God, showing the sincerity of his quest by the earnestness of his prayers and the tenderness of his heart. Such teaching is similar to the Puritan doctrine of 'preparatory works', and led to similar practice in counseling troubled souls: it is a far cry from Dutch Arminianism.[27]

As for Wesley's views on justification, again we shall see as we examine them in his sermons, he spoke of Christ's atoning death in penal and substitutionary terms. He insisted that it was on the grounds only of that once-and-for-all atonement that we are accepted by God. In 1765 he declared, '*I have believed about justification for 27 years just as Mr Calvin does.*'[28] Harrison further comments that this was the theme by which Wesley introduces his standard sermons, i.e. '*By grace ye are saved through faith and that not of yourselves it is the gift of God.*'

His own faith he recognised as God-given and no one more steadily refused to attribute to human merit any share in the work of salvation. His affirmation of the grace of God as the centre of his universe was as strong as any that can be found in the writings of Luther or Calvin. We are not surprised, therefore, to find him saying at the 1745 Conference that—*'The true Gospel touches the very edges of Calvinism'.*
He wrote to his Calvinistic friend Howell Harris, Aug 6th 1742,

> We agree
> (1) that no man can have any grace except it be given him from above.
> (2)That no man can merit anything but hell, seeing other merit is in the blood of the Lamb. Why then need there be this great gulf fixed between us?[29]

Writing to one, John South, in 1746,

> I believe firmly that in the most literal sense that without God we can do nothing; that we cannot think or speak or move a hand or an eye without the concurrence of the divine energy.[30]

No one could ever charge John Wesley with Pelagianism. In the 19th century, even a theologian as orthodox as R. L. Dabney could point to Wesley's sermons as sound teaching on justification by faith alone.[31]

Wesley's Doctrine of Prevenient Grace.

Robert C Monk comments,

> A synergism is qualifiedly admitted here but still within the Reformation context; even the restored human ability to respond is dependent on God's initiative and grace.

He continues

> In this formulation Wesley affirmed a Protestant doctrine of original sin, with its insistence upon total dependence on the mercy of God, and sought to avoid the pitfalls of a Pelagian inherent free will, at the same time, restoring a measure of responsibility to humanity. Responsibility thus renewed by prevenient grace carried with it as a corollary the ability to distinguish right and wrong, good and evil. Part of the gift of prevenient grace was, then, human

conscience. Through prevenient grace a believer not only was empowered to respond faithfully to God's grace offered in Christ but also to become a responsible moral agent.[32]

Whilst Wesley is renewing a traditional Anglican pattern here we can readily agree with Monk that he most likely imbibed this teaching through his reading of the Puritan Richard Baxter.

> It may surprise some to learn that it also had its precedent among Puritans. Richard Baxter could not accept an interpretation of God's grace that restricted it to a select few elected persons, so he insisted on the universality of what he termed 'common grace'. According to David Shipley, Baxter's description of common grace is a striking precursor of what is found in Wesley's conception of efficacious, prevenient grace. Baxter, like Wesley, insisted on the universality of 'common grace' that enables humans to respond personally to God's offer of saving grace, thereby making one responsible for co-operation with God's grace. Baxter, using an uncredited quotation from Augustine, affirmed that, 'He that made us without us, will not save us without us...'[33]

We see from this section that not only was Wesley free from the Arminianism of Archbishop Laud and his 18th Century successors, but that it is impossible to rightly charge him with believing or teaching any form of Pelagianism. He totally rejects the notion of man's inherent free-will and traces the source of salvation to grace alone; faith being the only channel through which grace comes and faith being defined in terms of trust and reliance on Christ. Rational Arminianism denies the doctrine of the Fall, the doctrine of imputed righteousness, and the substitionary atonement; it is important to see that Wesley denied none of these. Some argue that he denied imputed rightousness, so we look at this first.

1. Wesley's position in respect to the doctrine of Christ's imputed righteousness

There seems to be ambiguity, indeed controversy, in the minds of some regarding Wesley's beliefs at this point. Huntington, in his *The Funeral of Arminianism,* charges Wesley with declaring, '*Imputed Righteousness, imputed nonsense*', however fails to give his source.

Whether or not it is true that Wesley made such a statement seems to have been discussed since the 1760s and never resolved. When discussing this subject we need to be aware of the teaching of some of the Hyper-Calvinists at this point. Some asserted the doctrine of 'imputed sanctification'. According to this view, when believers are accepted by Christ, they are not only accounted righteous in justification, but they are also credited with holiness without any co-operation with the work of the Holy Spirit to make their lives actually holy. Robert Hawker, vicar of the parish of Charles near Plymouth from 1784-1827, was one who held to this opinion. He refused to preach the need for holiness of life, informing Charles Simeon that the only reason the Apostles had done so, was because of the then infant state of the church. The believer was as much sanctified at the start of his union with Christ as at its consummation.[34] . Charles Simeon was one who denounced this kind of teaching as undermining morality. Wesley's statements on imputed righteousness need to be understood as being a guard and corrective against such teachings. In regard to the doctrine of imputed righteousness, the highly respected Reformed theologian James Buchanan states that the Methodists believed the essence of the doctrine of imputed righteousness.

...although from some confused or mistaken apprehension of its meaning, they might still hesitate to adopt, in its full sense, the doctrine of imputed righteousness.

The germ of that doctrine is really involved in what they believe—for they held the substitution of Christ in the room of sinners—the imputation of their sins to Him—and His bearing the punishment which these sins deserved; they further held, that what He did and suffered on the Cross is imputed to believers for their justification—not what He suffered merely but what He did, when He became 'obedient unto death.'

Obedience was involved in His sufferings—and if this was believed to be imputed for us for the pardon of our sins, as constituting, along with His sufferings, the satisfaction which He rendered to the law and justice of God, then they admit the principle of His vicarious righteousness, which needs only to be extended so as to include His active obedience in fulfilling the precept, as well as the penalty, of the divine Law.[35]

Buchanan further adds:

> Wesley's sentiments on this point seem to have been influenced,
> to some extent, by his fear that the doctrine of imputed
> righteousness might be perverted into Antinomian error. In his
> letters to Hervey, he admits the doctrine, but demurs to the
> phraseology in which it has often been taught; and urges many
> of the usual objections to it. Yet no Calvinist could desire a clearer
> or fuller statement of it than is to be found in one of his 'Hymns
> and Spiritual Songs',

> > Join, earth and heav'n to bless
> > The Lord our Righteousness.
> > The mystery of Redemption this,
> > This, the Saviour's strange design,
> > Man's offence was counted His
> > Ours, His righteousness divine.

> > In Him complete we shine;
> > His death, His life, is mine;
> > Fully am I justified,
> > Free from sin, and more than free,
> > Guiltless, since for me He died;
> > Righteous, since He lived for me.

> In these lines, the active and passive obedience of Christ—that
> of His life and that of His death—are distinctly recognized: and
> both are represented as concurring to a full justification.[36]

What always made Wesley hesitant was the fear of
Antinomianism. He often had half an eye on Richard Baxter with
whom he shared the same fear. Following Amyrault, and indeed the
rationalistic Arminians, Baxter replaced the doctrine of Christ's
imputed righteousness with the doctrine of 'new obedience', i.e. neonomianism. Baxter thus made the obedience of faith the ground for
our justification rather than the empty hand which receives the free
gift of salvation. Wesley published in his *Christian Library* Baxter's
Aphorisms of Justification and John Goodwin's *Treatise on
Justification* in both of which these opinions are clearly advanced.
At the same time however, in his sermon on *The Righteousness of*

Christ, preached Nov 24th 1765, he states categorically the following (evidently in order to refute a false accusation against him)—

> I therefore no more deny the righteousness of Christ, than I deny the Godhead of Christ, and a man may fully as justly charge me with denying the one as the other. This is another unkind and unjust accusation. I always did, so still continually affirm that the righteousness of Christ is imputed to every believer.

In his *Journal* written on the same day he wrote:

> I preached on the same words in the lesson for the day. 'The Lord our Righteousness'. I said not one thing that I have not said at least fifty times this twelvemonth. Yet it appeared to one entirely new, who much importuned me to print my sermon supposing it would stop the mouths of all gainsayers. Alas for their simplicity. In spite of all I can print, say or do, will not those who seek occasion of offence find occasion.

Further of course we can quote Wesley's translation of Zinzendorf's great hymn:

> Jesu Thy blood and righteous
> My beauty are, my glorious dress;
> Midst flaming worlds in these arrayed,
> With joy shall I lift up my head.

Or, of course, there is Charles Wesley's great anthem of Methodism, *And can it be?*

> No condemnation now I dread;
> Jesus, and all in Him, is mine!
> Alive in Him, my living head,
> And clothed with righteousness divine,
> Bold I approach the eternal throne,
> And claim the crown through Christ my own.

In the sermon referred to above, Wesley says of the hymns:

> The hymns republished several times, (a clear testimony that my judgment was still the same) speak full to the same purpose of my belief in the imputed righteousness of Christ.

In the same sermon Wesley also refers to his *Treatise on Justification,* published a year earlier in 1764. He states,

> If we take the phrase of imputing Christ's righteousness, for the bestowing (as it were) the righteousness of Christ, including His obedience, as well passive as active, in the return of it, that is, in the privileges, blessings, and benefits purchased it; so a believer may be said to be justified by the righteousness of Christ imputed. The meaning is, God justified the believer for the sake of Christ, both his active and passive righteousness, is the meritorious cause of our justification, and has procured for us at God's hand, that, upon our believing, we should be accounted righteous by Him.

We can see the same also expressed in the sermon on *The Wedding Garment,* 1790.

Wesley clearly saw the way that some had abused the doctrine and guarded against that abuse, but I believe it is impossible to hold that Wesley denied the doctrine of the imputed righteousness of Christ.

2. Wesley's position on the doctrine of the Fall of man and the freedom of the will

In this area we see another of the fundamental differences between Wesley's Arminianism and that of the Remonstrants. John Fletcher of Madley, writing in *The first Check to Antinomianism, 1771,* wrote, that

> If the Arminians deny that man's nature is totally corrupt, and assent that he hath still a freedom of the will to turn to God, but not without the assistance of grace, Mr. Wesley is no Arminian, for he strongly asserts the total fall of man, and constantly maintains that by nature man's will is, only free to evil, and that divine grace must first prevent, and then continually further him, to make him willing and able to turn to God.[37]

This is significant given that Fletcher, but for his untimely death, would surely have been Wesley's successor as leader of the movement. Packer comments,

> The two Arminianisms divided over the question whether capacity for response to God had been wholly lost at the Fall. Wesley said

it had, but held that it was now restored to every man as a gift of grace. The Remonstrants (not it seems, Arminius himself) said it had never been wholly lost, and 'total inability' had never been a true diagnosis of man's plight in Adam. Sin, said the Remonstrants, in effect, has made man weak in the moral and spiritual realm, but not bad; he still has it in him to reach out, however sluggishly, after what is right, and God in fact helps him, powerfully if not decisively, in each particular right choice. Wesley agreed that God helps to actualize an existing capacity in every right choice, but maintained that this capacity only existed now because it had been supernaturally restored to all the race in consequence of the cross. While accepting Remonstrant synergism, in the sense of seeing man's cooperation in right action as something distinct from, and independent of God's energizing.

Wesley insisted that the capacity to cooperate was itself a love-gift from God to sinners, and that the Calvinistic doctrine that original sin involves loss of this capacity entirely had not been a whit too strong.[38] _Packer_

3. Wesley's view of the doctrine of substitutionary atonement

Rational Arminianism tended towards Socinianism and those who do not distinguish between the various forms of Arminianism, and have not studied carefully Wesley's particular beliefs have accused him of this heresy. Socinius taught that God's giving of pardon does not square with the need for satisfaction. He denied that the transfer of punishment from the guilty to the innocent was just. He totally rejected the concept of penal substitution and said that it would be an unlimited license to sin. Socinius taught that God forgives sin only on the condition of our repentance.

Wesley on the other hand taught the classic Reformation doctrine of penal substitution. As we shall see in Chapter 6 this theme runs through his Oxford University sermons, which became the manifesto of Methodism, and other sermons that followed that became the expository models for all Methodist preachers and a summary of Methodist teaching. For example, Sermon 5 states:

> To him that is justified or forgiven. God will not inflict on that sinner what he deserved to suffer, because the Son of his love hath suffered for him.

We might take a further example from Wesley's *Explanatory Notes on the New Testament,*

> Whom God set forth—before angels and men a propitiation—to appease an offended God. But if, some teach, God never was offended there was no need of this proposed propitiation. And if so, Christ died in vain. (Rom 3:25)

Wesley's strength of feeling on this issue was clear in his response to Andrew Ramsay. Ramsay, in his *Principles of Religion,* rejected the belief that the death of Christ was designed *'to appease vindictive justice and avert divine vengeance'.* This view he said was based upon *'frivolous and blasphemous notions'.* Wesley objected strongly; stating that these so-called frivolous and blasphemous notions he received as the precious truths of God. Moreover, he stated that those who said such things verily denied the Lord that had bought them. It is also to be noted that one of the reasons why Wesley eventually turned away from the writings of William Law was because of Law's rejection of the doctrine of substitutionary atonement.

4. Wesley's stated adherence to the authority of Scripture and the principles of the Reformation

At the opening of the City Road Chapel, London, Wesley said,

> Methodism, so called, is the old religion, the religion of the Bible, the religion of the primitive church, the religion of the Church of England.
>
> The old religion, the religion of the Bible, for Wesley, Methodism was synonymous with Scriptural Christianity.[39]

We might quote the memorable words from the preface to the *Standard Sermons:*

> To candid reasonable men, I am not afraid to lay open what have been the inmost thoughts of my heart. I have thought, I am a creature of a day, passing through life as an arrow through the air. I am a spirit come from God, and returning to God; just hovering over the great gulf; till, a few moments hence, I am no more seen; I drop into an unchangeable eternity! I want to know one thing—the way to heaven; how to land safe on that happy

shore. God himself has condescended to teach the way; for this very end he came from heaven He hath written it down in a book. O give me that book! At any price give me the book of God! I have it; here is knowledge enough for me. Let me be *homo unius libri*. Here then I am, far from the busy ways of men. I sit down alone: only God is here. In His presence I open, I read His book; for this end, to find the way to heaven....If any doubt still remains, I consult those who are experienced in the things of God; and then the writings whereby, being dead, they yet speak. And what I thus learn, that I teach.

Or to take another example from the sermon, The witness of our own spirit:

The Christian rule of right and wrong is the Word of God, the writings of the Old and New Testament; all that the prophets and 'holy men of old' wrote 'as they were moved by the Holy Ghost'; all that scripture which was 'given by inspiration of God', and which is indeed 'profitable for doctrine', or teaching the whole will of God; 'for reproof' of what is contrary thereto; for 'correction'of error; and 'for instruction', or training us up, 'in righteousness' (2 Tim. III: 16).

This is a lantern unto a Christian's feet, and a light in all his paths. This alone he receives as his rule of right or wrong, of whatever is really good or evil. He esteems nothing good, but what is here enjoined, either directly or by plain consequence; he accounts nothing evil but what is here forbidden, either in terms, or by undeniable inference. Whatever the Scripture neither forbids nor enjoins, either directly or by plain consequence, he believes to be of an indifferent nature; to be in itself neither good nor evil; this being the whole and sole outward rule whereby his conscience is to be directed in all things.

Or from the *Journal*, Thursday 5th June 1776,

My ground is the Bible. Yea, I am a 'Bible-bigot'. I follow it in all things, both great and small.

Clearly, the Bible was Wesley's constant and ultimate source of knowledge and authority. His creed was *I am a man of one book*, and this was manifest throughout all his sermons and works. There is historical significance, as Franz Hildebrandt observes,[40] in the reflection that he was born in 1738, exactly 200 years after England had the open Bible from the hands of Tyndale.

The evangelical revival is nothing else but a new edition of that first opening of the Word to the people in their own mother-tongue.

CHAPTER THREE

WHY DID WESLEY CALL HIMSELF AN ARMINIAN?

We may offer the following as suggestions, without altogether resolving the puzzle:

a. The influence of his mother.

Packer speaks of Wesley's fear of Calvinism as partly resulting from a life-long haunting by the ghost of Susanna. Susanna Wesley was in turn no doubt haunted by the memories of bitter harangues over the questions of duty-faith and free-offer of the Gospel, which stifled the gospel vitality of late seventeenth century Calvinism. One can only regret that Wesley held to a caricature of true Calvinism for the whole of his life, in spite of contact and friendship with the outstanding Calvinists of his day. He always described Calvinism as:

> tending to antinomianism, making holiness needless, restraining the preaching of God's love to the world, and fatalistic.

b. Fear of limiting the free-offer of the gospel

Iain Murray comments

> Calvinism, as Wesley misunderstood it, meant no proclamation of the love of God for all men.[1]

There are, however, ample illustrations from the writings of John Calvin to illustrate that this is not what he taught.

> Jesus Christ offers himself generally to all men without exception, to be their redeemer and that love extends to all men, inasmuch as Jesus Christ reaches out his arms to call and allure all men both great and small, to win them to him.[2]
>   And when he says the sin of the world, he extends this kindness indiscriminately to the whole human race, that the Jews

might not think the Redeemer has been sent to them alone....John, therefore, by speaking of the sin of the world in general, wanted to make us feel our own misery and exhort us to seek the remedy. Now it is for us to embrace the blessing offered to all, that each may make up his mind that there is nothing to hinder him from finding reconciliation in Christ, if only, led by faith, he comes to him.[3]

Yet I approve of the ordinary reading, that he alone bore the punishment of many because on him was laid the guilt of the whole world. It is evident from other passages, and especially from the 5th chapter of the Epistle to the Romans, that 'man' sometimes denotes all.[4]

God commendeth to us the salvation of all men without exception, even as Christ suffered for the sins of the whole world.[5]

Wesley seems to have accounted for Whitfield's Calvinism by believing that Whitfield was inconsistent in his Calvinism.[6]

c. The fear of antinomianism

Antinomianism was
- (a) The belief that once in Christ the Law was no longer binding on the believer.
- (b) The further false deduction from this premise that, in effect, the believer could live as he liked.

d. A wrestling with the principles of particularity and universality

We need to bear in mind not only Wesley's reaction to the narrow exclusivity of the Calvinism of his childhood, or perhaps we should say, his mother's childhood, but also the democratic influence of the Enlightenment and the fact that Wesley, unlike many of his contemporaries, was well-travelled. His motto was of course *The World is My Parish*. One can well imagine Wesley pondering long and hard over the issue of maintaining the truth of God's sovereignty in salvation and the universal suitability and application of the Gospel. The *'we are a garden walled around'*, mentality of much of the contemporary Calvinism he met, did not match or seem a suitable vehicle for bringing about the vision the Lord had given to him. There are lessons here for all of us.

These considerations present us with the need to ponder the fact that something needs to be said in defence of Wesley's 'misconception' of Calvinism. Iain Murray observes,

> The Reformers and Puritans had never to deal with Hyper-Calvinism, that is to say, with an outlook which allows for no divine compassion for the non-elect, no universal duty to believe on Christ for salvation and no need on the part of preachers to desire the salvation of their hearers...
>
> ...Wesley's itinerants were often opposed by Hyper-Calvinistic ministers for preaching that God is loving to every man. (Murray points us to examples of this in the Journal of John Nelson.) [7]

We conclude this section with the words of Franz Hildebrandt, whose writings have done a great deal in recent years to show us that the revival of the 18th Century was a revival of Biblical and Reformation Principles; and not a revival of Arminianism as such.

> 'Arminianism' on the part of Wesley must therefore primarily be understood as a corrective, an antidote to the ill-effects of predestinarian and antinomian teaching; and Dr. Croft Cell is undoubtedly right in keeping any Arminian reading of Wesley within this limit. He is also right in reminding us that 'his quarrel was not as much with historic Calvinism as with a degenerate species, and that a similar distinction has to be drawn between Arminius and the later Arminians.'
>
> In fact the history of Calvinism leaves no ground for Wesley's suspicion that 'every branch of it (i.e. that doctrine) has a natural, genuine tendency, without any wresting, either to prevent or obstruct holiness'. Whether one can go further and on account of 'the religious evaluation of activity in the world' link Wesley more closely with Calvin than with Luther and call him 'at heart, and what is more, openly, avowedly a Calvinist'; is open to serious doubt. It is one thing to count Wesley among the Reformers, holding to the 'Luther-Calvin idea of a God-given faith in Christ'; it is another to identify the spirit of Epworth and Aldersgate with that of Geneva. To us, Wittenberg appears to lie much nearer! Without any attempt to minimize the common ground of the three Reformers, which separates them from humanists and heretics, and fall into the deplorable habit of 'labelling', we may yet take

notice of the significant fact that in one of the chief controversial issues between Lutheranism and Calvinism—the doctrine of the Sacrament is another, Wesley, though, 'on the very edge' does not 'come down' on the side of Calvin. His brother's hymns against the Calvinist 'Moloch' would, both for their contents and tenor, find unqualified applause (and quite a few parallels!) in the Lutheran camp.[8]

CHAPTER FOUR

WESLEY'S PRE-CONVERSION BELIEFS DURING HIS TIME AT OXFORD

It is popular today to speak of Wesley as one who combined High Church beliefs with an evangelistic preaching ministry. Others like to see him as paving the way for 19th century Anglo-Catholicism. These opinions are far from the truth. A study of Wesley's pre-conversion beliefs and a right appreciation of the nature of High Church Anglicanism of that period help us to understand why. In this chapter therefore we will consider the influence of Oxford University, William Law, and the Mystics, and seek to define the 18th Century's use of the term High Church.

First we may note that Oxford was, in the main, out of step with the Whig politics and Latitudinarian theology of the day. The atmosphere remained neo-Jacobite and neo-Laudian. Oxford, and the Anglicanism it represented, had also abandoned Puritanism and fallen back upon the teaching of the Caroline Divines and set loyalty to the king as its chief goal. Green comments,

> Their theology was basically patristic, ponderous, learned and orthodox; Grabe and Potter, Cave and Beveridge formed their guides. Their devotional life was nourished in the works which formed the spiritual nurture of the young Wesley: the poems of George Herbert, the writings of his later successor at Bemerton, John Norris, and the works of the neo-Catholic mystics like Castiniza. With all this there went a fundamental respect for the Crown which became after the Hanoverian succession an indiscreet but never ultimately significant preference for the Jacobites.
>
> The religious life of the University and colleges was free of enthusiasm interpreted in a technical sense. It was founded on the Book of Common Prayer, once more enforced in 1662. Morning and evening prayers were said in the college chapels; the Holy Communion was regularly, if infrequently, celebrated there.

College accounts recorded the sums paid for the purchase of wine for the Communion and the washing of the surplice. There were, of course, no hymns in the services and, except in the chapels of the bigger colleges, no organs either; at Christ Church the choir sang anthems. There was a University sermon every Sunday in St Mary's which seems to have been well attended.

The University was essentially an Anglican institution, still one of the chief training grounds for the ministry of the Church of England (though it might be argued that the actual training was minimal), and open only to its members. All who sought membership of the University had to accept the Thirty-nine Articles. The majority of the dons were in Anglican orders, in the main destined for town or country parishes.[1]

In general the period was a time of reaction against the excesses of sectarian intolerance that had marked the final decades of the 17th Century. By the time of Wesley's birth in 1703 there was a broad acceptance of the necessity to escape from 'the smell of faggots'. The mood of the times was towards a liberal breadth of doctrine and practice, hence the term *Latitudinarian* to describe the stance of the Whig-Anglican party of the day. There were however some dissonant voices such as The Non-Jurors, those Anglican clerics who, having vowed loyalty to James II, had refused to go back on that loyalty and own allegiance to William and Mary. There was some noisy excitement in Queen Anne's reign when Dr Sacheverell, a violent opponent of toleration, roused High Churchmen and the London mob against the Whig government, accusing them of betraying the Church by over-leniency towards Dissenters. It was this later spirit which prevailed at Oxford. V.H.H. Green describes Oxford at this time—

If it is possible to generalize, Oxford after the Glorious Revolution settled within a framework of Tory politics and High Church Anglicanism, tinctured with non-juring views. Something of this can be seen in the university's treatment of Arthur Bury. Bury, a friend of Sheldon and rector of Exeter College, had in his book *The Naked Gospel*, published in 1690, 'pushed to an extreme Chillingworth's principle of the harmony of Scripture with natural reason, rejecting all the unnecessary complications introduced by the Fathers.' The fellows of his college, already at loggerheads with him over other matters, appealed to the Visitor, Jonathan Trelawny, Bishop of Exeter. Bury was faced with a variety of charges, ranging from heresy to the sale of college offices, and was subsequently deprived and declared to be excommunicate if he did not leave the college by 1st of August. An unfortunate chaplain who was one of his supporters dared to read Evening Prayers in the chapel in spite of his suspension and was excommunicated forth-with. A number of Oxford masters petitioned for a condemnation of *The Naked Gospel*; after some weeks' delay Convocation passed a decree to this effect and the book was burned in the quadrangle of the Schools. Bury retired to his vicarage at Bampton and indeed was recalled to preach before the University at St Mary's on New Year's Day, 1691 (which suggests that he had some sympathizers); but the episode underlined the rigidity of Oxford theological opinion. In another more innocuous fashion, this was to be illustrated by the patristic studies,[2] which engaged the attention of some of its leading patristic scholars. Oxford theology, in the main unaffected by the more illuminating ideas of the Cambridge Platonists and Latitudinarians, remained quietly, if solidly and learnedly, conservative and patristic, developing within a steadily hardening frame of High Anglican Politics.[3]

Distinguishing the 18th Century use of the term 'High Church' from that of today

The nature of High Church beliefs and practices in this period needs careful definition. Attempts have been made to trace a direct line between the High Church of the 18th Century to that of the High Church Oxford Movement of the 19th Century; however, close scrutiny of the two positions makes such a claim invalid.

The 18th Century High Churchman honoured the Reformation, and certainly did not regard it as a mistake or an unmitigated disaster, as the leaders of the Oxford Movement tried to portray it. There were amongst those who would call themselves High Churchmen, Calvinists such as John Pearson (1613-1686), Bishop of Chester; James Ussher (1581-1656), Bishop of Armagh; John Williams (1636-1709), Bishop of Lincoln; Joseph Bingham (1668-1723), College Tutor at Oxford; Thomas Wilson (1663-1755), Bishop of Sodor and Man; William Jane, Prolocutor of the Convocation of 1689, and Jonathan Edwards,

Principal of Jesus College, Oxford. Wesley was therefore, in justifying his own position in regard to doctrine, later confident in writing in 1748 to the Bishop of Oxford, *'It is the faith of our first Reformers which I by the grace of God preach'.*[4]

Wesley had no sympathy with Roman Catholic practice. Bett tells us:

> When he was at Mainz, in 1738, he copied out the notice of an indulgence which was posted on the door of the Cathedral, in the following terms: 'His Papal Holiness, Clement the XII, hath in this year, 1738, on the 7th of August, most graciously privileged the Cathedral Church of St. Christopher, in Mainz; so that every Priest, as well as secular and regular, who will read mass at an altar for the soul of a Christian departed, on any holiday, or on any day within the octave thereof, or on two extraordinary days, to be appointed thereof, or on two extraordinary days, to be appointed by the Ordinary, of any week in the year, may each time deliver a soul out of the fire of Purgatory.'[5]

Wesley added, 'now I desire to know, whether any Romanist of common sense can either defend or approve of this?'

He spoke out on many occasions in the strongest and clearest of tones against the idolatry and superstitions of the Church of Rome.[6] Henry Bett gives various examples:[7]

> In August 1739 when adverting to the charge that he himself was a Papist—a charge made, he says, generally either by 'bigoted Dissenters, or, (I speak without fear or favour) ministers of our own Church'—he takes occasion to quote a letter which he had written to a Catholic priest; giving his 'serious judgment concerning the Church of Rome'.
>
> In this he says that Romanists are guilty of adding to the things which are written in the Book of Life, and specifies amongst these things the doctrines of the seven sacraments, of transubstantiation, and of purgatory; and such practices as indulgences, prayer to the saints, the veneration of relics, and the worship of images, along with the claims made for the priority and universality of the Roman Church, and for the supremacy of the Pope. On the Papal claims Wesley remarks, in the Notes on the New Testament, in his

comment on 2 Thess. ii. 3, that 'while the man of sin, the son of perdition, eminently so called, is not come yet, nevertheless in many respects the Pope has an indisputable claim to these titles', since he 'increases all manner of sin above measure', and `has caused the death of innumerable multitudes', and claims `the prerogatives which belong to God alone'.

In another place he says that the doctrines and practices which are peculiar to the Church of Rome 'were not instituted by Christ—they are unscriptural, novel corruptions'. Elsewhere he speaks bitterly of the persecutions of which the Church of Rome has been guilty, and of 'that execrable slaughter-house', the Romish Inquisition, and 'those holy butchers' the inquisitors.

In the lines 'Written after Walking over Smithfield' Charles Wesley celebrates the 'glorious names' of the Protestant martyr:

'Who nobly here for Jesus stood,
Rejoiced, and clapp'd your hands in flames
And dared to seal the truth with blood!'

In another hymn he describes the Church of Rome as:
That most straiten'd sect

'Who every other sect disown
Who all beside themselves reject
As heaven were bought for them alone.'

Wesley and his brother were not, therefore, 'High Churchmen in the modern sense' in so far as that implies (as it so often does) the adoption of Roman cults and usages, a wistful gaze directed toward Rome with a hope of recognition and reunion, and a general tendency to depreciate the Reformation.

With this in mind, we totally disagree with Dr. Croft Cell's well known proposition, *'That Methodism is a unique synthesis of the Protestant ethic of grace and the Catholic ethic of holiness.'* [8] We would add with Franz Hilderbrandt,

It is an open question whether one may go further and describe this trend of Wesley's theology as 'Catholic retroversion', or as 'an original and unique synthesis of the protestant ethic of grace with the Catholic ethic of holiness'. There are undeniable similarities between his life and that of St Francis; there is the strong influence of the Anglican Mother-Church, unbroken even after 1738, there is the emphatic declaration 'that faith itself, even Christian faith, of God's elect, the faith of the operation of God, still is only the handmaid of love.'

Yet the Catholic spirit of Wesley, while full of charity towards individual 'papists' remained adamant against the Romanist position; he never recanted, or repented of, his 'Reformation principles, and his corrections of Luther, or indeed of any other teachers of the church, arose—as in the redefinition of 'faith and love'—not from the difference of tradition, but from his reading of the New Testament. 'Synthesis is not the proper word for what, to Wesley, was the living unity of faith-holiness, there was no need for him to 'add' the one to the other, 'when we so preach faith in Christ as not to supersede but to produce...all manner of holiness, negative and positive of the heart and of the life'. The proof of this, and the relation to Luther, will be seen in the doctrine of Christian Perfection'.[9]

Wesley, though identifying himself in early years as a High Churchman, was never so in any sacerdotal sense

Peter Nockles says that the 18th century High Churchman, whilst laying emphasis on the doctrine of sacramental grace, both in the Eucharist and in baptism, nevertheless normally eschewed the Roman principle of *ex opera operato*.[10] Horton Davies in his book, *Worship and Theology in England,* claimed that Wesley was always a high sacramentalist, but this is to be challenged. We may allow that he was a 'ritualist' insisting on having the communion wine mixed with water, but he certainly did not believe in any real and corporeal presence of the Incarnate Christ, in or under the sacramental elements, whether by transubstantiation or consubstantiation, as is now taught by High Anglicans. In this he was typical of the High Anglicans of the day. Again, following Henry Bett, we may look at Wesley's revision of the *Book of Common Prayer*, especially his *Sunday Services of the Methodists.* This ran through three editions—the 1784 American edition, and two English Editions of 1786 and 1788. The fact that he undertook such a revision is in itself highly significant, in respect to his 'High Anglicanism'.

The changes he made are very significant indeed, though he himself said in the Preface that he had made '*little alteration*'—which is also significant. He goes on to say that the principle changes are

The Holy Club, from which Methodism emerged. John Wesley addressing his friends. He is standing at the end of the table. Immediately on his right is George Whitefield, with Hervey, author of *Meditations*, beside him. The figure whose hands rest upon the closed Bible at the other end of the table is Ingham, who founded the Inghamites, and immediately on his left is Charles Wesley. Morgan, Visitor of Prisons, is seated at Charles's left hand. Broughton is seated at the extreme right of the picture.

LINCOLN COLLEGE OXFORD

these, that most of the 'holy days' (so called) are omitted, as at present answerable 'to no valuable end'. The Sunday service is considerably shortened (this no doubt to allow longer time for preaching). Some sentences in the Offices of Baptism and for the Burial of the Dead are omitted. But there are other important changes as well. The Absolution and the Athanasian Creed disappear, and in every case 'minister' or 'elder' is substituted for 'priest'. In baptism, the sign of the cross is omitted, and also the sentence 'that it hath pleased God to regenerate this infant with His Holy Spirit'. The Order of Confirmation is left out altogether, and so is the Order for the Visitation of the Sick. Protestant High Churchman Wesley was before Aldersgate St. but certainly he was not so afterwards.

The ecclesiastical environment described above clearly influenced John Wesley's reading in preparation for ordination during the period 1720-1735.

John Wesley entered Christ Church College in 1720, was ordained deacon 1725, and became a student tutor in 1725-1735. During this period Wesley's diaries show that he read a total of six hundred and ninety-one books. Of these, one hundred were read at meetings of the Holy Club. It would seem therefore that they were not only read but discussed and appraised. Another factor is that Wesley made many extracts and abridgements from seventy-five of these. Later fifty-one of these were published either in full or edited form. All of which suggests that Wesley's acquaintance with these volumes was more than casual.

The full list of these works can be found in V.H.H. Green's *The Young Mr. Wesley*. Of these we may select the following as having the most significant influence upon him, an influence that prepared him for an acceptance of the evangelical doctrine of justification by faith, showed him the need for practical holiness, and, in a negative sense, opened his eyes to the dangers of mysticism.

The writings of William Wake and justification by faith

William Wake was Archbishop of Canterbury from 1715-1737 and, as a Patristic scholar, published works on the Apostolic Fathers and the Church Catechism. He is described by C. J. Abbey in *The English Church*[11] as a—

> Moderate High Churchman heartily attached to the tenets and constitution of his church, and greatly valuing all such bonds of affinity as connected with that early post- apostolical era of which he had made a special study.

The main and predominant element in Wake's thought was that the fundamentals on which all true Christians agree ought to overrule all lesser difficulties, these difficulties being no grounds for violating the general unity of the Church. He therefore took great interest in all that might tend to bring more nearly together Christians of varying opinions, while he resented, almost with intolerance, whatever seemed likely to set and harden the existing differences. It was with great concern that he watched the failure of the hopes which had been entertained of bringing a large proportion of the Dissenters into the pale of the National Church.

> The same craving for unity led Wake to keep up constant communications with the Protestant churches of the Continent. 'It may be affirmed that no prelate since the Reformation had so extensive correspondence with the Protestants abroad, and none could have a more friendly one.' His name was well-known and his influence frequently felt among the leading Lutheran, Reformed, and Moravian pastors of Berne and Geneva, Nismes and Piedmont, Denmark and Holland, Hungary and Lithuania. One especial correspondence was Turretin: the 'second founder of the Genevan Church,' who did much to tone down the harsh supra-lapsarianism of Calvin and Beza, and to bring about a closer union between Lutheran and Reformed. The Archbishop's special object in these letters was not only to express his earnest sympathy with the work of those who were bringing the Protestant churches more nearly together, but also to take counsel with him on the question of subscription to the Helvetic Confession. His own opinion was that although such subscriptions were unfortunately a necessary safeguard, great care should be taken that the use of them must not be needlessly multiplied, and that men should by no means be interfered with in the private exercise of their judgment on difficult questions.

About the same time Jablouski, a principal leader of the Polish Lutherans, was consulting him on the possibility of any sort of union or common action between the Roman and Evangelical Churches. Wake replied that in his own opinion the pride, the tyranny, the pretensions of the Romans were such as would prove an absolute bar to any such attempts. The respective Churches could only treat on terms of perfect equality. Then, and then only, could be distinguished the fundamentals on which they were agreed, and how far on other points a concordat could be come to or mutual toleration admitted, and whether a liturgy could be framed which would admit of united worship. Unless such preliminaries were firmly insisted upon and willingly accepted, all conciliatory advances could end in nothing but failure, or concessions in which truth would suffer. But whatever Jablonski and his coadjuters might attempt, he had perfect confidence not only in the wisdom and learning with which he would carry on his endeavours after peace, but also in his firmness and love of truth.[12]

Wake attempted to forge a union between the Anglican and the French Gallican Church. This also did not succeed. For his part he demanded that they break with the See of Rome; for their part they demanded a closer adaptation of the Anglican standards to those of The Council of Trent. Wake believed that *The Thirty Nine Articles* were of the very essence of the true faith and therefore non-negotiable and the talks broke down. These discussions give us a very useful insight into the doctrinal beliefs of the High Church party at that time. Wake saw both good and bad in the Church of Rome;

The popish religion, though I could never enter into the belief of its doctrines, yet suited with my temper too much in many particulars. Their monastic way of life, somewhat like our collegiate only more strict, took mightily with me. The beauty and ornaments of their churches; the solemnity of their services; their care and decency in the performance of it; the zeal I observed them generally to have towards their priests and superiors of all kinds; their nunneries for single women to be bred up religiously and to retire into in their age; besides some other observations which I then thought were too easily parted with at the Reformation, gave me so far a great esteem and value for their church.

But the plain and notorious idolatry and uncharitable spirit which I saw with my eyes allowed and practiced among them; their narrow and uncharitable spirit in confining salvation only to their own church and party; their rigour in requiring a blind submission to everything that is either to be believed or done by them; their unchristian persecution of all that differ from them in matters of religion; their Latin service; their half-communion; papal supremacy; and, which in the course of my correspondence I too much discovered, the skepticism and infidelity of their greatest scholars as to many of the tenets and practices of their church; these gave me no lesser dislike to their religion and abundantly secured me against the danger of being seduced by them.[13]

In approaching the question of the difference between the Church of Rome and the Church of England, Wake laid down the following broad principles on which his argument was based, 'The opinions we charge the Church of Rome with, are plain and confessed, the practice and prescription of the chiefest authority in it', and that whilst the Church of England holds 'the ancient and undoubted foundation of the Christian faith', the Church of Rome has innovated. Upon the first principle of the offering of religious worship to God only, he observed that, 'though we do not think that there is now any sensible or material sacrifice to be offered to Him under the Gospel, as there was heretofore under the law; yet do we with all antiquity suppose the sacrifice of prayer and thanksgiving to be so peculiarly His due that it cannot without derogation to His honour be applied to any other.'

Wake appealed to the Fathers: Basil, Ambrose, Chrysostom, Jerome and Augustine, in the matter of the invocation of the saints. Those who argued that this was an honour done to them, would find that the above taught the contrary, constantly insisting that it was a honour belonging only to Almighty God. He therefore considered that the Roman Catholic practice in this respect to be subject to the censure of Article 22 as 'a fond thing vainly invented, and grounded upon no warranty of Scripture, but rather repugnant to the Word of God'. Further affirming that, 'there was no need for the Christian to go to intercessors which God has nowhere appointed, and which we can never be sure our prayers shall come up to.' He stated that 'We must confess we cannot but think these addresses to be too full of hazard and uncertainty to venture any requests at all, much less so many as they do every day upon them', citing, in order to substantiate his argument, passages from authorized Roman Catholic services and addresses to saints.

In respect to justification by faith, Wake taught—

The Church of England teaches that justification is the remission of sins; 'We,' he says, 'distinguish it from sanctification which consists in the production of the habit of righteousness in us.' 'We,' he says, 'teach that our sins are pardoned only through the merits of Christ imputed to us. And for the rest, we say that this remission of sins is given only to those that repent; that is, in whom the Holy Spirit produces the grace of sanctification, for a true righteousness and holiness of life.'

'The Church of Rome comprehends under the notion of justification, not only the remission of sins, but also the production of that inherent righteousness, which we call sanctification. They suppose with us, that our sins are forgiven only by the satisfaction of Christ. But then, as they make that inward righteousness a part of justification too; so by consequence they say our justification itself is wrought also by our own good works.' Here Wake is stating the classic Reformation doctrine of justification by faith as opposed to the teaching of the Church of Rome.

The three chief devotional writers who influenced Wesley at this period

Wesley himself tell us in his, *A Plain Account of Christian Perfection, 1765* that the three were Jeremy Taylor, in his *Holy Living and Holy Dying*; Thomas à Kempis, in his *De Imitatione Christi*, (which Wesley entitled *The Christian Pattern*); and William Law, in his *Serious Call to a Devout and Holy Life*.

I. Taylor's *Holy Living and Holy Dying*

Wesley wrote of Taylor's work;

> In reading the several parts of this book, I was exceedingly affected; that part in particular which relates to purity of intention.

Instantly I resolved to dedicate all my life to God, all my thoughts,
and words, and actions; being thoroughly convinced there was no
medium; but that every part of my life (not some only) must either
be a sacrifice to God, or myself, that is, in effect, to the devil.[14]

Two extracts from letters to his mother, (both quoted by Wood[15])
reveal Wesley's dissatisfaction with Taylor's teaching on assurance,
and throw light on Wesley's understanding of the meaning of faith.
In the former he refuses to accept Taylor's teaching that we cannot
know that God has forgiven our sins.

If we can never have any certainty of our being in a state of
salvation, good reason it is that every moment should be spent
not in joy but in fear and trembling; and then undoubtedly in
this life we are of all men most miserable! God deliver us from
such a fearful expectation as this![16]

The second letter was dated 29th July 1725, and on this letter, Wood
comments,

Wesley understood faith to be 'an assent to any truth upon
rational grounds.' He was not prepared to swear that he believed
anything unless it was demonstrated to him in logical fashion.
This was how Wesley viewed faith at the outset of his quest.
Without abandoning his conviction that faith must rest on a basis
which is not repugnant to reason, he was to discover that
justifying faith goes far beyond a mere subscription to
prepositional truth.

However, what he went on to explain was something which
required no revision. 'I call faith an assent on rational grounds,
because I hold divine testimony to be the most reasonable of all
evidence whatever. Faith must necessarily be resolved into
reason. God is true; therefore what He says is true. He hath said
this therefore this is true. When any one can bring me more
reasonable propositions than these, I am ready to assent to them;
till then, it will be highly unreasonable to change my opinion. In
terms of apologetics, that was unexceptionable.[17]

What is clear from Taylor's influence on Wesley was that, in spite
of its defects, it was used of God to convict him of his need for inward
holiness.

What is not often recognized is that Taylor though theologically a rational Arminian nevertheless taught ethical Puritanism. The first Oxford Diary contains an entry dated October 1st 1726, of two words: Idleness slays. It introduces us to the beginning of Wesley's lifelong battle against idleness. The process by which he trained himself and others in the habit of ceaseless diligence began in a fierce fight against the sin of ill-used time. The clue to this is found in a work by Bishop Taylor, who, as we know, was a great authority for Wesley and a principal fountain of his vocational idealism: 'The first general Instrument of Holy Living is Care of our Time.' All idleness is sin! It is better to plow on Sunday than to do nothing. The life of every man may and must be so ordered that it may be a perpetual serving of God. No man can complain that his calling takes him off from religion: his calling itself, i.e. his very worldly employment in honest trades and offices, is a serving of God. Plowmen, artisans, merchants are in their calling ministers of the Divine Providence. And God has given every man work enough to do, so that there shall be no idleness. In this conception of life, work and duty become synonyms.

Wesley adopted thus early the fundamentals of Taylor's *Holy Living and Dying*, built his own life upon them and consecrated every moment and every faculty of his being to the high calling of inducing others to do the same. These fundamentals—they are the essentials of Calvinistic ethics—are three: stewardship, subordination of life, every detail of it, to the glory of God, and the practice of the presence of God, that is, every moment is lived under God's watchful eye. They comprise the means and the methods of a holy life. 'Holiness means that all our labours and care, all our powers and faculties, must be wholly employed in the service of God and even all the days of our life.' Now among Taylor's twelve articles of a holy life and also the 'twelve signs of grace and predestination' we find two of high import for our subject. There is enjoined an ascetic self-discipline of life as a means to an inner lordship over the world linked with a clear orientation of life on eternal values. Further, justice in dealings and diligence in one's calling are set down as one, of the signs of grace and predestination. Therefore fruitful acquisitive activity or profitable productive industry and enterprise are a sign of active faith, are an assurance of one's calling and election.

On this basis the production of surplus values and increase in goods become a religious duty. It is the Puritan apotheosis of work 'as the most comprehensive human obligation from which there can be no exemption'. The corollary of this principle it may be noticed, is the labour theory of values which appears to be also a deposit of Calvinistic ethics in economic thinking. 'Work,' says Petty, 'is the father and active principle of wealth, as land (that is natural resources) is the mother.'[18]

2. Kempis's *Imitation of Christ*

The first impact of this book upon Wesley caused him to write,

> I began to see that true religion was seated in the heart, and that God's law extended to all our thoughts as well as words and actions.[19]

As with Law, Wesley had certain reservations in respect to à Kempis, and he wrote to his mother on the 28th May 1725, that he considered à Kempis too strict,

> I can't think that when God sent us into the world, He had irreversibly decreed that we should be perpetually miserable in it.

But if he did have reservations, there is on the other hand no doubt that the book stirred him—

> 'I began to alter the whole form of my conversation, and to set in earnest upon a new life'.[20]

It is worth noting that *The Imitation of Christ* formed part of his library whilst in Savannah, for during 1736 he spent some time reading it, perhaps daily. He used it as part of his visitation ministry and read portions of it to the sick.[21] It is surmised that it was Sally Kirkham who introduced Wesley to à Kempis.[22]

Professor Outler comments,

> 'From these great mentors in piety he learned that faith is either in dead earnest or just dead.'[23]

For Wesley the relentless search for salvation continued, but the light had not yet dawned. Wesley rightly saw in this book a description of that perfection that every Christian ought to seek to aspire to. He published his own translation of it in 1735. However

Wesley eventually came to reject mysticism, and said, 'Mysticism is not the Gospel of Christ'.[24]

3. William Law's *Serious Call to a Devout and Holy Life* (1729) to which is linked the *Treatise on Christian Perfection* (1726)

Wesley spoke in glowing terms of the profound influence these two books had upon his life and of the way that they led him to give his all to Christ. Some of this influence we see acknowledged and developed practically in his work, *A Plain account of Christian Perfection*.

Wesley met Law in person in 1735. He was so impressed by *The Personal Call* that he took the book with him to Georgia, and in fact read extracts from it to the passengers on board the *Simmonds* as daily devotions. He also read some of what he called the 'most affecting parts' to 'Miss Sophy' (Sophia Hopkey), niece of Mr Causton, the chief magistrate of Savannah, in between seeking to persuade her not to return to England. Obviously he liked and approved of what he read and considered that it had spiritual value both for himself and for those to whom he read it. However, a few weeks before the Aldersgate experience (24th May 1738), Wesley wrote a very severe, if not discourteous letter to Law, repudiating his teaching and blaming him for his agony of spirit, and went so far as to advise him in respect to his own spiritual condition. Law replied more graciously but did not appear to take Wesley too seriously.

Brazier Green comments,

> His correspondence with Law at this period shows that the two men were now speaking a different language.[25]

For twenty-two years Wesley's contact with Law ceased, until 1756, when again he published an open letter criticising his teaching. Wesley, however, did recognize Law's strengths and commented in a sermon of 1788,

> *The Serious Call*, a treatise which will hardly be excelled if it be equalled, in the English tongue, either for beauty of expression, or for judgment and depth of thought.

On the influence of Law's writing on Wesley personally, and his doctrine of Christian perfection, Wesley himself comments,

A year or two after Mr. Law's *Christian Perfection* and *Serious Call* were put into my hands. These convinced me more than ever of the absolute impossibility of being half a Christian. And I determined, through his grace (the absolute necessity of which I am deeply sensible of), to be all devoted to God,—to give Him all my soul, my body, and my substance.

W.B.Fitzgerald[26] comments that the central teaching of Law's *Serious Call* is

...nothing godly can be alive in us but what has all its life from the Spirit of God, living and breathing in us.

This emphasis emerges in Wesley's doctrine of sanctification as we shall see later.

I conclude this section on the nature of the High Church Movement in Wesley's day with the following quotation:

The Evangelical movement was a revival of personal religion. In the England of the eighteenth century this was most likely to begin by taking a High Church form. Most of the English Presbyterians, since 1719, had abandoned all insistence on any orthodox confession. They were moving through an Arian phase into a Unitarian position. Even the Independents, under the posthumous influence of Milton, whose poetic reputation was at its height, were warping towards Arianism.

The Quakers had already lost their early ardour, and were shrinking into a small middle-class sect. The Baptists had not yet begun to expand into the new industrial districts. A number of Presbyterians who had come under orthodox influences were returning to the Church of England. Bishop Butler and Archbishop Secker were by no means the only Anglican clergymen educated at Presbyterian academies. But High Church hostility to Dissenters' baptisms, and to any kind of recognition of presbyterial orders, was an obstacle to the return of Nonconformists to the Church. A revival of orthodox religion and piety, infused by Moravian influences with a new tincture of enthusiasm, must either accept the High Church rigidities and reject all assistance from Nonconformists, or accept what would now be called an undenominational basis.

By a strange paradox the Wesleys not only rebaptised Dissenters in Georgia and in England, but continued to defend the practice against criticism from Gibson after they had embarked in May 1738, on the foundation of a new religious society in London, whose rules did not include any provision for the conformity of all its members to the Church of England. This was probably done 'by the advice of Peter Boehler' the Moravian leader in London, in order to enable Moravians to be members. At this time Archbishop Potter, in accordance with earlier traditions, accepted the validity of Moravian orders. But the door was accidentally opened for English Nonconformists and Non-jurors.

The 'orders' of the new society provided for mutual discipline at weekly meetings in small bands, where each member confessed his faults and spoke 'the real state of his heart, with his several temptations and deliverance, since the last time of meeting'. The older religious societies had provided similar opportunities for mutual spiritual discourse, but with this difference, that in them the aim of practical holiness was normally pursued under direction from some clergyman, and directly related to preparation for Holy Communion. The Methodists were advised to communicate at their parish churches as often as opportunity offered, but the Methodist organisation from the very first overstepped parochial, diocesan, and denominational boundaries.

Perhaps the underlying reasons which made the Evangelical revival not a High Church movement will be clearer if we consider the case, not of Wesley or Whitefield but of William Law. Wesley and Whitefield were itinerant preachers, whose mission to souls burst all boundaries. At any time and in any Church they would have given trouble to the authorities. Law was a quiet soul who wrote devotional books.

He was ordained deacon in 1711 as a Fellow of Emmanuel College, Cambridge, but did not proceed to the priesthood for some years. He gave up his Fellowship in 1715 rather than take the oath of adjuration but he was not ordained priest until 1728, when he reluctantly received priest's orders from a Non-juring bishop. In his case we may well suspect that he was unwilling to exercise his ministry in opposition to the parish clergy. In the disputes among the Non-jurors about their precise relation to the rest of the Church of England, about the liturgical usages proposed by Collier and Brett, and about the authority of their College of Bishops, he found himself more and more out of place. His pacific endeavours offended all parties. The fact is that while Law could never overcome his scruples sufficiently to take the oaths, he could not conceive the small Non-juring communion, still less any part of it, as the only true Church of England. His experience of the logic of extremes, as expressed by such doctrinaire contestants as Roger Lawrence, or Thomas Deacon and his 'Orthodox British Church', compelled him to qualify not only his convictions about the claims of the Non-jurors, but his older High Church views about the exclusive claims of Episcopal Churches. His wide reading in ascetic theology gave him a grasp of the discipline of the spiritual life which saved him from Wesley's temptation to act on sudden impulses. He remained in spirit a mystical High Churchman. His piety, like Bishop Wilson's, was acceptable to the Tractarians, but his contemporary influence was felt rather in Evangelical than in 'High and Dry' circles.[27]

Such is a summary of the theological, ecclesiastical and devotional influences on Wesley during his time at Oxford. The influence of mysticism and his later rejection of its teaching we now need to examine more fully.

Mysticism, its Influence on John Wesley and His Latter Rejection of It

Alongside his famous *Journal* John Wesley kept a diary. On 19th March 1739 he entered the following note, 'At Agutter's, writ preface, read Luther.' Mr. Agutter was one of the gentleman pensioners of Charterhouse and provided a quiet room in which he could rest, write sermons, correct proofs and write letters.[28] J.S.Simon expresses the opinion that this entry has reference to the preface of Wesley's *Hymns and Sacred Poems*, published in 1739. The significance of this preface in relation to the present subject is that in it Wesley explains his position in respect to Mysticism. He states that at one time he was greatly affected by its teaching but that he went on to reject it. He speaks of 'those common writers', who claim to be justified in the sight of God for their deeds of outward righteousness, and of the mystics who claim to be justified in the sight of God for the sake of their inward righteousness. He then clearly states that claims of inward or outward righteousness on the part of fallen man can never be the grounds of his acceptance with God. The sole cause of our acceptance with God, he states, is the righteousness and the death

of Christ, who fulfilled God's Law and died in our place. As to the
condition of our justification in the sight of God, he stated,

> It is not our holiness, either of heart or life, but our faith alone;
> faith contra-distinguished from holiness as well as from good works.

Holiness of heart and holiness of life are not the cause of our
justification but the fruit of it. As Simon comments,

> With Luther on his table, and the vivid memory of his own
> experience in his mind, we can understand the meaning of his
> uncompromising statement.

Having demonstrated mysticism's failure rightly to understand
the nature of true Christianity, he goes on to criticize the whole
structure of mysticism. It is generally taught by the mystics that
there are five stages to the Christian life.
  1. Awakening
  2 Purgation
  3 Illumination
  4 The Dark Night of the Soul
  5 Union with God

> The mystics, said Wesley, cry, 'to the desert, to the desert, and
> God will build you up,' and adds, numberless are the
> commendations that occur in all the writings, not of retirement
> intermixed with conversation, but of an entire seclusion from men
> perhaps for months or years in order in order to purify the soul.

J.S.Simon adds,

> Wesley wrote with special emphasis on this point for the
> recollection of the motives that drew him to Georgia was within
> him. As against the mystics who had misled him he asserts,
> 'According to the judgment of our Lord, and the writings of His
> apostles, it is only when we are knit together that we have
> nourishment from Him, and increase with the increase of God.'

Whatever may be thought of the justice of his indictment, there can
be no doubt that, when he was writing in the room in Charterhouse,
his conviction against the practice of a 'solitary religion' was confirmed.
He was not inclined to condemn the love of quietness that leads a

man to seclude himself for a time in order that he may examine himself, and by meditation and prayer become more completely conscious of God. In the hymn book he was about to publish, there is a poem from the Latin, entitled *Solitude* and a *Farewell to the World*, from the French, which seem out of harmony with the assertions of the preface. They reveal the influence of the best 'mystic divines'; but Wesley's own convictions are unmistakable. He says,

> The Gospel of Christ knows of no religion but social; no holiness but social holiness. Faith working by love is the length and breadth and depth and height of Christian perfection. This commandment have we from Christ, that he who loves God loves his brother also; and that we manifest our love by doing good unto all men, especially those of the household of faith. And, in truth, whosoever loveth his brethren not in word only, but as Christ loved him, cannot but be zealous of good works. He feels in his soul a burning, restless desire of spending and being spent for them. My Father, will he say, worketh hitherto, and I work; and at all possible opportunities he is, like his Master, going about doing good.[29]

Wesley's reaction against mysticism is a timely warning for today when many are attracted to it, both in its Christianised and non-Christian forms.

> It is customary in the anarchic state of current Christian thought to identify mysticism outright with Christian experience. But we find in Wesley a thoroughgoing, experimental understanding of the Gospel with a militant opposition to mysticism of every name and nature.
> The reaction of Wesley against naturalistic humanism in religion, whether the philosopher or the moralist of the mystical variety, was radical, deep, and complete. The Wesleyan doctrine of faith does recognize and retain the truth-values in humanism; but it utterly transcends every primarily intellectualistic, moralistic or mystical version of the Christian faith. A religion of ideas, a religious experience whose primary trust is in considerations of natural reason or floats on the changeful tides of emotion or limits its confidence to a round of good works, is not the Wesleyan type, but its antithesis.
> Considerations of natural reasons and systems of opinion,

codes of conduct and work-righteousness, the wind and weather of subjective states and feelings, are radically subordinated therein to the objectivity of Christian experience and the Christian faith, to that of revelation and the atonement. The reference in Christian faith to a living and saving God is what really counts. All else is emptiness. An egocentric religion might have everything for sinful humanity but the power of saving faith and moral goodness in it.[30]

The extent of Wesley's reading is well known. Whilst at Oxford in the 1730s he was greatly influenced by Law's writings and plunged himself into the mystics. He later confessed to a total fascination with 'the noble description of God and internal religion made by the mystic writers.' His retreat from mysticism was a gradual one, but perhaps reached its climax in Savannah, Georgia. In a letter written 23rd November, 1736, he wrote,

> I think that the rock on which I had the nearest made shipwreck of the faith, was the writings of the mystics; under which I comprehended all and only those who slight any of the means of grace.[31]

Cell comments:

> Wesley's criticism of the mystics was thorough-going. The starting point was the radical conflict which he discovered between mystical principles and his religious evaluation of the Church. It was Wesley's deep feeling as a Churchman that was first wounded by the mystics. But his deep churchy feeling was abundantly more than blind attachment to an institution. It sprang from early perception and growing insight into the practical dependence of the basic Christian experience upon the Church and the means of grace. Saving faith simply does not arise without the influence of and some form of interaction with the believing community. Wesley's doctrine of Christian experience accepted the church form of Christianity as fundamental. Now Wesley early reached the conclusion that the mystics cancelled out of the doctrine of Christian experience the idea of all mediation in religion. All intermediaries are to be set aside and excluded. But this cancels out of religion the idea of

the Church and means of grace and finally undermines even the mediatorial office of Christ.

Wesley's idea that all and only those are mystics who slight any of the means of grace points not simply to a logical consequence, but also to the actual fact that mysticism by its very nature, impugns the essential historical and social character of Christianity and collides with the Christian idea of saving faith as given by the reconciling ministry of Christ and the Church.[32]

CHAPTER FIVE

WESLEY'S CONVERSION AND THE INFLUENCE OF THE MORAVIANS

The Moravians were the immediate instruments under the Spirit of God in bringing Wesley to evangelical faith. The Moravian church was first established in Bohemia in the year 1457. Forty years previously, John Huss had been burnt at the stake as a heretic on the shores of Lake Constance. During this period the beginning of bitterness and dissatisfaction rose up amongst his followers against the ways and practices of the Roman Church. So intense did this become that finally, in 1457, a number of the most serious and spiritually minded of them separated themselves from the Roman Church and united together into a religious brotherhood known as Fratres Legis Christi, (Brethren of the Law of Christ), later known as the Unitas Fratrum, (United Brethren). This later developed into a Church on New Testament lines, with the Bible as the sole standard of authority in all matters of faith and practice. Many from all stations and ranks of society joined the Church. Their spiritual leaders were originally ex-priests, but being an Episcopal Church the need soon arose to ordain a new generation of ministers.

The Church approached the bishops of the ancient Waldensian communion to ordain for them ministers of their own.

The Waldensians were a pre-Reformation Church, the oldest Protestant organisation in Europe north of the Alps. From the very outset of its course it was not only evangelical, but also evangelistic. It rekindled the lights that had died down in many places, and carried it into other parts still lying in darkness. Beyond the borders of Bohemia it extended its teaching and influence on organisation into the neighbouring countries of Poland and Moravia. Thus it embraced three nationalities, each distinct in race, in speech and government. Yet there were not three churches but only one. The three provinces, as they were called, formed something more than a federation, they were the component parts of an organic unity.[1]

Martin Luther made the following tribute to the Church of the Bohemian Brethren (*Unitas Fratrum*):

> Since the days of the Apostle, there has existed no Church which in her doctrines and rights has more clearly approximated to the spirit of that age than the Bohemian Brethren.

The Church suffered severe persecution during the difficult times of the Counter Reformation along with all the Protestant churches on the Continent. It suffered especially during the horrors of the 30 Years War, when the whole of Rome's powerful resources were concentrated to crush the Protestant churches.

Rome sought to exterminate the *Unitas Fratrum*. So severe was that persecution in Bohemia that the population was reduced from that of three million to a mere eight hundred thousand. As a result of this, the Church disappeared from Bohemia, though a remnant remained in Poland. So severe was the opposition to this small remaining group, that it seemed doomed to inevitable destruction. In 1656, when the town of Lissa, then its headquarters, was sacked and burned, its surviving Bishop, John Amos Comenius, fled to Holland, from where he was afterwards invited over to England by some Members of Parliament to improve and reorganise the English education system. He was regarded as being the leading authority on the subject then living. He was a man of encyclopaedic knowledge and left behind him a series of valuable writings.

The account of the sufferings of the Bohemian Church engendered much sympathy in England in the days of Oliver Cromwell and £600,000 was collected towards their relief. Later, in 1683, as a result of an appeal on their behalf by Charles II endorsed by the then Archbishop of Canterbury Sancroft, another large sum of money was raised for their relief. Several members of the Church at this time passed through the University of Oxford notably the two grandsons of Comenius. One of these, Daniel Ernst Jablonsky was consecrated Bishop of the Polish Moravian church in 1714. All through his life he kept up a close connection with many of the most prominent Anglicans of that period, especially Dr Potter who afterwards became

Archbishop of Canterbury. Meanwhile the Church, which had survived in spite of bitter persecution, was strongly stirred by the Spirit of God. This resulted in many leaving the restriction of their own country abandoning their homes and many of their possessions and fleeing across the border into Saxony where they found refuge on the estate of Count Ludwig Von Zinzendorf. Their settlement was called 'Herrnhut'—the Lord's Watch. Others of like mind flocked to this place of refuge, largely from Moravia (hence the name 'Moravians' attached itself to this community).

> The little colony grew rapidly; and here the ancient church was renewed, the old doctrines and discipline were again adopted, the old principles of church government were revived, and the episcopacy was restored, after having been providentially preserved at the Prussian court, where Jablonsky was one of the royal chaplains. And just as the infant church in Jerusalem in apostolic days had its Pentecost, from which its members went forth to be Christ's witnesses 'both in Jerusalem, and in all Judea, and in Samaria, and unto the uttermost parts of the earth,' so had this church also its own experiences of the quickening power of the Holy Ghost, when in 1727 He came upon its members gathered at the Table of the Lord and baptised them all into one body, and filled them with a strong, unquenchable passion to execute the Saviour's great commission, and to let all mankind know of His Cross and of His salvation.[2]

This event is often seen as the beginning of the modern missionary movement. It was as a result of this that the Moravians first came to England, not coming with any idea of settling here, nor of interfering with the existing work of the Gospel amongst the Protestant churches, but simply seeing it as a stopping off place on their journey to lands yet un-evangelised. God had a work for them here, however, of which they themselves could not have dreamt. The Society for the Promotion of Christian Knowledge, and its sister society, The Society for the Promoting of the Gospel in Foreign Parts, became interested in the work and asked for representatives to be sent over to give information.

Meanwhile in Germany, Herrnhut had become not only a missionary centre but also a refuge for Protestants suffering under the relentless persecution of Roman Catholicism. Many turned to Count Zinzendorf for help and, in order to enable some of these find a new home abroad, he applied on their behalf for permission for them to settle in the recently founded British Colony of Georgia, in America. The English authorities and the Georgian Trustees, under General Oglethorpe, the governor, readily responded to this request; particularly because it was part of their plan to make Georgia a strong Protestant bulwark against the Spaniards in Florida to the south, and the French in the west. These plans, however, never came to fruition.

At the last moment the Moravians changed their minds and established their settlement in the Quaker State of Pennsylvania. They did though establish extensive mission work amongst the Red Indians around Savannah in Georgia. In order to further this missionary outreach, one of the community's foremost leaders Von Spangenberg was sent to London. In London he attended and addressed the gatherings of some of the religious societies and a cordial link was established between the Moravians and believers in this country. It was Moravian missionaries on their way to Georgia that, in the providence of God, John Wesley met on board the *Savannah* in October 1735. Hasse records this event as follows:

> In his own wonderful way God was bringing together from distant parts the men whom he had prepared and appointed for affecting his gracious work of revival. 'They that go down to the sea in ships, that do business in great waters; these see the works of the Lord.' So the Jewish Psalmist sang long ago; and it was out on the stormy ocean, amid the raging of a tempest that terrified most of the passengers on an Atlantic liner of 175 years ago [the voyage taking them from October 1735, to February 1736], that John Wesley saw something of the working of the grace of God which mightily impressed and influenced him. He and his brother Charles, along with two of the Oxford friends, Benjamin Ingham and Charles Delamotte, both of them afterwards closely connected with the Moravians, were on the vessel, going out to convert the Indians, whilst still themselves uncertain as to their own conversion.

> On board they met other missionaries, Moravians, with the Bishop, David Nitschman, at their head, bound on the same errand,

BISHOP ASBURY'S HOUSE

WESLEY PREACHING IN GWENNAP PIT, CORNWALL

THE MOBBING OF JOHN WESLEY AT WEDNESBURY
Marshall Claxton (1813–1881)

but with such a strong assurance of faith that, amid that awful
gale, in spite of the very real perils of the deep, yea, in face of death
itself, they were perfectly calm, 'Knowing whom they had believed,
and being persuaded that he was able to keep that which they had
committed unto him.' This was a new experience in Wesley's life, a
new acquaintance which was destined to produce great results.'[3]

John Wesley and Peter Bohler

Wesley's mission to Savannah was a disaster, though probably it
is true that none amongst those hard-working colonists worked so
hard as their chaplain. He preached in French to the French
settlers, in Italian to the Vaudois from Piedmont, in German to
the Germans, and on top of this learnt Spanish that he might talk
to his, as he called them, with a certain Anglican inclusiveness,
'Jewish parishioners.' The Jews probably didn't count themselves
amongst his parishioners but he laboured for their salvation just
same. He wrote in his journal:

> Some of these Jews seem nearer the mind that was in Christ
> than many of those who call Him Lord.

In spite of all this, Wesley's ministry showed no success in Georgia.
The initial tide of popularity turned against him, and he stood
almost without a friend.

> Dr Burton of Oxford, who had urged Wesley to accept the call to
> America, sent his friend off with this caution ringing in his ear:
> 'Remember your parishioners are babes. Feed them with the milk
> of the Word, not with strong meats.' Dr Burton knew this man,
> and had only one fear for him,—that his zeal for Church forms
> would hurt his influence among men who neither knew nor cared
> for such things. But John Wesley's, shall we call it,
> conscientiousness, or his bigoted High-Churchism saw the world
> through vestry windows—John Wesley's unreasoning insistence
> upon the mere 'beggarly elements' utterly spoiled his work. For
> example, he insisted upon baptism by immersion, as the apostolic
> and therefore the only proper method. He actually refused to
> baptise if the parents would not agree to his demand. He declaimed
> against expensive dresses and jewels which some ladies wore to

church. Probably for this rebuke there was ground; and indeed it checked the extravagance for a time. He refused to admit dissenters to communion unless they denied the validity of their baptism and submitted to the rite at the hands of one Episcopally ordained. He refused to read the burial service over a dissenter.[4]

On the 22nd December 1737 Wesley left America having experienced the failure of many hopes but having learned many useful and painful lessons. It was during the storm on his return voyage that he also discovered the great fear of death in his heart, and the discovery of that fear very much disturbed him, for he knew that a Christian should not be afraid to die. He wrote in his journal:

I went to America to convert the Indians; but, oh! Who shall convert me? Who is he that will deliver me from this evil heart of unbelief? I have a fair summer religion; I can talk well; nay, and believe myself, while no danger is near: but let death look me in the face, and my heart is troubled, nor can I say, 'to die is gain.'

The ship that brought Wesley back to England was called the *Samuel*, and after an arduous voyage finally arrived at Deal. He noted on landing, '*I could do nothing for four days.*' He immediately after this, however, continued in his pursuit of a justification by works.

I now renewed and wrote my former resolutions:
1. To use absolute openness and unreserve with all I should converse with.
2. To labour after continual seriousness, not willingly indulging myself in any the least levity of behaviour, or in laughter— no, not for a moment.
3. To speak no word which did not tend to the glory of God; in particular, not a tittle of worldly things. Others may, said he, nay, must. But, what is that to me?
4. To take no pleasure which did not tend to the glory of God; thanking God every moment for all I took, and therefore rejecting every sort and degree of which I felt he could not thank Him in and for.[5]

On his return to London he met another Moravian, Peter Bohler (twenty-six years old at the time), on his way to carry out missionary work in Carolina. Garth Lean describes this meeting and its resultant effect as follows:

> Wesley's first interview with Bohler was on the 7th February and from then until 4th May, when Bohler left for Carolina, they were often together. 'My brother, my brother,' the graduate of Jena said to the Oxford don, 'that philosophy of yours must be purged away.' Wesley was mystified but willing to learn. He asked Bohler whether, being without faith, he should give up preaching. 'By no means. Preach faith till you have it; and then, because you have it, you will preach faith,' said Bohler—and on 4th March Wesley did so. Bohler's diagnosis of the Wesley brothers is told in a letter to the Moravian leader, Count Zinzendorf, at this time:

> 'I travelled with the two brothers, John and Charles Wesley, from London to Oxford. The elder, John, is a good-natured man: he knew he did not properly believe on the Saviour and was willing to be taught. His brother is at present very much distressed in mind, but does not know how he will begin to be acquainted with the Saviour. Our mode of believing in the Saviour is so easy to Englishmen that they cannot reconcile themselves to it; if it were a little more artful, they would much sooner find their way in it. Of faith in Jesus they have no other idea than the generality of people have. They justify themselves; and, therefore, they always take it for granted that they believe already, and try to prove their faith by their works, and thus so plague and torment themselves that they are at heart very miserable.'[6]

Bohler showed Wesley that saving faith is given in a moment. Wesley was forced against all his previous convictions to agree. He wrote:

> 'I was now thoroughly convinced, and by the grace of God I resolved to seek it unto the end.
> 1. By absolutely renouncing all dependence in all or in part upon my own works or righteousness on which I had really grounded my faith and salvation, though I knew it not, from my youth up.
> 2. By adding to the constant use of all other means of grace, continual prayer for this very thing, justifying saving faith, a full reliance on the blood of Christ shed for me, I trust in him

as my Christ, as my sole justification, sanctification and redemption.'[7]

On Wednesday the 24th May 1738, John Wesley got up at his usual hour of 5 a.m. and opened his Bible at the text, 'Whereby are given unto us exceeding great and precious promises, that by these ye might be partakers of the divine nature' and just before he went out, opening it again and reading, 'Thou art not far from the kingdom of God.' That morning he went to St Paul's Cathedral where he heard the anthem sung, 'Out of the depths have I called unto Thee, O Lord! Lord, hear my voice... For there is mercy with Thee, therefore Thou shalt be feared. O Israel! Trust in the Lord.' And then, as every Methodist knows:

> In the evening I went very unwillingly to our Society in Aldersgate Street, where one was reading Luther's preface to the Epistle to the Romans. About a quarter before nine, while he was describing the change which God works in the heart through faith in Christ, I felt my heart strangely warmed. I felt I did trust in Christ, Christ alone, for salvation; and an assurance was given me that he had taken away my sin, even mine, and saved me from the law of sin and death... I then testified openly to all there what I now first felt in my heart.
>
> But it was not long before the enemy suggested, 'This cannot be faith; for where is my joy?' Then was I taught that peace and victory over sin are essential to faith in the Captain of our salvation; but that, as to the transports of joy that usually attend the beginning of it, especially in those who've mourned deeply, God sometimes giveth, sometimes withholdeth them, according to the councils of His own will'.

After this John Wesley joined with his brother Charles and others; Charles having found salvation a few days previously joined in singing:

> Where shall my wondering soul begin?
> How shall I all to heaven aspire?
> A slave redeemed from death and sin,
> A brand plucked from eternal fire,
> How shall I equal triumphs raise,
> Or sing my great Deliverer's praise?

> Outcasts of men, to you I call,
> Harlots, and publicans, and thieves!
> He spreads His arms to embrace you all;
> Sinners alone His grace receives:
> No need of Him the righteous have;
> He came the lost to seek and save.

This is known as Charles Wesley's Conversion Hymn.

This was the beginning of the revival, and Peter Bohler the Moravian had been the Lord's instrument to light the flame. James Hutton wrote of Bohler's doctrine:

> It was new to our ears, but it found its way into our hearts and made us joyful; for most of us had been labouring in our own strength against sin, but without effect. Of this blessed theme nothing was heard from our pulpits; it was stifled by the breath of Pelagianism, and dry morality prevailed almost everywhere. Hitherto we had been far from Christ. This proved to be the commencement of true evangelical preaching in England.[8]

Like every other revival ancient or modern it had Calvary for its centre and the atoning blood of Christ for its theme. The influence of the Moravians certainly played a large part in bringing this about.

The influence of the Moravians of course carries us back to the teaching of the Reformation. It is surely also of the greatest significance that Wesley's conversion came about whilst one was reading aloud *Luther's Preface to the Epistle to the Romans*.[9]

We have traced so far the ancestral links of John Wesley showing him to be born of distinguished Puritan stock. We have taken note of the High Church influence through which he passed prior to his conversion, showing that these influences are to be distinguished from the modern concept and use of the term High Church. The High Church party of Wesley's day was anti-Roman in character and clearly had those within it who still taught the doctrine of justification by faith, though the majority had lost sight of it. Wesley himself did not see savingly evangelical truth until he met the Moravians, though prior to his meeting them he may have had some intellectual knowledge of the truth.

CHAPTER SIX

THE *FOUR OXFORD SERMONS*:
THE MANIFESTO OF THE NEW MOVEMENT

Almost immediately after his conversion Wesley began his great life work. The *Four Oxford Sermons* can be seen as announcing the main theme or the manifesto of that work. The *Four Oxford Sermons* were preached in the years 1738, 1741, 1742 and 1744.

Their titles were:

Salvation by Faith—June 11th 1738

The Almost Christian—July 25th 1741

Awake Thou that Sleepest—April 4th 1742

Scriptural Christianity—August 24th 1744

These sermons, we would argue, formed the manifesto of the revival. G C Cell comments:

> They assailed boldly the dead theology and decadent Christianity of Oxford circles and of the Church at large. They depicted the current religion as a 'nominal Christianity', no better than 'the faith of a devil and the life of a heathen'. Its adherents were called 'Saints of the World', or 'baptised heathen' whose religion is only 'a poor superstition' or 'mean pageantry'. This nominal Christianity is handed over as the lawful prey of a destructive criticism. But at the same time these Revival manifestoes do much more than picture the decay of religion; they raise the standard of reformation. They are sure 'a return to the principles of the Reformation' can alone avert national disaster. They culminate in the prayer, 'Be glorified in our reformation, not in our destruction!'[1]

As a clergyman of the Church of England, Master of Arts, and Fellow of Lincoln College, it was required of him that he preach before the University every third year. These sermons were preached from the historic pulpit of St. Mary the Virgin, Oxford.

The obligation was binding for both parties, 'no clergyman can avoid his turn, nor could the University refuse.' However Wesley was only called upon to preach on these three occasions. Such was the controversy unleashed that he was never called again.

The First Oxford Sermon on Salvation by Faith, which was the first manifesto of the Revival, was preached on the 19th day after his conversion experience. Its doctrinal importance as a document of Wesley's theology cannot be overestimated. Writing on the 34th year of his conversion Wesley reminded the critic who accused him of being a chameleon in his theology, that he had published in 1738 the sermon on Salvation by Faith, commenting, 'every sentence of which I subscribe to now.' This statement by Wesley, often reiterated and never retracted, should put an end once and for all the opinion, sometimes entertained, that the Oxford sermon on Salvation by Faith represents Wesley in the earlier and immature stage of his theology and was probably written in America. The fact is that it represents him in the epoch of his maturity. The preface of the first volume of *Standard Sermons*, 1746, states that the *Four Oxford Sermons* were placed first 'as the strongest answer to the assertion frequently made that we have changed our doctrine of late'. The *Journal* statement for September 1st, 1778, is very strong:

> Forty years ago I knew and preached every Christian doctrine which I preach now.

The general stability of Wesley's doctrinal ideas from his acceptance in 1738 of Luther's religious understanding of the Gospel, is not open to question. The sermon opens with the following bold affirmation of the absolute necessity of the grace of God in salvation:

> All the blessings which God hath bestowed upon Man, are of His mere grace, bounty, or favour; this free, undeserved favour; favour altogether undeserved; man having no claim to the least of His mercies. It was free grace that 'formed man of the dust of the ground, and breathed into him a living soul', and stamped on that soul the image of God, and bought all things under his feet. The same free grace continues to us, at this day, life, and breath, and all things. 'For there is nothing we are, or have, or

do, which can deserve the least thing at God's hand.' All our works, 'Thou, O God! hast wrought in us' these, therefore, are so many more instances of free mercy: and whatever righteousness may be found in man, this is also the gift of God.

A perusal of this sermon brings us to the same conclusion as that expressed by Cell, that what we have here is a return to the principles of the early Reformation. What Wesley was doing in setting out this manifesto was designed to challenge the current Christianity of his day which he claimed had degenerated into a 'false religion', a religion of mere opinions, forms and words, a kind of 'practical atheism'. Cell describes it as follows:

> Instead of patronising this godless, Christless Christianity of the age, the sermon is a bold challenge, an ultimatum. It represents every man utterly dependent on God, and then too a sinner in dire need of a saviour. Wesley's message humbles man and confronts him, prostrate in the dust and ashes of repentance, with the fact of a living and saving God.It recognises the infinite gulf between man's sin and God's holiness over which man's utmost resources cannot, only the almighty grace of God can, throw a bridge. The crucial points are the inclusion of all the cosmic activities of God under the principle of grace and the strict deduction of all moral goodness in man direct from divine agency. For 'sinful man simply cannot atone for any the least of his sins'.He simply does not have it in him of himself to do anything good. Whatever of righteousness may be found in man, that is also, all of it, the gift and work of God. If indeed any of our works have the least salt of saving holiness in them, they cannot be our own works, but God's work. 'All our works, Thou, O God, hast wrought in us.'[2]

Wesley is here expressing his own faith in Christ alone for salvation. The Aldersgate Street experience is the source of the spiritual life that was to become the characteristic of the revival. As that experience came 'as one was reading from the Preface of Luther's *Commentary on the Epistle to the Romans*' so we see Wesley again expressing the central thesis of the early reformers, that salvation is by faith alone, through grace alone. God is everything, man is nothing.

Cell continues:

> This manifesto would have gladdened the heart of a Luther and
> of Calvin too, and of all the early reformers. It voices the profound
> reaction in the soul of Wesley against the current humanist,
> libertarian theology prevalent in the great bulk of Anglican and
> in much Nonconformist preaching. The Christian consciousness
> has once and again reacted and protested against a futile
> 'laborious self-salvation'. It was the precise nature of the reaction
> in Wesley's own conversion-experience. But the 'self-salvation'
> of natural religion against which this manifesto pointedly and
> powerfully protests was not at all 'laborious'; it was morally lazy
> and religiously indifferent to the last degree.
>
> A religion of human freedom, self-help and moralistic
> salvation, and of natural moral goodness, was duly advertised
> in that age by its fruits, not at all as Christianity in earnest, but
> its antithesis. Into this climate of practical atheism came Wesley,
> confronting man with the fact of God and proclaiming with early
> Reformation accents that 'a continual sense of our total
> dependence on God for every good thought, or word or work' is
> the very pulse and life-principle of the Christian consciousness.[3]

**The Second Oxford Sermon was entitled 'The Almost
Christian'** and preached from Acts 26:28, *'Almost thou persuadest
me to be a Christian.'* Cell comments on this sermon:

> As a commentary on 'the sure testimony of experience', an open
> reference to Wesley's experiment 'for many years' (1725-1738) with
> a moralistic, intellectualistic, mystical achievement of 'the life of
> God in the soul of man'. He has described (I,13) the laborious self-
> salvation that diverted his mind from the objective reality of the
> Word of God and fixed his attention upon subjective experiences
> instead of upon the sole, full, final revelation in Jesus Christ of a
> living and saving God. It is to be noted that the differential of the
> almost and the altogether Christian is said to be the experience
> of saving faith that has in it the power of God, and this experience
> is referred to 'Thus saith His Word', 'Thus saith our Lord' and
> 'the Oracles of God'. Here again it is the objectivity of revelation
> and of Christian experience that is the great foundation.[4]

Cell continues:

> The reference in this Oxford Sermon of 1741 to his own experimentation and progress from the almost Christianity of several varieties to the altogether Christianity of revelation links up the outcome of the experience indissolubly with his acceptance of Luther's doctrine of faith and the Word of God. It was this insight of his conversion experience that shifted the centre of gravity in his preaching, altered the whole course of his life and sent him forth upon those magnificent, long pilgrimages of Gospel passion that place him in the front rank of Apostolic evangelism. Wesley's analytic judgment passed on his thirteen-year experiment in religion is as follows: 'I did go thus far for many years, as many of this place can testify; using diligence to eschew all evil, and to have a conscience void of offence; redeeming the time; buying up every opportunity of doing all good to all men; constantly and carefully using all the public and all the private means of grace; endeavouring after a steady seriousness of behaviour, at all times, and in all places; and, God is my record, before whom I stand, doing all this in sincerity; having a real design to serve God; a hearty desire to do His will in all things; to please Him who called me to 'fight the good fight', and to 'lay hold on eternal life'. Yet my own conscience beareth me witness in the Holy Ghost, that all this time I was but almost a Christian.'

In this sermon, having declared that many are but 'almost Christians', he goes on to state and define what true Christianity is as follows:

> 'The right and true Christian faith is [to go on in the words of our own church], not only to believe that Holy Scripture and the Articles of our faith are true, but also to have a sure trust and confidence to be saved from everlasting damnation by Christ. It is assured trust and confidence which a man hath in God, that, by the merits of Christ, his sins are forgiven, and be reconciled to the favour of God; whereof doth follow a loving heart, to obey His commandments' (Vol. II section 5)

This sermon was originally published as a separate pamphlet entitled 'True Christianity Defended', written in June 1741. In it two of the greatest Anglican divines of the 17th century: Tillotson and Bull, were cited as deviating from the Reformed faith. Cell comments:

> He seems to have had this situation in mind when a little later he remonstrated against 'running away from Calvinism as far as ever we can' when as a matter of fact 'the truth of the Gospel lies within a hair's breadth of Calvinism.'[5]

The Third Oxford Sermon was from the text Eph. 5:14, 'Awake, Thou that sleepest', and was actually preached by the Rev. Charles Wesley, though the sentiments expressed are fully in line with those of his illustrious brother. I mention it here as it is included in the *Four Sermons* that introduce Wesley's collection, and which were obviously so included as to set out the fundamentals of Wesley's faith and the message of the revival.

The Fourth Oxford Sermon, 'Scriptural Christianity' was from the text in Acts 4:31 'And that they were all filled with the Holy Ghost'. The best and most moving description of this sermon that I have come across is to be found in W. B. Fitzgerald's *The Roots of Methodism*. I quote it not only for its graphic description, but also because it gives the traditional Methodist interpretation of this event, *i.e.* Wesley was here continuing in the old Puritan spirit of his grandfather and great-grandfather.

> It is St. Bartholomew's Day August 24th, 1744, the day when Bartholomew Wesley and John Wesley, the Puritan ancestors of the founder of Methodism, both distinguished Oxford men, were ejected from their livings and now the inheritor of their courage and spirit, a fellow of Lincoln, preaches in St Mary's. Down the aisle of the famous old church move in stately procession all the dignitaries of the University,—first the beadles carrying the vice-chancellor's insignia of office, then the vice-chancellor himself, and behind him a little clergyman, decidedly under the average height, and yet a man who at once attracts the eyes of those about him. A young undergraduate, afterwards a famous Hebrew scholar, looks down from the gallery and feels that he is in the presence of a strong individuality. 'His black hair, quite smooth

and parted very exactly, added to a peculiar composure in his countenance, showed him to be no ordinary man.'

Following the preacher are the proctors and doctors of divinity, and as these take their places the preacher ascends the pulpit, reads the quaint bidding prayer, and very quietly and slowly announces his text.

'And they were all filled with the Holy Ghost.'

The sermon opens with a beautiful description of primitive Christianity, but as the preacher goes on to apply this early teaching to university life, a hush falls upon the congregation. Some of the heads of houses stand up, leaning forward as though they would not miss a single word. Seldom have weightier words fallen from St Mary's pulpit. One can imagine the sea of upturned faces, swept by amazement, anger, shame, resentment, as the bold indictment is developed. 'What example is set us by those who enjoy the beneficence of our forefathers? By Fellows, Students, Scholars, more especially those who are of some rank and eminence? Do ye, brethren, abound in the fruits of the Spirit, in holiness of mind, in self-denial and mortification, in seriousness and composure of spirit, in patience, meekness, sobriety, temperance; and in unwearied restless endeavours to do good to all men? Is this the general character of Fellows of colleges? I fear it is not. Rather have not pride and haughtiness, impatience and peevishness, sloth and indolence, gluttony and sensuality been objected to us, perhaps not always by our enemies, nor wholly without ground?

Once more: What shall we say of the youth of this place? Have you either the form or the power of Christian godliness? Are you diligent in your easy business, pursuing your studies with all your strength? Do you redeem the time, crowding as much work into every day as it can contain? Rather, are ye not conscious that you waste day after day either in reading what has no tendency to Christianity, or in gaming, or in—you know not what? Are you better managers of your fortune than of your time? Do you take care to owe no man anything? Do you know how to possess your bodies in sanctification and honour? Are no drunkenness and uncleanness found among you? Yea, are there not many of you who glory in your shame? Are there not a multitude of you that are forsworn? I fear a swiftly increasing multitude.

> Be not surprised, brethren—before God and this congregation
> I must own myself to have been of the number solemnly swearing
> to observe all those customs which I then knew nothing of, and
> all those statutes which I did not so much as read over, either
> then, or for a long time afterwards. What is perjury, if this is
> not? But if it be, oh, what a weight of sin, yea, sin of no common
> dye, lieth upon us! And doth not the Most High regard it?
>
> May it not be a consequence of this that so many of you are a
> generation of triflers with God, with one another, and your own
> souls? Who of you is, in any degree, acquainted with the work of
> the Spirit, His supernatural work in the souls of men? Can you
> bear, unless now and then in the church, any talk of the Holy
> Ghost? Would you not take it for granted if anyone began such a
> conversation that it was hypocrisy or enthusiasm? In the name
> of the Lord God Almighty I ask, what religion are ye of?[6]

After the sermon John Wesley is joined by his brother Charles
and one of two other friends and they leave the church alone. They
are marked men. Wesley will never again speak in the University
Church. The manifesto of the revival had nevertheless been sounded
out. These sermons do much more than describe the decay of
religion; they recall their hearers back to the teaching of the
Reformers. Broadly speaking they are a return to the doctrines of
the first Reformers and it is not without significance that they end
with the prayer, *'Be glorified in our Reformation.'*

Wesley understood the revival to be: 'God's design, not to form
any new sect; but to reform the nation, particularly the church;
and to spread scriptural holiness over the land.'[7] It is important to
see that the 18th-century revival was in the Reformation tradition.
This understanding has been challenged recently by David
Bebbington, in his book *Evangelicalism in Modern Britain.*
Bebbington seeks to make out the case that the Revival was the
child of the Enlightenment. In answer to this Gary Williams has
made the following perceptive comments:

> If we think that Evangelicalism began in the 1730s, then Wesley
> and Edwards became its most important fathers. This means
> that modern Evangelicalism was from its origin equally divided
> between Reformed and Arminian theology; neither could claim

to be the mainstream doctrinal position. In this sense it is easy to see how Bebbington's analysis serves to give a strong foothold to Arminianism within the evangelical movement by making foundational one of its most noted proponents. If, however we reconsider the origins of Evangelicalism and find that it is a Reformational and Puritan phenomena, then the picture looks very different. The Magisterial Reformers on the Continent and in England during the 16th century and the Puritans of the 17th century were almost without exception (e.g. Melanchthon) committed to a Reformed account of the doctrine of election. Evangelicalism considered as continuous from the 16th century becomes aboriginally Reformed on the doctrine of election rather than divided, and the position taken by John Wesley on election becomes a minority report much like that of Arminius. With such an historical perspective, Reformed theology constitutes the authentic, evangelical mainstream of three centuries, and the historical case for the foundational status of Arminianism is undermined.[8]

This statement gives focus to one of the main points of this theses *i.e* that if we count John Wesley as being broadly within the Reformation tradition, we maintain and strengthen the premise that Evangelicalism is rooted in the doctrines of the Reformation. Evangelicalism does not have two roots as Bebbington maintains.

CHAPTER SEVEN

THE WESLEYAN REVIVAL—A REACTION AGAINST
THE HUMANIZING INFLUENCES OF ARMINIAN ANGLICANISM

In this chapter we set out in greater detail to challenge the oft-repeated assertion that John Wesley taught an updated version of the Laudian-Anglicanism and was in fact attacking the last residue of Calvinism in the Church of England.

Harking back to the four Oxford sermons of the previous chapter, we can identify some of the terms Wesley used to describe the religion of his day: 'Saints of the world,' 'A religion not more than human.' These well described the humanistic, moralistic Arminianism of his day that held sway within the established church.

Perhaps the most universal tradition about John Wesley as preacher, pastor and, superintendent of the Revival above all, as its doctrinal guide, has been that he was the arch foe of Calvinism, root and branch. His doctrinal convictions are supposed to have been in their origin and development a radical Arminian reaction against the influence of Geneva in English Christianity. He is therefore the true historical successor and finisher of the work begun by Archbishop Laud (1573-1645) who found the Anglican Church saturated with the doctrines and practices of Geneva and set himself to redeem the Church of England from the influence of Calvinism. He undertook to break the blood bond between the Reformation and English Christianity and to restore the Catholic tradition. Laud's anti-Calvinism passed through the Wesleys into the structure of Methodism. Wesley's influence in the modern church has done more than anything else to discredit Calvinism.

This is in bold outline the historical account generally given of the origin and essence of Wesley's theology. It is scarcely necessary to point out that this radical anti-Calvinistic view of

Wesley holds undisputed sway in the secondary sources and in most recent interpretations of Wesley is almost axiomatic. What exposition of Wesley does not begin, continue, and end with his anti-Calvinism? This bias reaches the limit of paradox in the assertion that Methodism has no particular theology except opposition to Calvinism and that Wesley's teaching was at all points the antithesis of Calvinism. He can not be pictured in history as standing on the shoulders of Luther and Calvin. It is now quite the fashion to represent him as originally, i.e. from 1738 onward, the antithesis of Calvinism, as thinly affiliated with Luther, but deeply rooted, grounded and steadfast in the Catholic tradition of the Anglican Church. This total reversal of the facts reaches then the limits in the recent attempts to represent Wesley as a reaction against genuine Protestantism and at heart a High Churchman not far from the Catholic fold. He did indeed say of himself that he had been, prior to 1738, without knowing it, a Catholic humanist; but he has also said that he found himself out and broke radically alike with the Catholic conception of the Church and with the humanistic conception of faith.

Likewise we can note that:

Wesley's conversion experience is ... in no sense to be construed as a reaction against Calvinism. It was in its origin and principal character a reaction against the current religion of the Church of England. The facts are that Wesley not only rejected the Arminian divines of the Anglican Church as untrustworthy expounders of Christianity, but he arraigned them as, 'betrayers of the Church, sappers of the foundations of the faith and miserable corrupters of the Gospel of Christ.' He saw in their doctrines a common apostasy from 'the fundamental doctrine of all the Reformed churches'. He brought under this condemnation not only most of the living teachers of the Anglican Church but also 'the general stream of writers and preachers'. Indeed very few can we find who simply and earnestly teach and preach the faith of the first Reformers. He cited in his sermon on 'True Christianity Defended' (a significant title), written in June 1741 to be preached at Oxford, the greatest Anglican divines of former times, Tillotson and Bull, as examples of this Arminian apostasy from the Reformed faith. (See chapter 6)

The comprehensive issue between Wesley and Arminian Anglicanism, after he perceived its fatal gravitation toward humanism, experienced his evangelical reaction against its intellectualism, moralism, mysticism, and went back to the faith of the first Reformers, was as Wesley himself stated it, the idea of a God-given faith in Christ or the work and witness of the Holy Spirit as the first principle of all Christian experience.

What then was the opinion formed in the first decade of the Revival concerning Wesley's position by the general stream of writers and preachers, by the living teachers and leading minds of the Anglican Church, by the highest voices in the convocations, in the pulpits, and in university circles? Did his preaching impress them as moving securely in the Arminian paths their feet were accustomed to? Was there no other issue between Wesley and the Church of England in 1738 save only the most unusual manner and method of his ministry? Did they feel that he was in harmony with the Arminian mind and spirit of Anglican teaching and preaching? Or did he impress them (as we have noted before) as one of the leading bishops who always spoke of Wesley with respect, never with the rancour, said: 'You have gone back into the old and exploded Calvinistic expositions of the Christian faith.'[1]

This extended quotation from Cell is an important antidote for much of the modern teaching on John Wesley. Cell was writing before World War II, and focused particularly upon American Methodism. This enabled him to observe the older and more traditional Methodism, which he now saw being remoulded by those who had no sympathy with the principles of the Protestant Reformation. If I might add a personal note, I myself was brought up in a traditional Methodist family and personally observed and was taught that essential Methodism was in the Reformation tradition. Some writers since Cell's time have also confirmed this view, though they have been in the minority. They include Franz Hilderbrandt and A. Skevington Wood. Hilderbrandt says, in *Christianity According to the Wesleys*, (the Harris Franklin Rall Lecture of 1954):   (alone ?)

Justification by faith is the Cardinal doctrine, discovered by the Reformers and recovered by the Wesleys, in the New Testament;

and the truth of its contents is borne out by the fact that it is found in the Scriptures. 'I marvel that we were so soon and so entirely removed from Him that called us into the grace of Christ, unto another gospel. Who would believe our Church had been founded on this important article of justification by faith alone? I am astonished I should ever think this a new doctrine; especially while our Articles and Homilies stand unrepealed, and the key of knowledge is not taken away.'(Works X:491)[2]

The second writer of note is A. Skevington Wood who, in his book *The Burning Heart*, writes:

Now, whilst Wesley placed perhaps greater emphasis than did the Reformers on the need for an actual righteousness to be displayed as the evidence of saving faith, his teaching nevertheless remained strictly within Protestant categories, as Williams rightly affirms: 'Wesley's view is one of sanctification by faith alone. In other words, Wesley (*John Wesley's Theology Today*) put his doctrine within the Protestant framework of justification by faith, not within the Roman framework of justification by faith and works. He put it within the order of personal relationship to Christ, not within the order of a legal relationship to a moral standard.'[3]

We may also add Harold Lindstrom's comments from his book, *Wesley and Sanctification*:

At one with the Reformed outlook, he insists on the total corruption of natural man, grounding the tenet on the doctrine of original sin. 'Wherewithal then,' he says in the discourse which is the first testimony of the new alignment in his doctrine of justification, 'shall a sinful man atone for any of the least of his sins, with his own works? No. Were they ever so many or holy, they are not his own, but God's. But indeed they are all unholy and sinful themselves, so that every one of them needs of fresh atonement. Only corrupt fruit grows on a corrupt tree. And man's heart is altogether corrupt and abominable.' (Sermon on Salvation by Faith, 11th June 1738)

Later on he expands this line of thought. He says he is 'firmly persuaded, that every man of the offspring of Adam is very far gone from original righteousness, and is of his own nature inclined to evil; that this corruption of our nature, in every person born into the world, deserves God's wrath and damnation; that therefore, if ever we receive the remission of our sins, and are accounted righteous before God, it must be only for the merit of Christ, by faith, and not for our own works or deservings of any kind'. (*The Principles of a Methodist*, 1742 p.361.) In his Minutes for 1744 he explains how it is that Adam's sin can be imputed to the whole human race: 'In Adam all die; that is, (1) our bodies then became mortal. (2) Our souls died; that is, were disunited from God. And hence, (3) we are all born with a sinful, devilish nature. By reason whereof, (4) we are children of wrath, liable to death eternal. (Rom 5:18; Eph 2:3). Accordingly, he denies that natural man has free will or any power of his own to do good. His only hope is in the free grace of God.'

(See 1745 Minutes p.285 question 23 'Wherein may we come to the very edge of Calvinism? (1)In ascribing all good to the free grace of God. (2)In denying all natural free will, and all power antecedent to grace. And, (3) In excluding all merit from man; even for what he has or does by the grace of God.')[4]

Further, we can add the comments of Henry Bett in his *The Spirit of Methodism*, being the substance of the Fernley Hartley Trust Lecture 1937:

In the sermon on Free Grace Wesley teaches that the grace of God, which is the sole source of our salvation, is free in all and free to all. It does not depend on any power, or merit, or righteousness in man or anything that he has done, or anything that he is. These are not the cause of grace, but the effect of it. So far Wesley was at one with the Calvinists, and, indeed, it has been the insistence upon this positive part of the doctrine of grace that has always been the noblest strain in Calvinism.[5]

We might also look further back than Cell to writers firmly of the Calvinistic persuasion to further confirm this point that the Methodist teaching on justification by faith was in the great Reformation tradition. Take for instance Robert Lewis Dabney's discussion on 'The Moral Effects of Free Justification'. In it he demonstrates that the doctrine of justification by faith alone is an essential mark of all truly Protestant and evangelical denominations, and that free justification by faith alone produces good works. He regards essential Methodism's understanding of these matters to be plainly within that of a Protestant Reformed understanding.

George Park Fisher in his classic *History of Christian Doctrine* 1896, asks the question, 'In what way was Wesley's evangelical Arminianism different in its tone and practice from the Arminianism of Holland, and of his own English contemporaries?'

In the first place, the Dutch form of Arminianism was early modified by Socinian and other Pelagian elements. The central point in Wesley's creed was always justification by faith alone. Secondly, in Wesley it was not valued predominantly as an ethical theory, but as being identified, according to his view, with the interests of practical religion. The doctrine of the Holy Spirit, of his indispensable agency in conversion and sanctification, was never displaced or lowered in the Wesleyan creed. This faith in the living power of the Holy Spirit, not anything ascribed to unaided human agency, was the secret of the emphasis which was laid on assurance as a privilege attainable by all believers.[6]

This, incidentally, I think is why the first edition of the *Arminian Magazine* has etchings of three representative members of the Synod of Dort on its opening pages, *i.e.* Simon Episcopius, Johannes Bogerman and Johannes Uttenbogart. Bogerman was the Calvinistic President of the Synod, Episcopius one of the leading Remonstrants and Uttenbogart who is said to have been the compiler of the Five Points of Arminianism.[7] Wesley's intention seems to have been to get beyond the Socinian and Pelagian or humanistic Arminianism of his day to its true source.

CHAPTER EIGHT

ELEMENTS OF THE FIRST, SECOND AND THIRD CALVINISTIC CONTROVERSIES

The fact that Wesley and Whitefield came from very different backgrounds is well known. Whitefield's family had no pretensions to either saintliness or scholarly learning. Little is known of his parents except that they were the proprietors of The Bell Inn, Gloucester. Whitefield, we might say, entered into the Christian life with no previously acquired theological prejudices. We can trace the development of his Calvinism to the reading of Scripture with Matthew Henry's comments on his knees. J. C. Ryle tells us that the following books were influential in this way i.e. Henry Scougle's *The Life of God in the Soul of Man*, Joseph Alleine's *Call to the Unconverted*.[1] These influences were strengthened by his contact with the brothers Ralph and Ebenezer Erskine in Scotland.

Correspondence with the Erskine brothers began in May 1739. Tyerman says Whitfield's Calvinism was 'suddenly born in June 1739'. Our letter to Ralph Erskine dated 23rd of July 1739, expressed a thankfulness that Erskine approved of George's sermon. On the other hand, Erskine's own sermons were much consulted by George. Coupled with the Scottish influence, there was the growing friendship with Howell Harris, the Welsh preacher whose theology had swung from Arminianism to Calvinism. Writing to Harris in 1739, Whitefield admitted his Calvinism: 'Since I saw you, God has been pleased to enlighten me in that comfortable doctrine of Election, etc. At my return, I hope to be more explicit than I have been.' Naturally his subsequent visits to America and his friendship with the Calvinists, Jonathan Edwards, Gilbert and William Tennant, certainly strengthened the views Whitefield already had.[2]

John Wesley on the other hand came from a clerical family and a highly academic background. He was very much aware of the theological debates and disputes that had raged decades before his birth, and very clearly influenced by his parent's aversion to the high Supralapsarian and Antinomian Calvinism which characterised many of the Independent Churches in the last quarter of the 17th-century.

The form of Anglicanism the Wesley household recognised was very much influenced by the moderating influence of Bishop Burnett. Burnett's *Exposition of the Thirty-Nine Articles,* published in 1699, was the classic and standard commentary on the Articles at that period. Burnett's commentary on the 17th Article, that of Predestination and Election, can be summed up as follows:

> A Calvinist was taught by his opinions, to think meanly of himself, and to ascribe the honour of all to God. A Remonstrant or Arminian, on the other hand, was engaged to awaken and improve his faculties, to fill his mind with good notions, to raise them in himself by frequent reflection, and by a constant attention to his own actions—he would seek cause to reproach himself for his sins, and to set about his duty and purpose.
>
> As for the disadvantages, the Calvinist was tempted to a false security and sloth; the Arminian may be tempted to trust too much in himself and too little in God. If the Arminian was zealous to affect liberty, it was because he could not see how there could be good or evil in the world without it. A Calvinist seemed to break in on liberty because he could not reconcile it with the Sovereignty of God and the freedom of his grace.

Burnett continued to say that the common fault on both sides was, to charge one another with the consequences of their opinions, as if they were truly their tenets. They both spoke too boldly of God. It was very daring presumption to pretend to assign the order of all the acts of God, the ends proposed in them, and the methods by which they were executed.

The hardest thing to be digested in this whole matter, he said, was reprobation. Many Calvinists tried to avoid the logical reason for this if they held election, but rather than give up the latter, they would bear the responsibility of asserting the former. On the other side, those who persuaded themselves that the doctrine of reprobation was false, did not see how they could deny it, and yet ascribe a free election to God. Some had tried a middle way, of ascribing all that was good to God and all that was evil to man. 'Let us arrogate no good to ourselves, they say, and impute no evil to God,' is the way Burnett described this suggestion. So they allowed the matter to rest in a way which Burnett agreed, was lazy, yet safe.

Summing up, Burnett felt that the Article was against the Supralapsarians. It mentioned, nowhere, any reference to reprobation. It did assert the efficiency of grace but did not define it. It was very probable, he said, that those who wrote this Article meant that the decree of Predestination was absolute, but since they had not said it, no one was bound to believe that it was thus intended.

> Whilst the Arminian who did not deny that God had foreseen what all mankind would do or not do, could also subscribe to the Article, without renouncing their opinions on free will. However, the Calvinist had less ground for scruple as the article seemed to favour them.[3]

Certainly the Epworth home and its 1690's form of Anglicanism had a lifelong influence upon John Wesley. When he spoke of his rejection of Calvinism the influence of these formative years must always be borne in mind. The fact also that his parents rejected the hyper-Calvinism of their age also seems to have caused him to regard all Calvinism as of that type or as potentially tending towards it. The clearest evidence of this comes in his *Dialogue between a Predestinarian and his Friend,* 1741. The fact that the Calvinism of Whitefield and Hervey and even Toplady was not of this type does not seem to have been considered by him.

The first Calvinistic controversy within Methodism began in 1740 when John Cennick, a teacher in Wesley's Kingswood School in Bristol, confessed that he had embraced Calvinistic views.

> At this time, Cennick had ceased to preach Universal Redemption and led a party against the doctrine and against his patron. After useless attempts at reconciliation, Cennick had to be excluded. Cennick left Wesley and took with him about 90 of his followers and they joined Whitefield's movement. Cennick, however, found his true spiritual home soon afterwards, with the Moravians.[4]

but he did !

This led to the publication by Wesley of a sermon entitled *Free Grace*. The text was Romans 8:32. 'He that spared not his own son but freely gave him up for us all.' Interestingly this sermon is omitted from the *Standard Sermons* but in Benson's edition of *Wesley's Works* it appears at No. 55. To some degree the publication of this sermon went against Wesley's own advice and principle: 'Never in public or private use the term Calvinists as a term of reproach and try to prevent others from doing so.'

Whitfield urged Wesley not to publish the sermon; he wrote:

> Dear honoured Sir,
> If you have any regard for the peace of the Church, keep in your sermon on predestination.[5]

Whitfield's letter is a model of wisdom and brotherly love and worth quoting at length:

> My honoured friend and brother. For once hearken to a child, who is willing to wash your feet. I beseech you, by the mercies of God in Christ Jesus our Lord, if you would have my love confirmed toward you, write no more to me about misrepresentations wherein we differ. If possible, I am 10,000 times more convinced of the doctrine of election and the final perseverance of those that are truly in Christ than when I saw you last. You think otherwise. Why, then, should we dispute, when there is no probability of convincing? Will it not, in the end, destroy brotherly love, and insensibly take from us that cordial union and sweetness of soul which I pray God may always subsist between us? How glad would the enemies of the Lord be to see us divided! How many would rejoice, should I join and make a party against you! How would the cause of our common Master suffer by our raising disputes about particular points of doctrine! Honoured Sir, let us offer salvation freely to all by the blood of Jesus; and whatever light God has communicated to us, let us freely communicate it to others. I have lately read the life of Luther, and think it is no wise to his honour that the last part of his life was so much taken up in disputing with Zwinglius and others, who in all probability equally loved the Lord Jesus notwithstanding they might differ from him in other points. Let this, dear Sir, be a caution to us. I hope it will be to me; for, provoke me to it as much as you please, I intend not to enter lists of controversy with you on the

points wherein we differ. Only, I pray to God that the more you judge me, the more I may love you, and learn to desire no-one's approbation but that of my Lord and Master Jesus Christ.[6]

The controversy did not continue in this vein however and a division between the two followed with bitter words on both sides. During this period Whitefield built the Tabernacle in Moorfields Road. This was very near to Wesley's Foundry and the danger of a very serious rift threatened. Selina Countess of Huntingdon intervened to bring about a reconciliation:

> The two men held a union service at Whitfield's Tabernacle, in which the Lord's Supper was celebrated by over 1000 communicants, and the brotherly love thus restored bound their hearts together to the day of their death. Sometimes the old fire would suddenly flare up for a moment, when they began to talk of their respective opinions, but Whitfield would smooth it with his favourite saying, 'Well, brother, let us agree to disagree.'[7]

Out of this first Calvinistic controversy we are able to see something of Wesley's own views on the subject:

> During the year 1740 various anti-Calvinistic works were published by him. The years 1745 and 1751 also brought forth isolated works and then there was little until 1770 when the 'Minute Controversy' began. All these works showed the measure of importance Wesley attached to this subject. [8]

The first work was Serious Considerations concerning the Doctrine of Election and Reprobation. Extract from a Late Author (Isaac Watts) with an Address to the reader by John Wesley. London 1740. It was an extract taken from Watts' Essay, The Ruin and Recovery of Mankind; Question XIII: 'How far has the glorious undertaking of our Lord Jesus Christ provided any hope for the salvation of those who were not eternally chosen, and given into the hands of Christ to be redeemed and saved?' Watts had dealt with the subject quite reasonably and impartially, and, whilst it is difficult to see which school of thought it was to which he belonged, this criticism was mainly of the Calvinistic idea.[9]

Albert Brown Lawson quoted above seems to believe it difficult to see which side of the Calvinistic controversy Isaac Watts allied himself with. Disagreeing with Lawson I would contend that it was not unreasonable to say that Isaac Watts was a moderate Calvinist.

Early in 1741 there appeared another pamphlet entitled: *The Scripture Doctrine concerning Predestination, Election and Reprobation*, extracted from a late Author by John Wesley, London 1741.[10]

Herbert McGonigle, principal of the Nazarene College in Manchester, takes up this point and quotes Albert Brown Lawson.

> From texts which he quoted, the author said it was plain that, 'God chose some to life and glory before or from, the foundation of the world.' Just as Christ was actually not slain for thousands of years afterwards, so men could be said to have been 'elected from the foundation of the world' and not elected until their conversion. They were, as St Peter said, 'Elect according to the foreknowledge of God, through sanctification of the Spirit, unto obedience.' They were chosen to salvation through believing the truth which had to be proclaimed through the Gospel. According to Scripture, then, Predestination was: God's fore-appointing obedient believers to salvation, not without, but 'according to his foreknowledge' of their works, 'from the foundation of the world.' Just so he predestined or fore-appointed all disobedient believers to damnation, not without, but according to his foreknowledge of all their works.
>
> God, from the foundation of the world, foreknew all men's believing or not believing. And according to this, his foreknowledge, he chose or elected all obedient believers to salvation and refused or reprobated all disobedient unbelievers to damnation. There could of course have been the objection that the author held our faith and obedience to be the cause of God's electing us to glory. This, he answered, by declaring that faith in Christ producing obedience to him was the cause without which God elected none to glory. It could be shown like this:
>
> What is the cause of my obedience? My love to Christ.
> What is the cause of my love to Christ? My faith in Christ.
> What is the cause of my faith in Christ? The preaching of the gospel of Christ.
> What is the cause of the preaching of the gospel to us? Christ dying for us.

What is the cause of Christ dying for us? God's great love and pity wherewith he loved us, even when we were dead in trespasses and sins.[11]

The point however that Wesley was seeking to make here was not that of simple Arminianism *i.e.* that God foresaw good in men or faith in men, and on the strength of that foreseen good, predestined them to salvation. Wesley rather was attempting to prove that God does not give life and salvation to men on the basis of merit foreseen in them but on the basis of grace; grace alone brings forth faith, and such faith always produces good works. Wesley clearly believed in election, and that salvation is all of grace, his fear was of an outright avowal of unconditional election lest he open the door to antinomianism.

Later in 1741 there came a third tract. This was a re-publication of *Serious Considerations on the Absolute Predestination* by the Quaker author, John Barclay. This was followed in the same year by the work written by Wesley himself entitled, *Dialogue between a Predestinarian and His Friend* (previously referred to). Albert Brown Lawson comments,

The type of Predestinarian illustrated here was of the extreme Supralapsarian type. Whitefield, at his furthest extreme was certainly not one of these nor were those evangelicals such as Hervey and Toplady who were amongst Wesley's most bitter and extreme antagonists.[12]

Very significantly, when the heat of this first controversy died down and the reconciliation was made between himself and George Whitefield, Wesley wrote in his *Journal* for Wednesday the 24th of August 1743 that God may well have unconditionally elected some persons to eternal glory, however he could not bring himself to believe that those not thus elected must perish everlastingly. In the same way he speaks of Final Perseverance saying that he was inclined to believe that there was a state obtainable in this life, from which one could not finally fall. He that has attained this is one who could say, '*old things are passed away; all things are become new,*' but to believe that the elect would infallibly persevere to the end, he could not accept.

Wesley's strong reaction to Calvinism in this first controversy seems to have ended with some backtracking and, by the time we come to the 1744 Conference, we see further balancing with its statement:

Have we not then, unawares, leaned too much towards Calvinism?

Q. Have we not also leaned towards Antinomianism?

A. We are afraid we have.

Q. What is Antinomianism?

A. The doctrine that make void the law through faith.

Q. What are the main pillars hereof?

A. 1. That Christ abolished the moral law.

2. That therefore Christians are not obliged to observe it.

3. That one branch of Christian liberty is liberty from obeying the commandments of God.

4. That it is bondage to do a thing, because it is commanded, or forbear it because it is forbidden.

5. That a believer is not obliged to use the ordinances of God, or do good works.

6. That a preacher ought not to exhort to good works; not unbelievers, because it is hurtful; not believers, because it is needless.

Q. What was the occasion of St Paul's writing his Epistle to the Galatians?

A. The coming of certain men amongst the Galatians, who taught, 'Except ye be circumcised, and keep the Law of Moses, ye cannot be saved.'

Q. What is his main design therein?

A. To prove:

1. That no man can be justified, or saved, by the works of the law, either moral or ritual.

2. That every believer is justified, by faith in Christ, without the works of the law.

Q. What does he mean by the works of the law? Galations 2:16.

A. All works which do not spring from faith in Christ.

Q. What is meant by being under the law?

A. Under the Mosaic dispensation.

Q. What law has Christ abolished?

A. The ritual law of Moses.

Q. What is meant by the liberty? Galatians 5:1.

A. Liberty, from that law and from sin.

Thus was expressed Wesley's main objection to Calvinism, namely Antinomianism or the setting aside of the moral law as unnecessary. Wesley did not say that Calvinists taught Antinomianism, but simply stated that to the Calvinist it was a possible temptation and attitude.[13]

The Second Calvinistic Controversy

The second Calvinistic controversy centred upon the proposed publication and subsequent publication of James Hervey's, *Theron and Aspasio*. The stated purpose of the book was:

> The recommending to people of manners and polite accomplishments, the theology of Calvin and in particular, the doctrine of the Imputed Righteousness of Christ. I do not pretend, nor indeed do I wish to write one new truth. The utmost of my aim is to represent all doctrines in a pleasing light, and dress them in a fashionable and genteel manner.[14]

Wesley was asked by his friend Hervey to comment on the manuscript before publication. Wesley replied in modest terms suggesting a few alterations here and there. However, Hervey was not satisfied with this response and urged Wesley to assess his book in an open and candid way. This, sadly, Wesley did, and the thrust of this criticism centred upon the fear he always had of Antinomianism. He suggested that Hervey's presentation of Imputed Righteousness tended towards Antinomianism. Hervey states the classic Calvinistic understanding of imputed righteousness.

> By Christ's righteousness, I understand all the various instances of his active and passive obedience; springing from the perfect holiness of his heart; continued through the whole progress of his life; and extending to the very last pang of death. By the word imputed I would signify that of this righteousness, though performed by our Lord, is placed to our account; is reckoned, or adjudged by God as our own. Insomuch that we may plead it, and rely on it, for the pardon of our sins; for the adoption into his family; for the enjoyments of life eternal.

The second Person of the ever blessed Trinity unites the human nature to the divine; submits himself to the obligations of his people; and becomes responsible for all their guilt. In this capacity, he performs a perfect obedience, and undergoes sentence of death; makes a full expiation of their sin and re-establishes their title to life. By which means, the law is satisfied; justice is magnified; and the richest grace exercised. Man enjoys a great salvation, not to the discredit of any, but to the unspeakable glory of all, the divine attributes.[15]

Wesley in a letter to Samuel Furley written from Kingswood dated 14 October 1757 described Hervey as a 'deep-rooted Antinomian'. This was a very unjust assessment of Hervey and his work. Hervey in no way underestimated the moral law or the necessity to keep it. Indeed he went out of his way to stress obedience to the Divine Law.

As we have seen in a previous chapter Wesley did believe in the doctrine of Christ's imputed righteousness, although he did not like the term. Hervey in his correspondence with Wesley concerning this matter actually quotes Wesley's own words:

For neither our own inward nor outward righteousness is the ground of our justification. Holiness of heart, as well as holiness of life, is not the cause, but the effect of it. The sole cause of our acceptance with God is the righteousness and death of Christ who fulfilled God's law and died in our stead.[16]

Or as Albert Brown Lawson puts it:

There was no question of putting faith in the place of righteousness. Each took its proper place. The sole danger of speaking of the imputed righteousness of Christ, as Wesley saw it, was that a man could feel it was a cover for his unrighteousness. Here was the tendency towards Antinomianism and the more vulgar presentation of Calvinism namely: the elect of God were saved no matter what they might do subsequently, and the idea could encourage it.

He concluded with an appeal for the right use of the expression 'imputed righteousness', or if he saw the attendant dangers to employ an alternative. But he begged his readers not to do this to represent him as a papist or as an enemy to the righteousness of Christ.[17]

Interestingly and significantly however Wesley was never far away in his own beliefs from the Calvinism he criticized. We may note that Wesley defended Hervey's work from the criticisms of the Sandimanian writer who wrote under the pseudonym 'Palaemon', generally regarded to have been John Glass.[18] Wesley also quoted favourably from Hervey's *Works* on several occasions and Charles Wesley wrote a most moving poem in which he expressed his deep sorrow, on the occasion of the death of his friend James Hervey.

The Third Calvinistic Controversy

A minute taken at the 1770 Conference began what is generally known as the Third Calvinistic Controversy in the story of Methodism. It was the practice at the close of each Conference to publish the minutes. This was primarily for the convenience and use of the preachers, all of whom could not attend the Conference, and also to leave a permanent record of all that had been discussed and agreed. The only drawback with this system was that it made public the internal discussions and business of the denomination, and this was open to abuse and misunderstanding. This was particularly true of the never-to-be-forgotten minutes of that Conference. What was intended to be a corrective to what was perceived as an imbalance of emphasis, was seized upon by some, and taken quite out of context, and said to be a departure from evangelical orthodoxy. I quote the Minute in full:

> We said in 1744, we have leaned too much toward Calvinism. Wherein?
> 1. With regard to man's faithfulness. Our Lord himself taught us to use the expression. And we ought never to be ashamed of it. We ought steadily to assert, on his authority, that if a man is not 'faithful, if the spirit at work in him is that of unrighteous mammon', God will not give him true riches.
> 2. With regard to working for life. This also our Lord has expressly commanded us. Labour, literally 'work for the meat that endureth to everlasting life', and in fact every believer, till he comes to glory, works for, as well as from life.
> 3. We have received it as a maxim, that 'A man is to do nothing in order to receive justification'. Nothing can be more false.

Whoever desires to find favour with God should 'cease from evil, and learn to do well'. Whoever repents should do 'works meet for repentance'. And if this is not in order to find favour, what does he do them for?

1. Who of us is now accepted of God? He that now believes in Christ, with a loving, obedient heart.

2. But who among those who never heard of Christ? He that feareth God, and worketh righteousness according to the light he had.

3. Is not this the same with 'he that is sincere'? Nearly, if not quite.

4. Is not this 'salvation by works'? Not by the merit of works, but by works as a condition.

5. What have we then been disputing about for these thirty years? I am afraid, about words.

6. As to merit itself, of which we have been so dreadfully afraid; we are rewarded 'according to our works'! Yes, 'because of our works.' How does this differ from 'secundum merita operum', or as our works deserve? Can you split this hair? I doubt, I cannot.

7. The grand objection to one of the preceding propositions is drawn from matter of fact; God does in fact justify those who, by their own confession, neither feared God nor wrought righteousness. Is this an exception to the general rule? It is a doubt whether God makes any exception at all. But how are we sure that the person in question never did fear God and work righteousness? His own saying so is not proof; for we know how all that are convinced of sin undervalue themselves in every respect.

8. Does not talking of a justified or sanctified state tend to mislead many, almost naturally leading them to trust in what was done in one moment? Whereas we are every hour and every moment pleasing or displeasing to God, according to our works; according to the whole of our inward tempers and our outward behaviour.

It is easy to see that this minute, taken out of context, could be seen as a denial of the doctrine of justification by faith alone. However it must be seen in the light of Wesley's undoubted loyalty to the great Reformation doctrine of justification by faith alone that he had preached publicly now for more than 30 years. He had also, just prior to the publication of this minute, Sunday, November 18th, 1770, preached Whitefield's funeral sermon at the Tabernacle in Tottenham Court Road. In this sermon he had very forcefully and very clearly propounded this very doctrine.

> There is no power (by nature) and no merit in man—no, we are all dead in trespasses and sins—He (Christ) was delivered for our offences, and was raised again for our justification—But by what means do we become interested in what Christ has done and suffered? Not by works, lest a man should boast, but by faith alone.[19]

Albert Brown Lawson comments on this sermon:

> The very fact that Wesley preached this funeral sermon was by Whitefield's own request. This fact did not prevent his Calvinistic antagonists taking advantage of the occasion to further the controversy which was already beginning. Nor did the knowledge that, whilst Wesley and Whitfield had openly disagreed over doctrine to the very last, they had at least been reconciled and that there was a friendly spirit between them, seem to make any difference.
>
> Wesley preached this sermon on at least two more occasions and then published it in Dublin the same year. There came a quick attack on it in the *Gospel Magazine* to the effects that Wesley had uttered a great falsehood in saying that the 'grand fundamental doctrines which Mr Whitefield everywhere preached' were those John Wesley had specified.[20]

It was also true that Wesley had long been a preacher in the Countess of Huntington's chapels, and here also he had been faithful to the truth of justification by faith alone. However, when the said minutes were brought to the attention of the Countess there began a dispute which was to last at least six years. She took the minutes to be a fundamental attack upon the truth of the Gospel.

Wesley then took the tactless step of writing to her and telling her his innermost thoughts about her faults! He defended the minutes and reaffirmed his previous statement that he preached no other gospel than that which he preached thirty years ago. Naturally, Lady

Huntingdon resented this and opposed the minute with even greater fervour. The Hon. and Revd. Walter Shirley, her first cousin, also joined in the fray and proved to be Selina's greatest supporter in the affair. Lady Huntingdon decreed that all at Trevecca College who did not join her in opposing the minute should leave. Immediately Joseph Benson, an Arminian and a helper of Wesley, who was headmaster at the College, resigned. John Fletcher, in defence of Benson, followed suit and resigned as President of the Institution.

Wesley then sent her Ladyship a letter defending his minute and referring to his sermons on *Salvation by Faith* and *The Lord Our Righteousness* and protested his orthodoxy.[21] However, the Countess was not satisfied and issued a circular to which Shirley, with other Evangelical clergy and laymen appended their signatures. It ran as follows:

Sir,

Whereas Mr. Wesley's Conference is to be held at Bristol on Tuesday 6th of August next, it is proposed by Lady Huntingdon and many other Christian friends (real Protestants) to have a meeting at Bristol at the same time, of such principal persons both clergy and laity who disapprove of the underwritten minutes; and as the same are thought injurious to the very fundamental principles of Christianity it is proposed that they go in a body to the said Conference and insist upon the formal recantation, of the said Minutes; and in the case of a refusal that they sign and publish their protest against them. Your presence, Sir, on this occasion is particularly requested; but if it should not suit your convenience to be there, it is desired that you will transmit your sentiments on the subject to such persons as you think proper to produce them. It is submitted to you, whether it would not be right, in the opposition to be made to such a dreadful heresy, to recommend it to as many of your Christian friends, as well of the Dissenters as one of the established Church, as you can prevail on to be there, the case being of such a public nature.

I am, Sir,

Your obedient Servant,

Walter Shirley

Wesley did not appear unduly worried by this, but printed on 10th of July 1771 the defence of the minutes for the use of his preachers. He did however regard the impending visit of the Calvinists to his Conference as an unjustifiable imposition and remonstrated with Lady Huntingdon. She too saw the point of this, but it was too late for her to withdraw. She wrote to Wesley on the eve of the 1771 Conference trying to soften the proceedings. Shirley, too, on arrival, realised he was in an embarrassing position and he also wrote a letter to which John Wesley replied orally, stating that the protest group would be received on Thursday, the third day of the Conference. The protest party comprised of Shirley with two of the Countess' preachers and three laymen. The Conference was well attended, a fact due, no doubt to the prevailing controversy.

The reconciliation letters of the Countess and Shirley were read and it was proposed that they should be published just as their 'Circular' letter had been. Wesley defended himself against the accusation that he had not preached the doctrine of Justification by Faith. What was more, he declared that he felt that there was some personal hostility against him, but at this statement, Shirley affirmed his regard and goodwill towards Wesley. Shirley submitted a declaration that he had drawn up. After a few but not inconsiderable emendations made by Wesley, it was signed by 53 of his preachers, although two objected. These were Thomas Olivers, who was to feature prominently in the controversy in due course, and John Nelson, the former stonemason preacher from Birstall in Yorkshire. It must be noted too that Charles Wesley's signature was also omitted. The declaration ran as follows:

Whereas the doctrinal points in the Minutes of the Conference held in London, 7th August 1770, have been understood to favour justification by works; now the Rev. John Wesley and others assembled in Conference do declare that we had no such meaning, and that we abhor the doctrine of Justification by Works as a most perilous and abominable doctrine, and, as the said Minutes are not sufficiently guarded in the way that they are expressed, we hereby solemnly declare, in the sight of God, that we have no trust or confidence but in the merits alone of our Lord and Saviour Jesus Christ, for Justification or Salvation, either in life,

death, or in the day of judgment; and though no one is a real
Christian believer (and consequently cannot be saved) who doth
not good works where there is time and opportunity, yet our
works have no part in meriting or purchasing our salvation from
first to last, either in whole or in part.[22]

After the reading of the above statement Wesley demanded a public
acknowledgement from Shirley that he had misconstrued Wesley's
minute. Shirley, at first prompted by one of the laymen, reluctantly
agreed.

The purpose of the minute had once again been prompted by
Wesley's concern regarding antinomianism. The purpose was to
emphasise the necessity of good works after justification, not as a
means of justification, but as evidences that a work of God had
truly taken place in the heart.

The matter should have been brought to an end at this point
but, subsequent to this, five tracts were published by John Fletcher,
defending John Wesley's actions and further warning against the
dangers of antinomianism. Richard Hill, followed by his brother
Rowland Hill, John Berridge and Montague Augustus Toplady,
entered the controversy from the Calvinistic side and, as mentioned
above, the acrimony continued for the space of about six years.

It was not until the year 1779 that the last Calvinistic
Controversy could be said to have died down. Before this, other
attempts to reconcile the two parties had been made by such as
James Ireland and John Thornton, but without much success.
However the time had now come for the expression of regrets and
these were voiced between such as Fletcher and Richard Hill,
Berridge and Shirley.

Wesley himself did not emerge blameless from the dispute. His
Minute no doubt was justified as he needed to guard his societies
from the antinomianism and excesses that had suddenly crept into
them. However the opening statement of his Minute: 'We have
leaned too much toward Calvinism,' was not well thought out nor
expressed, and clearly gave offence to the Calvinists. His hasty
withdrawal after the 1771 Conference has also been criticised for
he ought, before leaving, to have made it his business to see that
the matter was closed without misunderstanding on either side,

and that his instructions to Olivers to cancel the publishing of Fletcher's first tract 'A Check to Antinomianism' was carried out. Reflecting on these controversies one cannot help but wonder if Wesley's fear of antinomianism had not progressed into becoming an obsession and also that, in his reaction to hyper-Calvinism, largely inherited from his parents, he fought too hard against men who were but 'a hair's breadth' away from his own opinions. What undoubtedly these controversies have done is to obscure the fact that Wesley was nevertheless a man following the essential principles of the English Protestant Reformation. This point is well summed up in the oft-repeated anecdote of the conversation which took place between Wesley and Charles Simeon:

'Sir,' said the young Simeon, 'Sir, I understand that you are called an Arminian; now I am sometimes called a Calvinist, and therefore, I suppose we are to draw daggers. But, before I begin to combat, with your permission, I will ask you a few questions, not from impertinent curiosity, but real instruction. Pray, Sir, do you feel yourself a depraved creature, so depraved that you would never have thought of turning to God, if God had not put it into your heart?'

'Yes,' said the veteran, 'I do indeed.'

'And do you utterly despair of recommending yourself to God by anything that you can do; and look for salvation solely through the blood and righteousness of Christ?'

'Yes, solely through Christ'

'But, Sir, supposing if you were first saved by Christ, are you not somehow or other to save yourself afterwards by your good works?'

'No; I must be saved by Christ, from first to last.'

'Allowing then, that you were first turned by the grace of God, are you not in some way or other to keep yourself by power?'

'No.'

'What, then? Are you to be upheld every hour and every moment, by God, as much as an infant in its mother's arms?'

'Yes, altogether.'

'And is all your hope in the grace and mercy of God, to preserve you unto his heavenly kingdom?'

'Yes, I have no help but in him.'

'Then, Sir, with your leave, I will put up my dagger again; for this is all my Calvinism, this is my election, my justification, my final perseverance. It is in substance all that I hold, and as I hold it; and, therefore, if you please, instead of searching out terms and phrases to be a ground of contention between us, we will cordially unite in those things wherein we agree.'[23]

Tyerman says the conversation was obtained from Dr Dobbin. It is not recorded in Wesley's *Journal*.

CHAPTER NINE

THEOLOGY OF WESLEY'S HYMNS

Wesley's voyage to Georgia in 1735 was a memorable turning point in the history of English hymnody as the Oxford Methodists soon became friendly with the Moravian fellow passengers. Canon Ellerton commented:

> John Wesley's impressible nature was especially touched by the bright faith and humble, cheerful piety of these good people who sang their beloved Lutheran hymns day by day through the most tempestuous weather. It was the first time that Anglicans and Lutherans, singers of psalms and singers of hymns, worshipped and travelled together in familiar intercourse; and one of the results of their fellowship undoubtedly was the large extent to which hymn-singing entered into the devotions of the future Methodist Societies.[1]

The history of hymn singing within the Moravian communion is well summed up in the preface to the Moravian Hymn Book 1914.:

> The Moravian church, or *Unitas Fratrum*, was the first of existing Reformed Churches to issue a hymn book in the language of the people. Appearing in various forms and in different tongues, it has been in use for over four centuries, and they therefore justly kept claim to be the oldest Reformed Book of worship in existence.
>
> The first hymnbook, in Bohemia, was issued by Bishop Luke, and printed at Prague in 1501. Subsequent issues followed one another up to the year 1659, and later included many of the Reformation Hymns, and in the edition of 1566, the Litany in the Lutheran form, was inserted. In these collections of the *Unitas* in its earlier days, the hymns are largely of an objective character, and marked by a rugged strength of expression. The hymn book rooted itself in the hearts and homes of the people; and in times

of persecution and oppression, as well as during the weary years of exile, it sustained the faith of the scattered members of the *Unitas*. Subsequently it formed one of the strong historic links between the Moravian church in its ancient and its modern form. After the Renewal of the church took place at Herrnhut in 1722, some private collections of hymns by Count Zinzendorf were made use of; but it was not till the year 1735 that a Church Hymn Book was issued. This also was compiled by Zinzendorf, and was, of course in German. Various supplements were added up to the year 1748. Its successor was the large and Catholic Collection known as '*Das Londoner Gesangbuch*', printed in London 1753-1755, with more than 3000 hymns. The first English Moravian Hymn-book appeared in London in 1741; it was entitled, 'A Collection of Hymns by several authors with several translations from the German Hymn-book of the ancient Moravian Brethren.'

It is an undisputed fact that a very accurate guide to the state and condition of a church is to be found in the hymn book that it uses. Its spiritual state and theological beliefs are to a very large degree governed by the psalms and hymns sung by the congregation. Dr Stoughton in his *Religion in England 1800-1850,* adds:

Psalmody and hymnody, which had been neglected in England beyond what some readers would suppose, the Wesleys took up from the beginning, with a clear-sighted view of its importance and with a zeal that ensured success. Methodism never could have become what it did without its unparalleled hymn book. That, perhaps, has been more effective in preserving the evangelical theology than *Wesley's Sermons* and his *Notes on the New Testament*. Where one man read the homilies and the expositions, a thousand sang the hymns. All divisions in Christendom have a stamp imprinted on their piety, by which they are easily known. As to the fervour of Methodism, there can be no mistake; of its owing largely to the concrete and personal character of its psalmody. It does not deal in the calm intellectual contemplation of abstract themes, however sacred and sublime; but in the experience of believers, as soldiers of Christ, fighting, watching, suffering, working, and seeking for full redemption. You catch in them the trumpet blast, the cry of the wounded, the shouts of victory, and the dirge at the warrior's funeral.

Indeed Wesley's hymn book is a most remarkable devotional treasury. In these hymns Methodism arguably possesses a collection of spiritual verse unsurpassed outside of divine inspiration.

It is interesting and significant to note, as far as the purpose of this thesis is concerned, that in April 1861, C.H. Spurgeon organised a Bible Conference to mark the opening of The Metropolitan Tabernacle, London. The theme of the Conference was 'The Doctrines of Grace.' In the opening lecture he made the following extended comments on the theology of Wesley's hymns:

> There are Calvinists in connection with Calvinistic Churches, who are not Calvinistic, bearing the name but discarding the system. There are, on the other hand, not a few in the Methodist churches, who, in most points perfectly agree with us, and I believe that if the matter came to be thoroughly sifted, it would be found that we are more agreed in our private opinions than in our public confessions, and our devotional religion is more uniform than our theology. For instance, Mr Wesley's hymn book, which may be looked upon as being the standard of his divinity, has in it upon some topics higher Calvinism than many books used by ourselves. I have been exceedingly struck with the very forcible expressions there used, some of which I might have hesitated to employ myself. I shall ask your attention while I recall verses from the hymns of Mr Wesley, which we can all endorse as fully and plainly in harmony with the Doctrines of Grace, far more so than the preaching of some modern Calvinists. I do this because our low doctrine Baptists and Morisonians ought to be aware of a vast difference between themselves and the Evangelical Arminians.

> Hymn 131, vv. 1,2,3.
>> Lord I despair myself to heal:
>> I see my sin but cannot feel;
>> I cannot, till thy Spirit blow,
>> And bid the obedient waters flow.

>> 'Tis thine a heart of flesh to give;
>> Thy gifts I only can receive:
>> Here, then, to thee I all resign;
>> To draw, redeem, and seal,—is thine.

With simple faith on thee I call,
My Light, my Life, my Lord, my all:
I wait the moving of the pool;
I wait the word that speaks me whole.

Hymn 133, v.4.
Thy golden sceptre from above
Reach forth; Lo! My whole heart I bow;
Say to my soul, 'Thou art my love;
My chosen 'midst ten thousand, thou.'

This is very like election.

Hymn 136 vv. 8,9,10.
I cannot rest, till in thy blood
I full redemption have:
But thou, through whom I come to God,
Canst to the utmost save.

From sin, the guilt, the power, the pain,
Thou wilt redeem my soul:
Lord, I believe, and not in vain;
My faith shall make me whole.

I too, with thee, shall walk in white;
With all thy saints shall prove,
What is the length, and breadth, and height,
And depth of perfect love.

Brethren, is not this somewhat like final perseverance? And what
is meant by the next quotation, if the people of God can perish
after all?

Hymn 138, vv. 6, 7.
Who, who shall in thy presence stand,
And match Omnipotence?
Ungrasp the hold of thy right hand,
Or pluck the sinner thence?

Sworn to destroy, let earth assail;
Nearer to save thou art:
Stronger than all the powers of hell,
And greater than my heart.

The following is remarkably strong, especially in the expression, 'force'. I give it in full:

Hymn 158

       O my God, what must I do?
       Thou alone the way canst show;
       Thou canst save me in this hour;
       I have neither will nor power:
       God, if over all thou art,
       Greater than my sinful heart,
       All thy power on me be shown,
       Take away this heart of stone.

       Take away my darling sin,
       Make me willing to be clean;
       Make me willing to receive
       All thy goodness waits to give.
       Force me, Lord, with all to part;
       Tear these idols from my heart;
       Now thy love, almighty show,
       Make even me a creature new.

       Jesus, mighty to renew,
       Work in me to will and do;
       Turn my nature's rapid tide.
       Stem the torrent of my pride;
       Stop the whirlwind of my will;
       Speak, and bid the sun stand still;
       Now thy love almighty show,
       Make even me a creature new.

       Arm of God, thy strength put on;
       Bow the heavens, and come down;
       All my unbelief o'erthrow;
       Lay th' aspiring mountain low;
       Conquer thy worst foe in me,
       Get thyself the victory;
       Save the vilest of the race;
       Force me to be saved by grace.'

Hymn 206. vv.1-2.

> 'What am I, O thou glorious God!
> And what my Father's house to thee,
> That thou such mercies hast bestow'd
> On me, the vilest reptile, me!
> I take the blessing from above,
> And wonder at thy boundless love.
>
> Me in my blood thy love pass'd by,
> And stopp'd, my ruin to retrieve;
> Wept o'er my soul thy pitying eye;
> Thy bowels yearn'd and sounded, 'Live!'
> Dying, I heard the welcome sound,
> And pardon in thy mercy found.'

To these observations Spurgeon adds the following:

> Permit me to say, that the strength of the doctrine of Wesleyan
> Methodism lay in its Calvinism. The great body of the Methodists
> disclaimed Pelagianism in whole and in parts. They contended
> for man's entire depravity, the necessity of the direct agency of
> the Holy Spirit and that the first step in the change proceeds
> not from the sinner, but from God. Does not the Methodist hold
> as firmly as ever we do, that man is saved by the operation of
> the Holy Ghost and the Holy Ghost only? And are not many of
> Mr Wesley's sermons full of that great truth, that the Holy Ghost
> is necessary to regeneration? Whatever mistakes he may have
> made, he continually preached the absolute necessity of the new
> birth by the Holy Ghost, and there are some other points of
> exceedingly close agreement; for instance, even that of human
> inability. It matters not how some may abuse us, when we say
> man could not of himself repent or believe; yet, the old Arminian
> Standards said the same.

To continue, it is sometimes said that Wesley misunderstood
the doctrine of repentance, and turned it into a legal preparation
for faith; the hymns however enable us to see that this was not the
case. Take for example, Hymn 105 in *The Collection of Hymns for
the use of the People called Methodists 1780.*

O that I could repent!
O that I could believe!
Thou by thy voice the marble rent,
The rock in sunder cleave!

Thou, by thy two edged sword
My soul and spirit part,
Strike with the hammer of thy word,
And break my stubborn heart!

Saviour, and Prince of Peace,
The double grace bestow;
Unloose the bonds of wickedness,
And the let the captive go:

Grant me my sins to feel,
And then the load remove;
Wound, and pour in, my wounds to heal,
The balm of pardoning love.

Or take the following Hymn 106:

Saviour, Prince, enthroned above,
Repentance to impart,
Give me, through thy dying love,
The humble contrite heart:
Give me what I have long implored,
A portion of thy grief unknown;
Turn, and look upon me Lord,
And break my heart of stone.

Or again Hymn 84:

Come, thou all victorious Lord!
Thy power to us make known;
Strike with the hammer of thy word,
And break these hearts of stone.

O that we all might now begin
Our foolishness to mourn;
And turn at once from every sin,
And to our Saviour turn!

Give us ourselves and thee to know,
In this our gracious day;
Repentance unto life bestow,
And take our sins away.

Conclude us first in unbelief,
And freely then release;
Fill every soul with sacred grief,
And then with sacred peace.

Impoverish, Lord, and then relieve,
And then enrich the poor;
The knowledge of our sickness give,
The knowledge of our cure.

That blessed sense of guilt impart,
And then remove the load;
Trouble, and wash the troubled heart
In the atoning blood.

Our desperate state through sin declare,
And speak our sins forgiven;
By perfect holiness prepare,
And take us up to heaven.

The hymns of Wesley are a perfect combination of the objective and the experiential. It is said that the 1780 *Hymn Book*, which with the supplement added in 1877, served the Methodist congregations until the early part of the 20th century. This book was, says Luke Wiseman, in *The New History of Methodism*, based on the order of Bunyan's *Pilgrim's Progress*. It, like all subsequent Methodist hymnbooks, until the present collection, begins with the hymn, 'O for a thousand tongues to sing, my great Redeemer's praise.' The picture is of Evangelist crying in the street calling sinners to repentance and faith in Christ.

My gracious Master and my God,
Assist me to proclaim,
To spread through all the earth abroad
The honours of thy name.

He breaks of the power of cancelled sin,
He sets the prisoner free;
His blood can make the foulest clean,
His blood availed for me.

After exhorting sinners to return to God, Evangelist goes on to describe:
1. The pleasantness of religion
2. The goodness of God
3. Death
4. Judgment
5. Heaven
6. Hell

He describes formal religion, and inward religion.

Hymns then suited to every stage of the pilgrims progress follow:

Convicted sinners praying for repentance
Mourners convinced of sin
Persons convinced of backsliding
Backsliders recovered
Believers rejoicing
Believers fighting
Believers praying
Believers watching
Believers working
Believers suffering
Believers seeking for full redemption
For believers saved
For believers interceding for the world

To this collection of experiential hymns, was also added the great doctrinally objective hymns of worship, such as, the great hymn of the nativity, *Hark the herald angels sing*, or the great hymn of the resurrection, *Christ the Lord is risen today*...

Wesley's hymns constantly emphasise his belief in the universality of redemption and yet, as we have tried to demonstrate in their description of the conversion experience, and indeed in their setting forth of the need of conversion, thoroughly Calvinistic.

CHAPTER TEN

JOHN WESLEY AND PURITANISM

Mention has already been made of John Wesley's Puritan ancestry, but the extent to which he himself was influenced by the Puritans is the subject of this chapter. Robert C Monk in his great work *John Wesley and his Puritan Heritage* begins by acknowledging that there has been a resemblance made between John Wesley's teachings and practices and those characteristic of the 17th-century English Puritans, since Wesley's own time.

> Among Wesley's contemporaries, Bishop Warburton identified the 'true character of Methodism', with the 'old Precisians, Puritans, and Independents'. Samuel Johnson and Horace Walpole similarly suggested such identification. Accusations that 18th-century Methodism was another form of Nonconformity were often heard during Wesley's ministry Late in his life, after he had become comfortable with the term Methodist, an admirer demonstrated that, though Wesley presumed the name had not been used before his own day, it had in fact been applied to certain of the 17th-century nonconformists (see Curnock's note on the subject in *The Journal of the Rev. John Wesley A M*, Epworth Press 1909 5:42). In the eyes of many of his contemporaries, Wesley revived the spirit and practice of Puritanism.[1]

Monk goes on to give us the following helpful definition of the meaning of the term Puritan:

> The most common reference to Puritanism in late 16th-century England denoted those who sought to continue the Protestant Reformation by establishing what they understood to be 'pure' forms of doctrine, worship, church polity, and exemplary Christian living within the English church. The political implications and consequences of these endeavours identified 17th-century Puritans

with the struggle for liberty and constitutional rights—Puritans
of varying ecclesiological persuasions were united in their
conviction that Christianity, based on a vibrant faith, involved
humanity in an experiential relationship with the God revealed
in Christ where all human existence was to be patterned after
Christ's teaching and example. For them religious authority found
its base in the Scriptures which became the primary rule and guide
for thought and action.

The usual conventional English dependence on Scripture
supplemented by church tradition and reason became suspect —
particularly dependence on tradition. As John Wilkinson points
out, their theological concentration was on the sovereignty and
righteousness of God and the all pervading character of human
sinfulness, buttressed by a deep concern for salvation. Their ethical
idealism grew out of these convictions, since no human action was
understood to be free from moral demands and consequences.
These attitudes combined to produce an emphasis on a serious,
circumspect, and disciplined daily life. Their insights into the basis
of such Christian living, and their instruction concerning it, were
things that specifically attracted John Wesley's attention.

Objective evidence of Wesley's great familiarity with Puritan
writings and practices of course comes from the large number of
Puritan works he saw fit to include in his monumental work, *The
Christian Library*. Where Wesley gained his knowledge and
acquaintance with these writings has been largely a matter of
conjecture. V. H. H. Green, in his book, *The Young Mr Wesley,* in
giving the lists of Wesley's reading in the period 1725-34, mentions
only a few of the more well-known works, Milton's *Paradise Lost*,
Bishop Hall's *Contemplations on the New Testament*, Isaac Watts'
On Predestination, and the works of Richard Baxter, Edmund
Calamy, and Samuel Clarke.

Wesley's Georgia Diaries show us that in the winter and spring
of 1737, he read such Puritan works as Bishop Hall's *Meditation
on Heaven*, Clarke's *Lives*, *The Works of John Owen*, Milton's
Paradise Regained, *The Life of Thomas Haliburton* and *The
Catechism of the Assembly* (presumably that of the Westminster
Assembly).

In the Autumn after Aldersgate (1738) he read Edwards's *Surprising Conversions*. In May 1739 he read Daniel Neal's *History of the Puritans*, and in October of that same year he read *Bunyan's Life*, as well as *The Pilgrim's Progress*, and repeated his reading of Milton's *Paradise Lost*.

This, though a significant and impressive list, still fails to account for that very wide familiarity with Puritan writers that is evidenced by *The Christian Library*. Monk suggests that once Wesley was willing to drop the prejudices of his education and background, he was open to materials from a far wider constituency. His concern for practical godliness must have brought him to find an early affinity with the Puritan writers. His insatiable reading habits could well account for the wide range of works he plundered.

> Wesley was willing to credit the Puritans with pre-eminence in the area of practical godliness, and, recognising this, he may well have made a thorough and exhaustive examination of their writings. However the inclusion may be explained, Wesley clearly was not only familiar with the tradition, but also willing to permit their insights concerning the Christian faith and life to play a vital role in the instruction of his own people.[2]

1. The Christian Library

The idea of forming the *Christian Library* may first have come from Wesley's father. As a leading member of the Athenian Society, Samuel Wesley was a major contributor to one of their publications, entitled *A Young Student's Library*, a work of extracts and abridgements.[3] On June 18th 1746, Dr Philip Doddridge, the principal of the Dissenting Academy in Northampton, responded favourably to Wesley's suggestion for such a work to be produced. In August 1748, writing to Mr G. Blackwood, a London banking friend, Wesley outlined his objectives in publishing *A Christian Library*:

> I have often thought of mentioning to you and a few others a design I have had for some years of printing a little library, perhaps fourscore or one hundred volumes, for the use of those that fear God. My purpose was to select whatever I had seen most valuable in the English language, and either abridge, or

take the whole tract, only a little corrected or explained, as occasion should require. Of these I could print 10 or 12, more or less, every year, on a fine paper, and large letter which should be cast for the purpose—As soon as I am able to purchase a printing press and types I think of entering on this design. I have several books now ready; and a printer whose desire is nothing more than food and raiment. In three or four weeks I hope to be in London, and if God permit to begin without delay.[4]

Work on the *Christian Library* began in 1749 and its first volumes contained material from the Early Church Fathers and extensive chronological accounts of the lives of exemplary Christians. Wesley prepared this in the face of an almost impossible workload snatching odd minutes here and there, often while travelling. Because of this there were generally few prefaces and introductions to his abridgements. However, there was an introduction to the rather large number of Puritan materials included in the library. Monk comments that this revealing preface provides us with his most extensive comment on the Puritans and their experiences.

> After an account of the lives, sufferings, and deaths of those holy men, who sealed the ancient religion with their blood, I believe nothing would either be more agreeable or profitable to the serious reader, than to add some extracts from the writings of those who sprung up, as it were, out of their ashes. These breathe the same spirit, and were, in a lower degree, partakers of the same sufferings. Many of them talk joyfully of a spoiling of their goods, and all had their names cast out as evil; being branded with the nickname of Puritans, and thereby made a byword and a proverb of reproach. I have endeavoured to rescue from obscurity a few of the most eminent of these: I say a few; for there is a multitude of them, which it would be tedious even to name. Nor have I attempted to abridge all the works of these few, for some of them are immensely voluminous. The works of Dr Goodwin alone would have sufficed to fill 50 volumes. I have therefore selected what I conceived would be of most general use, and most proper to form a complete body of Practical Divinity.[5]

The above statement clearly reveals Wesley's respect for the Puritans and their sufferings and states his reason for selecting their writings as being that they are pre-eminently works of practical Divinity. John A. Newton in his *Methodism and the Puritans* makes the following comments:

> Among those whose works he abridged were Robert Bolton, John Preston, Richard Sibbes, Thomas Goodwin, Thomas Manton, Isaac Ambrose, Nathaniel Culverwell, John Owen, Joseph Alleine, Samuel Rutherford, John Bunyan, Richard Baxter, John Flavel, Stephen Charnock, John Howe, and his own grandfather, Samuel Annesley.

It is an impressive list and shows that Wesley took very seriously the advice of Philip Doddridge, from whom he requested in 1746 a list of books of 'practical divinity' for his preachers to read. Five of the eight 'nonconformists of the last age', whose works Doddridge recommended, were duly included in the Christian Library, as well as Bolton and Sibbes from the six 'Puritans, and the Divines of the Separation'. Wesley read the history of the Puritans as well as their theology, and found himself moved to sympathy for non-conforming ministers of 1662.

As early as May 1739, he was reading Daniel Neal's recently published *History of the Puritans;* and he 'snatched a few hours' to dip into it again in 1747. He was amazed on this second reading, 'at the execrable spirit of persecution' which drove those venerable men out of the Church. By this date he had considerable experience of 'the execrable spirit of persecution' himself, and no doubt felt his kinship with the Puritans. Yet he was fair-minded and detached enough to be able to add a criticism of 'the weakness of those holy confessors, many of whom spent so much of their time and strength in disputing about surplices and goods, or kneeling at the Lord's Supper'.

So impressed was Wesley with Neal's work, that he included it among the textbooks for Kingswood School, so that the sons of his preachers should have some grounding in the history of the Puritan tradition. Some years later (1745), Wesley read another classic of Puritan history, Calamey's *Abridgement of Mr Baxter's Life*, and was forced to exclaim: 'What a scene is opened here! In spite of all the prejudices of education, I could not but see that the poor Nonconformists had been used without either justice or mercy; and that many of the Protestant Bishops of King

Charles had neither more religion, nor humanity, than the Popish Bishops of Queen Mary.'

Wesley's large scale republication of the great Puritan authors was a highly significant act. It was also symbolic of a comprehensive debt which the Methodists owed to the Puritans, a debt which may be summarised under the heads of Theology, Liturgy, Pastoralia, Family Piety and Ethics.[6]

Counting the authors that Wesley has included in the Christian Library, we see that authors in the Puritan tradition constituted the greatest part of the total, although a bare majority. Thirty-one are Puritan whereas twenty-nine are Church of England authors. Measuring the material by the volume of space taken up by Puritan writers we see that clearly these are in the majority. Monk reminds us that amongst those listed as Church of England men are some who displayed Puritan sympathies, even though they conformed to the Church of England in 1662. Archbishop Robert Leighton, the Scottish divine, would have qualified under Richard Baxter's classification as an 'old Presbyterian' who accepted real ordination while privately and knowingly understanding it in terms different from those of the officiating Bishop. Bishop Edward Reynolds who took part in both the Westminster Assembly and the Savoy Conference, was included. He conformed, evidently thinking that others would later join him, and accepted the Bishopric only after seeking the advice of Baxter, Calamy, and other Puritan leaders. Also included amongst the Anglicans were the Cambridge Platonists who were in general sympathy with the political aspirations of the Commonwealth, and were judged by the Westminster Assembly as 'fit to be fellows'. These differed at several major points with orthodox Puritanism but they shared the Puritan concern for vital personal religion displayed in everyday life. From this group Wesley included, Ralph Cudworth, Nathaniel Culverwell, John Smith, John Worthington, and Henry More.

One of Wesley's inclusions is of particular interest *i.e.* that of *The Westminster Shorter Catechism*. Here we might say, within the limits imposed upon it by its purpose, we have the major theological precepts of Puritanism set out. In the first place, the fact that Wesley saw fit to include it confirms the fact that he believed that 'the truth was within an hair's-breadth of Calvinism', and that he was a man within the great Reformation tradition.

Wesley's hostility to election and predestination are clearly seen however, in that he simply deletes all reference to them in the course of his abridgement. Likewise his belief that the doctrine of the Perseverance of the Saints tended towards antinomianism is seen in that he also dropped many of the references to this teaching in his *Christian Library* version. Monk highlights the fact that another important omission from Wesley's abridgement of *The Shorter Catechism* is in respect of its teaching concerning perfection.

> Question: Is any man able perfectly to keep the Commandments of God? No, but doth daily break them in thought, word and deed.
>
> The Westminster Divines, acknowledging the nature of sinfulness even in the elect, effectively rejected the possibility of perfection. Wesley no doubt believed that the catechism unduly limited God's grace that, in his understanding, could make a person perfect in love within one's earthly life.
>
> Wesley agreed with the framers of the catechism that sinfulness often remained in believers; but, at the same time, he insisted that God's grace could, even so, 'perfect' one's love. 'If love is the sole principle of action' and if the believer has 'the mind that was in Christ', all things are done in love. The perfect believer made 'mistakes' because of infirmities, ignorance, misjudgement, and so on, which are in fact morally imperfect; yet, because these are not contrary to perfect love, they are not 'sins.'
>
> For Wesley this meant that perfection was a possibility, through God's grace for every believer, although he never claimed to have received 'perfection' himself. Where the catechism denies the possibility of perfection Wesley, true to his own beliefs, had to change it.[7]

The issues of divine election of believers, the perseverance of the saints and the time and extent of human perfectibility are the issues that chiefly guided his expurgation and modification of Puritan material.

CHAPTER ELEVEN

JOHN WESLEY AND PURITAN THEOLOGY

Horton Davies, in his *English Free Churches,* comments:

> Methodist evangelical passion and experimental religion were a revival of Puritan religion.[1]

For John Wesley, religion could never be a mere formal assent to a set of doctrines or a system. As a younger man he had attempted to put himself right with God, through rigorous discipline, through a strict adherence to an ecclesiastical system, and miserably failed. Wesley sought for a heart religion and a personal relationship with God.

The Moravians pointed out to him his need of repentance and faith in Christ and this he found on 24th May 1738, when at a meeting in Aldersgate Street, London, as one was reading Luther's Preface to Paul's Epistle to the Romans, he felt his heart strangely warmed, and that he was trusting in Christ in Christ alone for salvation. Wesley wholeheartedly concurred with Bishop Joseph Hall when he wrote:

> There is nothing more easy, than to say divinity by rote—but to hear God speak it to the soul, and to feel the power of religion in ourselves, and to express it out of the truth of experience within, is both rare and hard—It will never be well with me—Till sound experience has really catechised my heart, and made me know God and my Saviour otherwise than by words.[2]

Richard Alleine described as a 'phanatick' the person who imagines he is a true Christian merely because he carries out the forms of religion in every detail.[3]

Wesley also recognised with the Puritans that there are dangers arising from a purely experiential religion. He, like them, recognised that experiential religion needs to be safeguarded by various checks and balances.

147

Emphasis upon the experimental nature of religion, particularly stress upon a personal inner relationship with God carries with it the danger of undercutting the authority of external form, practice, or tradition. Recognising this danger, Wesley accompanied his stress upon experiencing religion with an insistence that experience itself be tested by a variety of checks and balances. The truth about God taught in Scripture, the well tried doctrines formulated through tradition, the form of the Christian life as exemplified by other believers, and human reason itself all stood along with personal experience as authoritative criteria for the Christian life.

The Puritans were generally as anxious as Wesley to guard against the dangers of experimental religion without losing the thing itself—that real experience of God's love in the heart of the believer. More radical branches, particularly the Quakers, cast off the external authorities, insisting on the primacy of the Spirit. Most, however, affirmed that experience must be tested by other authorities. John Owen's *Exposition of the Doctrine of the Holy Spirit*, although written in another context, expresses his recognition of various 'authorities'. In the substance of what it delivered, I have the plain testimony of the Scripture, the suffrage of the ancient church, and the experience of them to sincerely believe and rest upon. For Wesley and the Puritans before him, external religious authorities were appropriated as a believer's own experience that kept them from being only irrelevant externals.'[4]

Essentially for both the Puritans and John Wesley, the test of genuine Christian experience was the infallible Scriptures.

1. Justification

What is emerging in our study of Wesley's doctrine is that in the essentials of the faith he is clearly in line with the great doctrines of the Reformation. In respect to the doctrine of original sin, Monk reminds us that Wesley's treatise on the subject was in part written as a defence of Isaac Watts' formulation of the doctrine.[5]

In the same treatise Wesley also draws extensively on John Howe's work, *The Living Temple*. In *The Christian Library*, Wesley includes several Puritan works on the subject of original sin *i.e.* Joseph Alleine's

An Alarm to the Unconverted (1662), Thomas Goodwin's *A Child of God Walking in Darkness* (1659), and John Flavel's, *Navigation Spiritualised, or A New Compass for Seamen* (1682). Monk adds:

> With the Puritans, Wesley offered a traditional Protestant understanding of humanity's original sinfulness, the human condition that called for salvation. He used their literature as a support of his own interpretation of this universal sin, even though this corollary doctrine of prevenient grace would have been rejected by most of them.[6]

The respected evangelical historian David G. Fountain, in his work on E.J.Poole-Conner, makes the following significant statement in regard to Poole-Conner's view of the theology of John Wesley.

> E.J.Poole-Connor quotes from Fletcher of Madeley, 'He (Wesley) is not an Arminian—for he constantly maintains that man is only free to do evil.' E.J.Poole-Connor used the word Methodist rather than Arminian, saying, 'Methodism does not share the Pelagian sympathies of Arminianism. It takes a darker view of original sin as more than a disease, as complete depravity. It attributes human freedom since the Fall not to any partial survival of original freedom, but to the direct prevenient grace of the Spirit of God in the individual soul. And it lays far greater stress upon definite conversion and regeneration as a necessary subjective experience for every man.'

It is also significant as Dr Fountain points out, that when drawing up the confession of faith of the original F.I.E.C., E.J.Poole-Connor was careful not to exclude the Wesleyan, but he did in fact exclude the Arminian. The relevant article includes the phrase:

> ...The utter depravity of human nature in consequence of the Fall and the necessity for regeneration.[7]

In the same way Wesley consistently expounded the necessity of faith as the one necessary condition of salvation also thereby putting him squarely within the Reformation tradition.[8]

Wesley was critical of the Church of England of his day for having preached, 'our holiness or good works, as the cause of our justification.'[9] He insisted that the Church of his day had moved away from the traditional Church of England doctrines as expounded in the *39 Articles* and *The Homilies.*

Scholars such as Albert Outler and Colin Williams expressed the consensus of much recent scholarship when they affirmed that Wesley's mature doctrine of salvation retained its Reformation base wherein justification and sanctification are both necessary and are both appropriated by faith through grace alone.[10]

At this point we may observe that Wesley's inclusion of Baxter's *Aphorisms of Justification* within *The Christian Library* seems largely to have been because of Baxter's attempt to guard the doctrines of free grace from the dangers of Antinomianism. Wesley recommends this book along with John Goodwin's *Treatise on Justification.*

There are several important strands to draw out here. One is of course to note that when John Goodwin wrote this thesis he was an avowed Calvinist; it was only in later life that he became an Arminian. Wesley was well aware of this and purposely quoted this work of Goodwin's in his controversy with the Calvinists over the true nature of Christ's imputed righteousness. As we have seen already, Wesley believed in the doctrine of Christ's imputed righteousness, though was constantly anxious to guard the doctrine from being used as a support for Antinomianism. In his preface to his abridgement of Goodwin's work he comments:

> Perhaps I should not have submitted, at least not so soon, to the importunity of my friends, who have long been soliciting me to abridge and publish the ensuing treatise had not some warm people published a tract, entitled, 'The Scripture Doctrine of Imputed Righteousness Defended,' by them judged it absolutely incumbent on me to publish the real Scripture doctrine. And this I believed I could not either draw up or defend better than I found it done to my hands by one who, at the time he wrote this book, was a firm and zealous Calvinist. This enabled him to confirm what he advanced by such authorities, as well from Calvin himself, as from his most eminent followers, as I could not have done, nor any who had not been long and critically versed in their writings.[11]

These instances are further proof that Wesley sought to identify his doctrine with that which he perceived to be that of the Reformers.

2. Assurance

Early in his ministry Wesley was willing to call the doctrine of assurance the 'main doctrine of the Methodists'. Later he affirmed:

—that this great evangelical truth has been recovered, which had been for many years well nigh lost and forgotten.[12]

Wesley was criticised and attacked for preaching this doctrine by his contemporary Church of England critics. Most of them only saw in it the danger of 'enthusiasm'. He was conscious also that in emphasising this doctrine he was walking in the steps of the Puritans. In response to critics of his position, in an open letter to the editor of *Lloyd's Evening Post* (December 20th, 1760), he replies:

You say: 'No Protestant divine ever taught your doctrine of Assurance.' I hope you know better; but it is strange you should not. Did you never see Bishop Hall's *Works*? Was not he a Protestant divine? Was not Mr Perkins, Bolton, Dr Sibbes, Dr Preston, Archbishop Leighton? Inquire a little further; and do not run thus hand over head, asserting you know not what. By assurance (if we must use the expression) I mean 'a confidence which a man hath in God that by the merits of Christ, his sins are forgiven and he is reconciled to the favour of God.'[13]

Monk further adds:

Wesley quite obviously believed that the doctrine of assurance he propounded was the same doctrine as had been taught by early Puritan divines as well as traditional Church of England representatives. In fact, in another letter he insisted that the doctrine was found among the early Reformers: 'Luther, Melanchthon, and many other (if not all) of the Reformers, frequently and strongly assert that every believer is conscious of his own acceptance with God, and that by a supernatural evidence.'

For Wesley the doctrine was not the 'property' of any Christian party or group. In his more elaborate defences of the doctrine against the charge of enthusiasm, he was concerned with showing that assurance was a legitimate part of the heritage of the Established Church. In *A Further Appeal to Men of Reason and Religion* (1745), and in the letters to Thomas Church (1746), and to Bishop Warburton (1762), extensive sections demonstrated the doctrine of assurance of adoption. These passages also suggested that one could find affirmation of an authentic witness of the Spirit among the teachings of the Church of England's most honoured representatives, particularly Bishop Pearson. He found the same doctrine in the church offices and sermons— particularly the Homilies. Even so, as this reference to the concept of a Presbyterian doctrine indicates, he was quite conscious the doctrine was strongly represented among the Puritans and that he found their presentation of it attractive.

With the exception of William Perkins (d.1602) all the 'Protestant divines' listed by Wesley in the passage just quoted were included in abridgements found in *The Christian Library*.[14]

Wesley's doctrine of assurance, however, differed from that of the Puritans in that they linked the doctrine of assurance with the doctrine of the final perseverance of the Saints. For them the doctrine of assurance was an assurance of eternal salvation. Wesley however spoke in terms of the assurance of 'present salvation'.

> For the Puritans the strength of present assurance was connected to the assurance of eternal salvation. Sibbes remarked: 'Our assurance is not only for the present, but for the time to come.' Perkins, chiefly concerned to distinguish true Christianity from that of the 'papists', normally interpreted assurance as that of eternal salvation, yet also emphasised the present element since the whole question revolved around whether a person might be 'certain of his own salvation' in this life'.[15]

These differences, however, should not allow us to miss the many similarities between Wesley's teaching on assurance and that of the Puritans. Together, they emphasised the personal experience of God, Wesley's conversion experience, 'my sins, even mine'. Together, they were well aware of the place of doubt, recognising that there were times when even the most faithful believer doubted his state of grace. Both the Puritans and John Wesley emphasised the necessity of assurance. Both also distinguish between two types of witness, that is the direct and the indirect witness. Wesley agreed with John Owen's statement:

The Spirit worketh—immediately by himself, without the imposition of any reasonings, or deductions and conclusions— he immediately works the minds of men to a rejoicing and spiritual frame, filling them with exaltation and gladness; not that this arises from our reflex consideration of the love of God, but rather gives occasion thereunto.[16]

Monk concludes:

Was Wesley correct in finding that his doctrine of assurance was the same as that taught among Puritans? Unquestionably a large measure of similarity is present between Wesley's presentation and that of the Puritan divines. In a sense Wesley's exposition of the doctrine places him midway between the Puritans, who, insisting on the Spirit's witness, often implied, as a corollary, assurance of eternal salvation, and his contemporary Church of England colleagues who rejected the reality of all witness because it might imply 'enthusiasm' and a firm assurance of eternal salvation. Wesley retained the important reality of the witness without necessarily implying eternal salvation.

At the same time, with the Puritans, he guarded against enthusiasm and presumption through joining the necessity of 'the witness of our own spirits', dependent upon fruits of the Spirit, with the witness of the Holy Spirit. Identification does not entail exact correspondence, and Wesley's doctrine does diverge at some points from that of the Puritans; nevertheless, identification of much of Wesley's presentation with that of exemplary Puritans may be sustained. Wesley clearly saw that what he pointed to, personal consciousness of salvation, which gives vitality and meaning to present life, was also affirmed by those of the Puritan tradition. This doctrine, a significant cornerstone in their affinity, points towards additional areas of relationship between Wesley and the Puritans.[17]

3. Covenant Theology

Using the Old Testament as a pattern Christians have traditionally seen Christ as a New Covenant of God's unchanging love and presence. A resurgent interest and emphasis on Covenant Theology seems to have come into prominence again during the 16th century, in the theologies of Zwingli, Oecolampadius, Bucer, Peter Martyr, and others. Covenant Theology, or as it came to be popularly recognised as 'Federal Theology', was a prominent feature of the Reformed churches. As early as the 1530s in England it found expression in the writings of William Tyndale and John Frith.

> In these works the covenant expressed the divine side of the relationship by seeing God's steadfast love as both a promise and a binding of God's mercy to the believer. On the believer's side love was appropriated through personal commitment and responsible living. It was then conditional; it depended on the believer's continuing faithfulness to the Gospel teachings.[18]

In the century following, Covenant Theology also became one of the central Puritan teachings. John Preston called it the point of 'greatest moment that a minister has to preach to his flock.'[19]

> Perry Miller suggests that the Puritan understanding of the covenant was an 'extension' of what Orthodox Calvinism implied. It preserves the sovereignty of God by retaining his unmerited initiative in salvation and, at the same time, provides a rationale for man's obligation in terms of faith and moral duty. (Perry Miller, *The New England Mind: The Seventeenth Century.* New York. Macmillan. 1939. p.367.) Faith and duty towards God in this interpretation are grounded in God's covenant promise, not human cooperation. It is this Calvinistic pattern of the covenant that becomes the dominant, though not exclusive, Puritan expression.[20]

In John Wesley's *Works*[21], in answer to critics of his teaching on the doctrine of assurance, he stated that his doctrine of assurance was the same as that taught by the early Puritans. One of those early Puritans cited was William Perkins. Here we might remember that Perkins had a considerable influence in regard to the teaching of Covenant Theology in the English Church. Perkins was a non-separating Puritan, on the one hand influenced by the high Calvinistic and speculative theology of Theodore Beza but also by the practical theology of Pierre de la Ramus (1515-1572), who at that time was lecturer at Cambridge. In his work *A Golden Chain or The Description of Theology* (London, 1591), he calls Scripture 'A teaching sufficient to live well'. Perkins followed a theology of usefulness. His aim was to bring the practical rather than the theoretical out of theology. He was committed to making the Bible's teaching and theology useful to mankind. The writings of Perkins were carried in the *Mayflower* and it is said that from these the American colonists drew their virtues of industry and thrift.

Whether or not Wesley read Perkin's writings on Covenant Theology is not known. However, these same principles were characteristic of Puritan teaching in general and it is known that Wesley drew on these writings. An emphasis on the practical out-workings of the Christian life and a total rejection of Antinomianism was one of the chief characteristics of Wesley's ministry.

> Wesley saw in this covenantal insistence upon the necessity of works issuing from faith an antidote to antinomianism. He also insisted one was bound to obey the commandments 'under the covenant of grace, though not in order to his justification'.[22]

John Preston's *The New Covenant* or *The Saint's Portion* was edited and published by Wesley in *The Christian Library*. Preston, as in line with all covenant theologians, emphasised the Reformation principle of salvation through divine grace alone rather than good works. As Monk points out by the 1580s, a 'double covenant' theory had emerged, a covenant of grace and a covenant of works. Preston expressed this as follows:

> The Covenant of Works runs in these terms, Do this and thou shalt live, and I will be thy God. This is the covenant that was made with Adam (in paradise) and the covenant that is expressed by Moses in the moral law, Do this, and live. The second is the Covenant of Grace, and that runs in these terms. Thou shalt believe, thou shalt take my Son for thy Lord, and Saviour, and thou shalt likewise receive an absolution for thy sins, for a reconciliation with me, and therefore thou shalt grow up in love and obedience toward me, then I will be thy God and thou shalt be my people.[23]

Monk further reminds us that Wesley's agreement with the chief lines of Preston's exposition of Covenant Theology is evidenced by his sermon on *The Righteousness of Faith*.

Wesley differed, however, from the main-line Puritan position in that, while he also recognised two covenants, that is the Covenant of

Works and the Covenant of Grace, he rejected the idea of a Covenant of Redemption; in this the Reformed theologians taught that God the Son entered into a covenant with God the Father in eternity past to the end that he would undertake to save the elect. Wesley commented:

> I have heard of another covenant which I understand not. I have heard 'That God the Father made a covenant with His Son before the world began, wherein the Son agreed to suffer such and such things, and the Father to give Him such and such souls for a recompense; that in consequence of this, those souls must be saved, and those only so that all others must be damned'. I beseech you, where is this written? In what part of Scripture is this covenant to be found? We may well expect a thing of this moment to be revealed very expressly, with the utmost clearness and solemnity. But where is this done? And if it is not done, if there is no such account in all the Bible; which shall we wonder at most, that any serious man should advance, or that thousands should believe so strange an assertion without one plain text of Scripture to support it, from Genesis to the Revelation?[24]

Mention must also be made, of course, of Wesley's use of the concept of the Covenant in the Methodist Annual Covenant Service. John A. Newton comments:

> In liturgy and worship, Methodism's main debt to the Puritans is embodied in Wesley's use of extempore prayer and preaching, in the inspiration and example of Watts' hymns and in the Covenant Service which derive from the writings of Richard Alleine. The Covenant was central to Puritan theology and basic to any understanding of the church as the elect people of God. In Puritan piety, however, to renew one's covenant was primarily an act of individual devotion. Wesley, while retaining a searchingly personal reference in his service, transformed the renewal of the covenant into a corporate act of the worshipping community. The service focused the societary nature of Methodism, its concern for Christian Fellowship and its earnest seeking after holiness. Finally, in this field of liturgy, Wesley was guided in his adaptation of the Prayer Book Services for the use of the American Methodist by the suggestion for revision put forward by the Presbyterians at the Savoy Conference in 1661.[25]

Wesley records the institution of the Covenant Service in his *Short History of the People called Methodists* as follows:

> August 6, 1755, I mentioned to our congregation in London a means of increasing serious religion, which had been frequently practised by our forefathers,—the joining in the covenant to serve God with all our heart, and with all our soul. I explained this for several mornings following: and on Friday many of us kept a fast unto the Lord; beseeching him to give us wisdom and strength, that we might 'promise unto the Lord our God, and keep it'. On Monday, at six in the evening, we met for that purpose at the French church in Spitalfields. After I had recited the tenor of the covenant proposed, in the words of that blessed man, Richard Alleine, all the people stood up, in token of assent, to the number of about eighteen hundred. Such a night I scarce ever knew before. Surely the fruit of it shall remain for ever.[26]

4. Sanctification and Perfection

Like the Puritans before him Wesley was intensely interested in the process of sanctification. For both, the relationship with God entered into through faith in Christ, stood for little if it did not take in the constant transforming presence of the Holy Spirit in the believer's life. Monk comments:

> The significant truth contained in the doctrine of sanctification was never lost in those branches of Protestantism most insistent on the priority and domination of justification by faith. The Reformed tradition consistently retained the distinction between justification and sanctification without losing the vitality of either. The English Reformation, in all its branches, understood sanctification as a core component of the Faith, so the sanctified, holy life was constantly emphasized and taught. Both Puritans and Wesley, in accenting this doctrine, typified the mainstream of their joint heritage. The parallels between the two traditions are most obvious in their elaborate instructions for Christian living, yet these arose out of their emphasis on sanctification and their understanding of the doctrine itself.
>
> For the Puritans and Wesley, sanctification was grounded on faith and not on human merit—to give it any other base would

be to reinstate salvation through an order of merit. John Owen declared, 'Faith is the instrumental cause of our sanctification; so that, where it is not, no holiness can be wrought in us. It is from faith in God through Jesus Christ, acting itself in obedience unto the Gospel, that we purify or cleanse our soul, which is our sanctification.' (*Concerning the Holy Spirit*, Works of John Owen, Vol. 2. p.488.) Robert Bolton's *The Saints Self Enriching Examination*, affirmed, 'Saving faith is the root and fountain of sanctification.' (London: printed by Anne Griffin for Rapha Harford 1634, p.132.) The similarity of Wesley's position and his clarity on this feature of the doctrine is seen in his sermon 'The Scriptural Way of Salvation'.

Faith is the condition, and the only condition of our sanctification, exactly as is justification. It is the condition; none is sanctified but he that believes; without faith no man is sanctified. And it is the only condition; whatever else he has or has not. In other words, no man is sanctified till he believes; every man, when he believes, is sanctified.[27]

It is at this point that we must radically differ from the view held by George Croft Cell and W. E. Sangster. W. E. Sangster comments:

Dr Cell, has called Wesley's doctrine, 'an original and unique synthesis of the Protestant ethic of grace with the Catholic ethic of holiness,' and we feel, with Dr Umphrey Lee, that this is 'a wise and just observation'.[28]

Cell believed that Wesley had established:

A necessary synthesis of the Protestant ethic of grace with the Catholic ethic of holiness. He has not deviated a hair's breadth from the Luther-Calvin doctrine of sin and salvation by faith. But he has joined with this, substituting it for the Predestinarianism of Luther and Calvin, the Catholic appreciation of the progressive imitation of Christ as the concrete meaning of Christian Perfection. The Wesleyan synthesis indicates therefore a more just appreciation of the whole human response to a realisation of the truth values of the Christian faith.[29]

Monk, quoting Colin Wilson, mounts an irrefutable challenge to this view when he says:

If it were true that Wesley accepted a Catholic doctrine of holiness, he must accept its essential elements: the ability of man, with the help of grace, to rise in a 'ladder of merit' and to reach the goal or level of perfection. In the case of general sanctification a believer would be able and required to reach a certain moral level before he or she could be saved. (In order to assure the possibility of this, the concept of purgatory had become an integral part of the system.) To accept these components of the doctrine, required one to accept the corollary doctrine of grace; grace becomes essentially a helpmate to the natural ability of humanity. Wesley rejected these concepts, insisting that no merit is required or possible for believers; that salvation is a free gift of God without consideration of a standard or level of holiness. In doing this he not only affirmed a Protestant doctrine of grace but also a Protestant doctrine of sanctification wherein sanctification is, like justification, dependent on God's unwarranted grace appropriated by humans through faith.[30]

Because the fact that Wesley was in the main line of Reformation teaching is so crucial an element in the understanding of his theology I give Colin William's quotation in full:

> The judgment of Cell and others is subject to real question. We have seen that the Catholic goal of perfection kept man tied to the order of merit and was held within the framework of the ladder of ascent, but we must also remember that the Catholic goal depended entirely upon grace. The difference of the semi-Pelagianism of Rome from the Protestant view does not lie in the extent of dependence upon grace. The difference lies in the fact that the Catholic doctrine sees man as enabled by grace to rise up the ladder of merit, and at last, justified by works by virtue of the proper use of God's grace, to reach the goal of perfection. To faith, which is the means for entrance into the Christian life, must be added the works made possible by grace through which perfection is reached. Because man must merit his salvation by reaching the required standard of holiness, purgatory is necessary in order to enable believers who have not reached the required standard to complete the process.
>   This Catholic view of holiness cannot be moulded onto the Protestant view of grace. In the Protestant view grace is the free

gift of God, and man can never merit his salvation. Purgatory is removed for the simple reason that man's salvation is not dependent on his reaching a required standard of ethical achievement but is the gift of God's free grace to be received by grace alone. If it is true that Wesley accepted the Catholic ethic of holiness, it must also be true that he accepted the Catholic and abandoned the Protestant view of grace.

In our examination of Wesley's doctrine of justification, however, we have seen that while he placed greater emphasis than the Reformers upon the transformation that should attend the faith relationship with Christ, he still remained within Protestant categories. The 'holiness without which no man shall see the Lord' of which Wesley speaks, is not a holiness that is judged by objective moral standards, but a holiness in terms of unbroken relationship to Christ the Holy One. The perfect Christian is holy, not because he has risen to a required moral standard, but because he lives in this state of unbroken fellowship with Christ.

Wesley's view is one of sanctification by faith alone. In other words, Wesley put his doctrine within the Protestant framework of justification by faith, not within the Roman framework of justification by faith and works. He put it within the order of personal relationship to Christ, not within the order of a legal relationship to a moral standard.[31]

We might also quote from the esteemed Methodist scholar, Gordon Rupp, in emphasising this point:

> The Methodist Gospel has a shape and coherence—It has sometimes been explained by saying that John Wesley combined the Protestant teaching of justification by faith with the Catholic concept of holiness. I do not find this an enlightening statement at all. In England it is almost always made by people slightly ashamed of Protestantism and I do not think it bears close inspection. What he had to say about holiness was bound together with what he believed about justification by faith. From beginning to end John Wesley believed and preached justification by faith only. Nevertheless it is true, as he put it, that holiness was his point. For him a Pauline doctrine of justification was closely linked with the Epistles of John and the doctrine of love.[32]

Wesley's doctrine of sanctification was entirely consistent with that of the Reformers and Puritans in that he saw it as a gradual and life-long process. His recognition of the importance of a gradual progressive work and the believer's own task in cultivating that work was evidenced in his comments to his brother Charles in 1776 when he said:

> Go on, in your own way, to what God has peculiarly called you to. Press the instantaneous blessing: then I shall have more time for my peculiar calling, enforcing a gradual work.[33]

The gradual or progressive work of sanctification in the life of the believer was a constant emphasis of the Puritans. John Owen says, for example:

> This work of sanctification differs from that of regeneration.— The work of regeneration is instantaneous, consisting in one single creating act. Hence it is not capable of degrees in any subject. No one is more or less regenerate than another; everyone in the world is absolutely so, or not so, and that equally, although there are degrees in their state on other reasons. But this work of sanctification is progressive, and admits of degrees. One may be more sanctified and more holy than another, who is yet truly sanctified and truly holy. It is begun at once, and carried on gradually. An increase and growth in sanctification or holiness is frequently in the Scripture enjoined to us, and frequently promised unto us.[34]

Owen goes on to describe how God's effectual grace calls forth our diligent obedience. 'It is God who worketh in us in order that we will work and act in accordance with his good pleasure.' Again the same teaching can be found in Wesley by examining several of his early sermons, *i.e.* 'The Circumcision of the Heart'(1733), 'On Grieving the Holy Spirit'(1733), and 'On the Holy Spirit'(1736).

> We are convinced, that we are not sufficient of ourselves to help ourselves; that, without the Spirit of God, we can do nothing but add sin to sin; that it is he alone who 'worketh in us' by his almighty power, either 'to will or do' that which is good—it being as impossible for us even to think a good thought, without the

supernatural assistance of his Spirit, as to create ourselves, or
to renew our whole souls in righteousness and true holiness.[35]

Or,

As all merit is in the Son of God—So all power is in the Spirit of
God;—all true faith and the whole work of salvation, every good
thought, word, and work, is altogether by the operation of the
Spirit of God.[36]

Although we see Wesley clearly in the Reformed and Puritan
tradition in regard to the doctrine of sanctification, we must
acknowledge his teaching in regard to the possibility of an
instantaneous 'present and entire sanctification' in this life, would
have been rejected by most Puritans. The Puritans taught that
holiness could not be consummated within this life. Entire
sanctification came only at or after death.

Monk and others have pointed out that there were some amongst
the Puritans who taught the doctrine of perfection of 'intent', or
'sincerity of heart', which may fruitfully be compared to Wesley's
own doctrine. Gordon Wakefield in his *Puritan Devotion* notes
William Dell as teaching, a doctrine of perfection, and others, such
as Richard Greenham, leaning towards this doctrine, without
affirming 'absolute unspottedness in this life'.

Albeit to that of perfection which the Scripture taketh for
soundness, truth, and sincerity of heart, which is void of careless
remissness we may come.[37]

Gordon Wakefield finds elements of perfectionism in John Preston's
The New Covenant included by Wesley in *The Christian Library*.

Preston expounds the Word of God to Abraham which the Geneva
Bible renders: 'I am God all sufficient; walk before me and be
thou perfect.' He says, 'every man is more or less perfect as he is
more or less persuaded of God's all sufficiency,' and after a
lengthy exposition of the similitude between the Christian's life
and a journey on foot, which occupies almost a whole sermon,
he comes to his next main point: 'whosoever hath an interest in
God's all sufficiency, must be a perfect man.' Perfection is in
integrity of heart, says Preston, and can exist along with those

infirmities which are an inevitable part of our humanity. Otherwise the second Adam would be less powerful to instil grace than the first to communicate sin, and the work of God in the new creation would come short of that in the beginning, when the Lord looked on everything that he had made, and behold it was very good. We dare not limit the redemption wrought by Christ. Preston recognizes that there are degrees of perfection: 'there is a perfection of the bud and a perfection of the flower'. This is a favourite metaphor of expositors of Wesley, and is paralleled in Preston's words: 'So this is true of the works of redemption, of the works of God in a man's heart of destroying the works of Satan, and setting up a new building, which is the work of Jesus Christ, and the end, for which he came; I say this is true of it, it is perfect, it wants only growth: As, you may say, it is a perfect seed, when it is ripe it will be a perfect flower; for it is a perfect plant, when it grows up, it will be a perfect tree, it is perfect in all respects. Such a perfection is in the works of Redemption, and, if the heart of man be not entire, and the work of grace be not throughout, if there be a defect in the principle, and constitution of it, there should be a defect in the works of Redemption, which indeed cannot be.[38]

According to Preston, Romans 7 could be the experience of a perfect man:

A sheep may fall into the mire as soon as a swine, for the commission of sin, and so likewise for the omission of duties; an apple tree may have a fit of barrenness and unfruitfulness, as well as a crab tree, or any other, but the difference is great in the manner of them as we shewed: but still the main difference is to be remembered, that he that hath a perfect heart, is still cleansing and purifying himself; the other do not that, but so fall back to sin, that they wallow in it, as a swine doth in the mire.[39]

At this point it will be useful to have before us Wesley's definition of Christian Perfection, as set out in his work, *A Plain Account of Christian Perfection*.

They are not perfect in knowledge. They are not free from ignorance, no, nor from mistake. We are no more to expect any living man to be infallible than to be omniscient. They are not free from...... infirmities, such as weakness or slowness of understanding, irregular quickness or heaviness of imagination. Such in another kind are impropriety of language, ungracefulness of pronunciation; to which one might add a thousand nameless defects, either in conversation or behaviour. From such infirmities as these none are perfectly freed till their spirits return to God; neither can we expect till then to be wholly freed from temptation; for 'the servant is not above his master'. But neither in this sense is there any absolute perfection on earth. There is no perfection of degrees, none which does not admit of a continual increase.

Wesley indeed has, like Preston, a perfection that is imperfect. Monk sums up this subject as follows:

> One may question whether Wesley had really moved beyond what Preston was attempting to formulate in his presentation of the doctrine. Without affirming complete moral perfection, Preston recognises a perfection of personal commitment that produces love and service and goes beyond occasional moral failures. That he called these failures sins, and Wesley did not consider himself obliged to do so, is not of major consequence. Both were concerned with an overarching perfection of the whole person, a perfection that becomes the motivating force of one's personality and that discounts occasional failures. Neither could accept a perfection of degree which failed to demand continual increase. Thus, although Wesley's perfection was a present possibility, it still had to improve or increase in love, just as Preston demanded a constant increase in love. Preston's concept of perfection, on the other hand, certainly allowed some sense of present perfection by his concentration on purity of intention of dedication present at any moment in the believer.
>
> Both authors sought a very similar, if not identical, end product—a pure, perfect, or sound heart in the believer, a desired end is not perfect obedience to a standard of conduct; it is perfect conformity to a model of divine orientated virtue. Being restored in the image of God is basic to the whole process. The same sense of value could equally be applied to Preston's formulation.
>
> The following passage exemplifies how close Wesley's concept corresponded to Preston's interpretation of the essence of a perfected

heart. As can be seen, Wesley cut the passage extensively but retained the core of the message. The passage vividly illustrates how Preston conceived what Wesley termed 'humanities corruptible infirmities' and their place in the life of the perfected person.

'Now what is it to be pure? That which is pure is full of itself, and has no other hetero genial thing mingled with it; so, that heart is pure, which hath no sin in it, which is holy, which hath a renewed quality of grace, which hath an inward regenerate man, that which will mingle with no sin, that is full of itself and admits not the mixture of any sin. My beloved, I must be warily understood, here I say, it admits not the mixture of any sin. It is true, sin may cleave, and adhere to man, as dross doth to the silver, but it mingles not with the regenerative part, nor that constitution of a man's heart, it is not weaved into the texture of his heart; it is no ingredient of the very frame and fabric of it, but though sin be here, yet the heart still casts it out of itself, it resists it, and rejects it, and purifieth and cleanseth itself from it; this is properly a pure heart.'[40]

To conclude, whilst it is going too far to say that Wesley's doctrine of entire sanctification or perfection, was wholly drawn from Puritan sources, notably Preston's, nevertheless it needs to be acknowledged that this teaching was something not wholly different from one section, though a minority section, of Puritan teachers.

We might also add at this point that Wesley's emphasis upon the goal of the Christian life being the pursuit of perfection is, when considered dispassionately, perfectly at one with the spirit of Calvinism. Dean Inge wrote of Calvinism:

The consciousness of election to salvation, instead of producing a paralysing fatalism, inspired a vigorous and confident energy—The elect is a chosen vessel in God's hands; his life is given him for a definite purpose. A strong and steady self-control, extending over the whole of life, is practised. Perfection is not an ideal for the few; it is an end which all the elect are bound to pursue. It is often brought against Calvinism that it is a brutal and prosaic creed, hostile to beauty, and art. This is really not true. Calvin was a Humanist and a fine scholar, and the Puritan was often a student, a connoisseur of art, an accomplished musician. A good example of the Puritan home is that of the Milton family. John Milton's father was a musician, who often regaled his family with madrigals of his own composing. The boy John sat up till midnight studying Greek, Latin, French, and Italian. Colonel Hutchison, the regicide, was a lover of the arts, a collector, and a musician. The Puritan dressed plainly, but well and carefully; they were very cleanly in their persons, more so than their opponents. Their dislike of ornament and symbolism in divine worship was due to their fear that the doctrines which they wished to exclude might be so reintroduced.

In Beard's words: 'It was the form of faith in the strength of which the Dutch Republic was sustained and the American Republic was founded; to propagate which Tyndale gave to the English people the Bible in their own tongue, and with it his life; which formed the Royal intellect of Cromwell, and inspired the majestic words of Milton.'[41]

Wesley's whole character and desire to live life to the glory of God, fits well into the above description and I believe proves the point that his emphasis on Christian perfection was not alien to the fundamental spirit of Reformation Calvinism.

Other considerations can be touched upon, indicating that Wesley's teaching in this area was not so far removed from the Reformed position as is often asserted. For example, Wesley spoke of sanctification being 'by faith'. It is sometimes asserted that this was a radical departure from Reformed teaching. David Bebbington, in his book *Holiness in 19th-century England*, states:

> There was a sharp contrast with the Reformed tradition, according to which unremitting effort was called for. Holiness, in the teaching of Calvinists such as Fuller, could be achieved only by dint of regular deeds that hardened into godly habits.[42]

However, the following quotation from an address given by Dr Moody Stewart at the close of the 1875 General Assembly of the Free Church of Scotland, entitled *Higher Holiness*, shows a position clearly within the Reformed tradition referring to the part of faith in sanctification not that dissimilar from Wesley's position and actually quoting from Wesley to illustrate the point:

> The means of attaining holiness—In the way of acquiring holiness, its attainment by faith has been spoken of as if it was

a new discovery, and also as if a man was sanctified by faith alone in the same sense in which he is justified by faith alone. It is true that many who look to Christ alone for their justification, have been looking partly to themselves for their sanctification; but this obliquity of view springs from a defective sight of justifying righteousness. Sin has no condemnation because we are not under the law, but under grace; and sin has no dominion because we are not under the law, but under grace; and according to our apprehension of free grace and our apprehension and experience of sin's no condemnation and sin's no dominion. In our Shorter Catechism, with its wondrous fullness and precision throughout, while our effectual calling is defined as the work of God's Spirit, our sanctification is described as a 'work of God's free grace', exactly as justification is an 'act' of the same free grace; not thereby setting aside the Spirit's work, but bringing out the great truth that sanctification comes from grace, and if from grace in God then through faith in us, for 'therefore it is of faith that it might be by grace'.

Practically it has brought a bright surprise to most believers when they have found that with the pardon of sin through the blood of Christ there has been the victory over it through the same grace that forgave it. But we are not sanctified at once as we are justified; we are never exhorted to perfect our justification, as we are called to be 'perfect in holiness'; and while sanctification is unto faith and never apart from it, it is likewise through trials, through mercies, through temptations, through deliverances; and in it we work out our own salvation, because God worketh in us to will and to do of his good pleasure.

But knowing these things, how far short we fall in doing them; with how little confidence we can say to our flocks, 'Be ye followers of me, even as I also am of Christ?' What a treasure of unused holiness is mine, is yours, in Christ; there for us, there possessed by us; but how guiltily content we are to have it in Christ, instead of drawing it out of his fullness as grace for grace to ourselves. We receive holiness by faith, but we obtain it also by intensity of prayer, of which Coleridge says most truly, that 'to pray with all the heart and strength, with the reason and the will—prayer with the whole soul—is the highest energy of which the human heart is capable'; and it is at the same time the most fruitful. If we prayed for holiness as for our very life we should find it above all our asking and thinking.

We obtain it, further, by solemn and unreserved dedication of ourselves to God in Christ, which with our fathers frequently took the form of a written personal covenant with God. Oh, that we did one and all, by the mercies of God, present our bodies, our entire persons, a living sacrifice, that so we may prove in ourselves, in our own hearts and lives, 'what is that good and acceptable and perfect will of God.'

But along with faith and prayer and self surrender, there are daily lessons to be learned in detail by us all. Our Lord Jesus Christ would himself live over again in the world in the person of each one of you, and in the place where he has planted each as his own representative in the earth. In the Marriage of the Lamb, the Bride will come to him washed in his own blood and clothed with his own righteousness; and also 'in raiment of needlework' wrought out through her own hands by God working in her to will and to do; in a clothing minutely beautiful as by the million-fold puncture of the needle—'stitch, stitch, stitch'—till her patient continuance in well doing is crowned with glory, honour, and immortality. In this trying, humbling, yet most glorious process, the soul is helped by all kinds of detail, such as are found in Thomas à Kempis: 'How littlesoever the thing may be, if it be inordinately loved and regarded, it defiles the soul and keeps it back from the supreme good. No man is safe to speak but he that willingly holds his peace. What thou art thou art; nor is it any use to thee to be accounted greater than what thou art in the sight of God.'

Or again, in the words of John Wesley, 'It is hardly credible how strait the way is, and of what great consequence before God the smallest things are. As a very little dust will disorder a clock, and the least grain of sand will obscure our sight, so the least grain of sin which is upon the heart will hinder its right motion toward God. And as the most dangerous winds may enter at little openings, so the devil never enters more dangerously than by little unobserved incidents, which seem to be nothing, yet insensibly open the heart to great temptations.'[43]

5. 19ᵗʰ Century changes to Wesley's doctrine of sanctification and perfection

There were substantial changes to Wesley's teaching on perfection and sanctification towards the middle period of the 19th-century. The first significant modifications came through the ministry of James Caughey, an American revivalist, who toured England four times between 1841 and the mid 1860s.

Caughey was a Northern Irishman of 'Scotch ancestry' whose family emigrated to the United States and settled in the district of Newburgh, New York. Historically, Caughey has languished in the shadows of the well-known revivalist Charles G. Finney, who preceded him in the first part of the century, and Dwight L. Moody who succeeded him in the latter. Nevertheless Caughey was an important figure in the history of revivalism in the USA and Britain.

Significantly he arrived in Britain at the time of the agitation within the denomination that finally resulted in the formation of a United Methodist Free Church. He took the side of ministers such as James Everett who was seeking to see old Methodism revived with new energy. Richard Carwardine in his *Transatlantic Revivalism*, perceptively observes that; 'there was more to Caughey than is suggested by this atavistic (reversion to original type) interpretation.' Though the large gatherings and excitement caused by Caughey's meetings echoed something of the early days of Methodism, what was not initially perceived by all was that Caughey was introducing a man-centred understanding of the traditional Wesleyan doctrine of sanctification.

Methodists were at this time engaged in a debate over means and human instrumentality that corresponded closely to the instrumentalist debate in contemporary Calvinism. Although their views on human ability were in theory more generous than the Calvinists, Methodist theology did not give man *carte blanche* over means. During the 1830s protracted meetings and penitent benches caught the imaginations of experimenters, and the incidence of 'special services' spiralled upward in the early and mid 1840s.

Caughey arrived in Britain when the more cautious Methodists were afraid that these new techniques savoured of 'getting up' a revival and undervalued the regular means. His holding of daily services for months on end condemned him on both counts. Though the revival prayer meetings of the late 18th and early 19th centuries have often gone on until the early hours of the morning for several days without cessation, they had been extended and repeated on an ad hoc basis, after the request of congregations that felt spiritually starved: sometimes in Branwell's meetings 'the enthusiasm excited was so great that the people would not go home'. Dow, one of the leaders of the Primitive Methodists arrangements, was notoriously impromptu.

Caughey's meetings, in contrast, were premeditated, part of a preconceived campaign to stir a religious awakening, more or less without regard to the initial receptiveness of the audience. Other elements of calculation and contrivance in Caughey's meetings: penitent benches, particularising in sermons, and repeated use of the same text came under similar attack, though the additional charges that he planted 'decoy penitents' at the front, to encourage the shy penitents to come forward, and that he deliberately regulated the interior lighting for dramatic effect were probably unfounded.

Under attack Caughey was unflinching. But despite his emphasis on prayer, it was difficult for him to escape the charge of revivalistic engineering; when, infrequently, he tried to adopt a non-instrumentalist explanation of revival as simply God-given, the argument rang hollow.[44]

Credit here is due to Jabez Bunting who, when it was pointed out to him by one of the preachers that Caughey's ministry was a danger to 'the credit of religion and the welfare of Methodism', led the Conference to exclude him. Under Caughey's type of preaching in the States, he was informed:

That the same people are converted again and again; and that if all the announced conversions could be found, the entire population of the States would be converted in four years; that they proceeded in this 'converting' work, as deliberately and mechanically, as a builder to raise a house: and nowhere is true and fervent and established piety more scarce, than when these proceedings are most frequent.[45]

Bebbington comments that;

Just as Finney remodelled the Calvinistic tradition in radical Enlightenment terms in order to maximise 'conversions', so Caughey remoulded the Wesleyan tradition. It was crucial, he believed, to encourage as many people as possible to enter the experience of sanctification.[46]

Caughey altered the traditional teaching in several respects.

Firstly, in that he declared that there was no need to wait to be sanctified, the previous norm of agonised wrestling towards experience was superseded.

Secondly, there was no need for any confirming awareness of having received the experience. Now the deliberate act of believing was enough to guarantee that holiness of heart had come. It was, as Caughey himself stated, a matter of, 'naked faith, stripped of all feeling.'[47] He further stated that, since long seeking and spiritual confirmation were no longer necessary, purity of heart need no longer be confined to a small number of enlightened souls, but was available to the multitudes on request.

A further area of consideration also needs to be raised at this point. That is a belief in some form of 'second blessing' held to by some within the Reformed tradition. Dr Martyn Lloyd-Jones comes to mind, and it is significant that he was brought up within Welsh Calvinistic Methodism. Although Dr. Lloyd Jones made it very clear that he believed the sealing of the Spirit to be an experience subsequent to conversion, he said that this sealing had nothing to do with sanctification.[48] He described it as:

> The Spirit of adoption, the Spirit of sonship; not the fact that we are sons, but our realisation of it; in other words this sealing is that direct assurance which the Holy Spirit gives us of our relationship to God in Jesus Christ.
>
> We have already seen that there are two other types of assurance which are good and excellent as far as they go—the assurance gained from the objective argument based on statements in Scripture and also the more subjective grounds of assurance deduced from the so-called tests of life found in the First Epistle of John. But it is possible for us to know that we have an assurance beyond that, namely, that which is given by this sealing of the Spirit. 'The Spirit himself testifieth with our

Spirit that we are the children of God.' Rom 8:16. This is a direct and immediate testimony borne by the Holy Spirit to us. It is no longer something which I reason out of the Scriptures; it is not the result of spiritual logic or deduction; it is direct and immediate. It does not mean that we hear any audible voice, or that we see some vision. Generally it comes as the result of the Spirit illuminating certain statements of Scripture, certain promises, certain assurances. He brings them to me with power and they speak to me, and I'm certain of them. These things become luminously clear to me and I am as certain that I am a child of God as that I am alive. This is something which happens to us in such a manner that we not only believe in general that all who are Christians are children of God, but the Holy Spirit tells me in particular that I am a child of God.

Dr Lloyd Jones goes on to quote John Wesley himself in relation to this:

'It is something immediate and direct, not the result of reflection or argumentation. There may be foretastes of joy, of peace, of love, and those not delusive, but really from God, long before we have the witness in ourselves.'
According to Wesley's teaching you can be a good Christian, and you could have experienced the operations of the Spirit in many ways, even including foretastes of joy and peace and of love from God himself, long before you have this direct witness of the Spirit, this overwhelming experience.[49]

I appreciate that a great deal more research would necessarily need to be done on this particular subject but this is outside the purpose of this book. My point here is merely that belief in some form of special visitation of the Spirit of God after conversion, has been held by some within the Reformed tradition, (though not my own personal view) and therefore belief in such an experience does not necessarily put one outside the pale of the Reformed tradition.

I also include here a helpful note by Benjamin Field, the respected 19th-century Methodist theologian, showing the difference between Wesley's teaching on Christian perfection and other perfectionist teachers:

1. The Perfectionism of the Mystics

This was taught by Thomas à Kempis, Macarius, Fenelon, Lucas, Law, Madame de Guyon, and other writers, Protestant and Papal. Their opinions glowed with the very sanctity of the Gospel. They presented in their writings such a portraiture of the perfect Christian as would awaken the noblest aspirations of a regenerate heart; but they taught that the perfect love of God would raise a man above those mental infirmities which are inseparable from our present state; and that these lofty attainments were to be reached by seclusion from the world, ascetic self-abnegation, and works of charity and benevolence. Wesley's statement of the doctrine differed from theirs as being far more clear, more consistent with our present state of infirmity and ignorance, and more readily attainable by present faith in a perfect Saviour. In a letter to one of his correspondents he says: 'I want you to be all love. This is the perfection I believe and teach; and this perfection is consistent with a thousand nervous disorders which that high-strained perfection is not. Indeed, my judgment is that to overdo is to undo; and that to set perfection too high is the most effectual way of driving it out of the world.' Moreover, he had no sympathy with the notion that the perfection of the Gospel could be reached by seclusion from the world and a long series of self-denying works. His words are: 'as to the manner, I believe this perfection is always wrought in the soul by faith, by a simple act of faith; consequently, in an instant. But I believe a gradual work, both preceding and following that instant.'

2. The Perfectionism of Pelagianism

It has been said that Wesley adopted the Pelagian scheme, but no statement can be further from the truth. Pelagianism presents a strictly legal perfection—perfect conformity to the law. But, denying the doctrine of man's depravity and of the direct influences of the Spirit, it holds that perfection may be attained through the efforts of mere natural ability. Wesley, on the other hand, set forth an evangelical perfection—perfect conformity to the terms of the Gospel. But, strenuously maintaining the doctrine of hereditary depravity and of the Spirit's influence, he held that this exalted state could only be attained through the merits of the Saviour's death, and by the power of the Holy Ghost.

3. The Perfectionism of the Oberlin School

The chief representatives of this school are Professors Mahan and Finney. In some respects their phraseology comes very near the Wesleyan view; and the illustrations of the doctrine, and the arguments employed to prove it, in general are the same as are employed by us. But, like the Pelagians, they make the original moral law of God the standard of perfection. Says Finney, 'nothing more nor less can possibly be perfection or entire sanctification than obedience to the law.' It is difficult to say precisely what he means by this language; but this is the point at which it is understood the Oberlin theory differs from ours. Wesley and Fletcher were always careful to make it clear that the perfection to which we are called 'is not perfection according to the absolute moral law; it is perfection according to the special remedial economy introduced by the atonement, in which the heart, being sanctified, fulfils the law by love (Rom. 13:8,10); and its involuntary imperfections, which are, in the sense, transgressions of the perfect law, are provided for by that economy, without the imputation of guilt'. When Mr Wesley thus explained his opinions to Bishop Gibson, the prelate exclaimed, 'Why, Mr Wesley, if this is what you mean by perfection, who can be against it?'[50]

Perhaps the main points of emphasis in this section ought to be that Wesley's doctrine of sanctification ought not to be exclusively limited to the instantaneous experience of the 'second blessing'. The fact that it also comprises of a gradual development of the Christian life is not generally realised. The mistake has meant that the importance of obedience and works in sanctification has been overlooked. This mistaken view we hope to rectify in the next section of our study. We have also seen that there were differences between what one might call the traditional Wesleyan view of sanctification and the holiness teachers of the mid and latter part of the 19th-century. One significant area of difference, not mentioned above but requiring a large amount of study, would involve an investigation of Wesley's concept of the kingdom of God, the pursuit of perfection, and his post-millennial view of history, and the more individualistic pre-millennial and dispensational views of the later holiness schools.

CHAPTER TWELVE

JOHN WESLEY AND THE PURITAN ETHIC

There has been an unbroken chain of opinion within the Methodist body, even up to the present day, that sees the traditional Methodist ethic as being firmly in the Puritan mould. Writing in the *Methodist Recorder*, March 23rd 1972, Dr Irvonwy Morgan, one time President of The Methodist Conference and Moderator of the Free Church Federal Council, wrote:

> The popular image of the Puritan conjures up a life-denying, and joyless fanatic, a follower of Swinburn's 'Pale Galilean' who turned the world grey with his breath. It pictures a man whom when he came to power banished 'cakes and ale' and substituted a sour Sabbatarian self-denial of anything which gave pleasure to the ordinary man.
>
> Nothing of course could be further from the truth, however not for the Puritan that 'one crowded hour of glorious life is worth an age without a name.' For the Puritan coveted a name, his own name written in the Book of Life, and he sought this heavenly registration with prayers and tears, in the certain hope that one day the trumpets of glory would sound for him on the other side.
>
> It was to this type of man that John Wesley appealed in the Introduction to his *Hymn Book* of 1779, on the grounds that it contained clear directions for making his calling and election sure. For however much it might appear that the Arminianism of Wesley and the Calvinism of the Puritan were antithetical models for presenting the Gospel, the fact is that the 'assurance' of Methodist theology and the 'election' of Puritan theology meant (effectively) the same thing, namely, the gift given to the believer in order that he might know that he is truly a redeemed child of God.

Of course the Puritan spirit has always created hostility, for unregenerate man tends to admire the carefree Cavalier with his elegant, hedonistic, laughter-loving enjoyment of the pleasures of life rather than the serious disciplined concern for godliness and righteousness of the Puritan warrior and pilgrim. To the worldly-minded man, such determined piety, such self-denying ordinances, such living godly only demonstrated a mistaken man who could pursue that will of the wisp of holiness, the *ingis fatuus* of salvation.

What offends the world in the Puritan witness is its concern for godliness, which by its nature is both a criticism of worldly aspirations and the denial of worldly wisdom. To put it in the words of John Preston, 'It is living godly that brings persecution, the being downright and balking at nothing, because the devil is our old enemy and will stir up men against us, to nibble at our heels, for the devil ignores those who are indifferent, but the Saints, who are his enemies, they are sure to smart for it.' If, as Jerislav Pelikan asserts, the core of Christianity is a pessimism about life but an optimism about God, then Puritans were most exemplary Christians. They were convinced that the world with all its prizes was merely vanity and a striving after wind, and other satisfactions of worldly ambition were not to be compared with the consciousness of having pleased God in godly living. It is theoretically possible to please God and please oneself, as the Methodist Covenant service has it, but such occasions are very rare, and not to be relied upon!

The same article goes on to acknowledge the true nature of man as being a fallen creature who without Christ's gift of salvation can only 'descend deeper and deeper into chaos and dark night'. It acknowledges man's responsibility to act as in the sight of God and to attend to our earthly duties with a heavenly mind; that the function of the Church was to remind men of their spiritual nature and to convey such helps as God had ordained for them to live holy lives. The article acknowledges the need for the Christian to observe the Sabbath day as the 'market day of the soul' and to feed on Christ in the ordinances that he had provided, to converse in spiritual things by prayer and the study of God's holy Word.

It is clear that the Puritan ethic of Wesley's Epworth home

remained with him throughout his life, and passed into the bloodstream of Methodism. It is also possible to trace the roots of Wesley's ethical principles beyond 17th-century Puritanism to the Reformers themselves and indeed to the fathers of the Reformation, notably William Tyndale, whom we may also note is often regarded as one of the fathers of Puritanism. John Wesley was politically a high Tory and believed in giving honour to those to whom honour was due. This side of his character is reflected in the famous Reformation Homilies of the Church of England, in the Homily on Obedience:

> Almighty God hath created and appointed all things in heaven and earth in a most excellent and perfect order. In heaven he hath appointed distinct and several orders of archangels and angels. In earth he hath assigned kings, princes and other governors, under them in all good and necessary order—every degree of people in their vocation, calling and office—hath appointed unto them their duty and order: some are in high degree, some in low, some kings and princes, some inferior, some subjects, priests and laymen, masters and servants, fathers and children, husbands and wives, rich and poor: and everyone hath need of other: so that in all things is to be lauded and praised for the goodly order of God without which no house, no city, no commonwealth can endure nor last.

In 1527 Tyndale wrote his *Obedience of a Christian man*. E. Gordon Rupp in his *Studies in the making of the English Protestant Tradition*, comments on Tyndale's work:

> Tyndale's exposition of the obedience of subjects and of the office of the Governor is embedded in the treatment of the duties of children and parents, masters and servants, husbands and wives. This sort is not of the State as a preservative against chaos, so much as the power of the executor of the law of God.
> The king is in the room of God: and his law is God's law, and nothing but the law of nature and natural equity which God engraved in the hearts of men. Heads and governors are ordained of God, and are even the gift of God, whether they be good or bad. And whatsoever is done to us by them, that doth God, be it

good or bad. God therefore hath given laws unto all nations and in all lands, and hath brought kings, governors and rulers in his own stead, to rule the world through them.[1]

These principles were essentially shared by John Wesley and find expression in the hymns of his brother Charles:

> Sovereign of all! Whose will ordains
> The powers on earth that be,
> By whom our rightful monarch reigns,
> Subject to none but Thee.[2]

The same is true of his thoughts concerning the upbringing of children:

> Father of all, by whom we are,
> For whom was made whatever is;
> Who hast entrusted to our care
> A candidate for glorious bliss:
>
> Poor worms of earth, for help we cry,
> For grace to guide what grace has given;
> We ask for wisdom from on high,
> To train our infants up for heaven.
>
> We tremble at the danger near,
> And crowds of wretched parents see,
> Who blindly fond, their children rear
> In tempers far as hell from Thee;
>
> Themselves the slaves of sense and praise,
> Their babes who pamper and admire,
> And make the helpless infants pass
> To murderer Molech through the fire.[3]

But for all Wesley's high Tory principles and autocratic hold upon the early Methodist societies, there was also a different side to Wesley's character. This is most evident in the fact that he was willing, though reluctant at first, to set aside the authority of the bishops of the Anglican Church and ecclesiastical rules and conventions when these seemed to impede the Holy Spirit's purpose in spreading the Gospel. Moreover, in embracing the Puritan ethic

Methodism also embraced the Calvinistic spirit of democracy. Ernst Troeltsch made the following observation;

> Calvinistic Puritan Pietism was somewhat different from Continental Pietism. It was the moral School of the English middle classes, and after the fluctuations of the great period of the Enlightenment in England, it reappeared as early as the 18th century—this time, however in the shape of Methodism, which was indeed in the line of the old Puritan tradition, though it also contained some essentially new elements. The Evangelical spirit which it produced, which repeatedly led the attack on the Enlightenment, in spite of various deviations, reveals even today the power of the Puritan Calvinistic spirit.[4]

These tensions within Wesley himself and early Methodism were later to manifest themselves in the 19th-century divisions within Methodism. We shall consider these in more detail later.

We can further see the Puritan spirit within Methodism in the well-known *Rules of the Society of the People called Methodists* first published on 1st May 1743.[5] John A. Newton comments that this emphasis may come partly from Wesley's High Church asceticism in the Holy Club phase; but the particular forms it took, for example, its strict Sabbatarian practice, suggest a more specifically Puritan origin. Many of Wesley's injunctions to his Helpers have a clear Puritan ring about them. In any form of ethical rigour there is in some the tendency for prohibitions to become predominant. Yet in both Puritanism and Methodism there is a constant, positive stress on the godly life, on practical religion, on Christianity in earnest, or as Wesley delightfully summed up the whole meaning of the Christian life, in the words of Paul, 'faith working by love.'[6]

We can also see the Puritan spirit exemplified *par excellence* in the way that the early Methodists faced death. John Wesley said, 'Our people die well.' This was clearly in the Puritan tradition. Richard Baxter in his *Dying Thoughts,* wrote 'Christian, make it the study and business of thy life to learn to do thy last work well.' And Matthew Henry wrote:

> When we see the day approaching, we must address ourselves to our dying work with all seriousness, renewing our repentance

for sin, our consent to the Covenant, our farewells to the world; and our souls must be carried out towards God in suitable breathings.

John A. Newton reflects on the fact that the Puritan would have been appalled at the modern tendency to surround the dying man with a conspiracy of silence, until drugged and insensible, he is able to 'shuffle off this mortal coil without ever really facing death'. As the Puritan was serious about living life so also he was serious about facing death. His attitude to death was positive, he saw it as a final deed to be done and an ultimate battle to be fought. He sought for fresh experiences of God, and fresh discoveries of God's mercies in his final illness, and he sought to glorify God in death as he had sought to do so in life.

> The enormous literature of Puritan funeral sermons makes clear the edification to be drawn from a believer's deathbed, either by those who witnessed his end, or by those who heard or read of it later. No doubt some of these sermons tend to idealise, to soften the harsh reality of a painful illness or a dying agony. Yet in some of the greatest descriptions of Puritan deathbed scenes, it is the verisimilitude that commands respect. Baxter could expatiate on 'the great difference between the death of a heavenly believer and of an earthly sensualist', and extol the former as 'a comfortable death'. But by 'comfortable' he did not mean a death void of physical pain, as the context of the phrase and the manner of his own dying both make plain. 'It wonderfully prepareth for a comfortable death,' he writes, 'to live in the fellowship of the sufferings of Christ;' and the day before he died he said to his friends, with the honesty that was ingrained in him, 'I have pain, there is no arguing against sense, but I have peace, I have peace.' (*Autobiography*, ed. Lloyd Thomas, p.266.)
>
> It was in this great Puritan tradition of holy dying that Susanna Wesley was found as she took her leave of the world. It was a tradition which her own father had adorned with his last words of triumphant faith: 'I'll die praising thee, and rejoice that there are others that can praise thee better. I should be satisfied with thy likeness; satisfied, satisfied! Oh my dear Jesus I come!' (*The Excellency of a Public Spirit*, Williams, p.146). The same

longing to give glory to God in 'articulo mortis' breaks out again in John Wesley's dying words—'I'll praise, I'll praise...' with unconscious happiness, Wesley's lips take up the words of one of the greatest hymns of the Puritan tradition, Isaac Watts' 'I'll praise my Maker while I've breath'.

No words could better express the strength and confidence of the God ward reference of Puritan faith than these; the resolve that, to the very last breath, life is to be expended *'ad maiorem Dei gloriam'*:

> I'll praise my Maker, while I've breath;
> And when my voice is lost in death,
> Praise shall employ my nobler powers;
> My days of praise shall ne'er be past,
> While life, and thought, and being last,
> Or immortality endures.[7]

We see therefore that, at the very end of his life, Wesley again joins himself to the Puritan succession of faith, and echoes, in a moving and wonderful way his grandfather's words of nearly a century before, 'I'll die praising thee.'

CHAPTER THIRTEEN

JOHN WESLEY AND AUTHORITY IN THE CHURCH

'Methodism, so-called, is the old religion, the religion of the Bible, the religion of the primitive Church, the religion of the Church of England.' These words were spoken by John Wesley at the opening of the 'New Chapel' in City Road, in November 1778. There can be no doubt that Wesley held to the classical Protestant position in regard to the Word of God, as recorded in the Articles and Confessions, that is, that it constitutes the final authority in all matters of faith and order. His position is expressed in the *39 Articles of the Church of England* as follows:

> Holy Scripture containeth all things necessary to salvation: so that whatsoever is not read therein, nor may be proved thereby, is not to be required of any man, that it should be believed as an article of the faith, or be thought requisite or necessary to salvation. In the name of the Holy Scripture we do understand those Canonical Books of the Old and New Testament, of whose authority was never in any doubt in the Church. (Article VI)
>
> The Church hath power to decree Rites or Ceremonies, and authority in controversies of Faith: and yet it is not lawful for the Church to ordain anything that is contrary to God's Word written, neither may it so expound one place of Scripture, that it may be repugnant to another. Wherefore, although the Church bear witness to and is the keeper of Holy Writ, yet, as it ought not to decree anything against the same, so besides the same ought it not to enforce anything to be believed for necessity of salvation. (Article XX)

By the term 'old religion' Wesley means the religion of the Bible; as Franz Hildebrandt put it, 'Methodism is synonymous with Scriptural Christianity.'[1]

Here we might recall the well-known words from the Preface to the *Standard Sermons*:

> To candid, reasonable men, I am not afraid to lay open what have been the innermost thoughts of my heart. I have thought I am a creature of a day passing through life as an arrow through the air. I am a spirit come from God, and returning to God; just hovering over the great gulf; till a few moments hence, I am no more seen; I drop into an unchangeable eternity! I want to know one thing—the way to heaven; how to land safe on that happy shore. God himself has condescended to teach the way; for this very end he came from heaven. He hath written it down in a book. O give me that book! At any price, give me the book of God! I have it: here is knowledge enough for me. Let me be '*homo unius libri*'. Here then I am, far from the busy ways of men. I sit down alone: only God is here. In his presence I open, I read his book; for this end, to find the way to heaven—If any doubt still remains, I consult those who are experienced in the things of God; and then the writings whereby, being dead, they yet speak. And what I must learn, that I teach.

By *homo unius libri* Wesley means the reliance upon the word of salvation given in the Scriptures. His point is that the final authority in matters of religion is the Bible, any other writings must therefore be judged in the light of this once-and-for-all revelation.

> The Scriptures are the touchstone whereby Christians examine all real or supposed revelations. In all cases they appeal 'to the law and testimony', to try every spirit thereby.[2]

Colin W. Williams comments:

> Wesley must be placed with the Reformers in his principle of *sola Scriptura*, in the sense that Scripture is the final authority in matters of faith and practice; not in the sense that tradition and experience have no value, but in the sense that this further source of insight must be congruous with the revelation recorded in Scripture. It is clear, that Wesley based his principle of *sola Scriptura* on a type of verbal inspiration theory.[3]

Many examples from Wesley's Works could be cited. One of the clearest states:

The faith of the Protestants, in general, embraces only those truths, as are necessary to salvation, which are clearly revealed in the oracles of God. Whatever is plainly declared in the Old and New Testament is the object of their faith. They believe neither more nor less than what is manifestly contained in, and provable by, the Holy Scriptures—The written word is the whole and sole rule of their faith, as well as practice. They believe whatsoever God has declared, and profess to do whatsoever he hath commanded. This is the proper faith of Protestants: by this they will abide, and no other.[4]

It is easy to prove that this strict adherence to Scripture as the only and final authority in the Christian life was deeply embedded in Methodism long after Wesley's demise, indeed throughout the 19th-century until finally eroded by Liberalism in the early 1930s. Quoting from a summary of Methodist doctrine in 1818 we read:

When it pleased God to raise up the Rev. John Wesley, to be the founder of Methodism; he resolved, through divine help, to make the Bible his only guide, in all the important doctrines which he embraced; and which he faithfully delivered to the people. His own language was, 'I designed plain truth for plain people; therefore, of set purpose, I abstain from all nice and philosophical speculations; from all perplexed and intricate reasonings; and as far as possible, from even the show of learning, unless in something citing the original Scriptures.'[5]

At the time of the Downgrade Controversy in the 1880s Spurgeon commented that the Methodists alone amongst the large denominations at that time had clung to the doctrine of the full inspiration, infallibility and supreme authority of the Scriptures.

It is sometimes observed that Wesley laid a great emphasis upon the place of experience in the Christian life; this is undoubtedly true. He wrote:

I am not afraid that the people called Methodist should ever cease to exist, either in Europe or America. But I am afraid, lest they should only exist as a dead sect, having a form of religion without the power. And this undoubtedly will be the case, unless they hold fast both the doctrine, spirit and discipline with which they first set out.[6]

However, Wesley was also careful to point out and teach that experience is the appropriation of authority, and not its source:

> For Wesley experience is not the test of truth, but truth the test of experience. Wesley feared any approach to doctrine or worship which overlooked the necessity of personal experience, but he equally feared any reliance upon experience which left the question of truth to the vagaries of individual or collected feeling. He knew the danger of the Christian faith being torn from its historical moorings by being subjected to the vagaries and limitations of human experience, and so he insisted upon the priority of the Word. Speaking in his *Journal* of the *Life of Mr Marsay*, he wrote: 'He was a man of uncommon understanding, and greatly devoted to God. But he was a consummate enthusiast. Not the Word of God, but his own imaginations, were the sole rule of his words and actions.' (Journal VI p.202.)
>
> Wesley knew that there is an irreconcilable variability in the operation of the Holy Spirit on the souls of men, more especially as to the manner of justification. Many find him rushing upon them like a torrent, while they experience the overwhelming power of saving grace. This has been the experience of many; perhaps of more in this late visitation than in any other age since the time of the Apostles. But in others he works in a different way:
>
> > He deigns his influence to infuse,
> > Sweet, refreshing, as the silent dews....
>
> Let him take his own way: He is wiser than you.(Letters VII p.298.)
>
> Because of this variability, no experience can be made normative, but all experience must be submitted to the touchstone of Scripture. Commenting on the Quakers, Wesley objects that they make Scripture 'a secondary rule, subordinated to the Spirit'. He answers that the Scriptures are the touchstone whereby Christians examine all, real or supposed revelations—For though the Spirit is our principal leader, yet he is not our rule at all; the Scriptures are the rule whereby he leads us into all truth.(Letters II p.117.) [7]

Oliver A. Beckerlegge has very helpfully collated from *Wesley's Journal*, a short article on *Church Order According to the Scriptures*. In Wesley's own words he lays down the following points in the introduction:

1. I lay this down as an undoubted truth: The more the doctrine of any Church agrees with the Scripture, the more readily ought it to be received. And, on the other hand, the more the doctrine of any Church differs from the Scripture, the greater cause we have to doubt of it.

2. Now, it is a known principle of the Church of England, that nothing is to be received as an article of faith, which is not read in the Holy Scripture or to be inferred therefrom by just and plain consequence. Hence it follows, that every Christian has a right to know and read the Scripture, that he may be sure what he hears from his teachers agrees with the revealed Word of God.

3. On the contrary, at the very beginning of the Reformation, the Church of Rome began to oppose this principle, that all articles of faith must be provable from the Scripture (till then received throughout the whole Christian world), and to add, if not prefer, to Holy Scripture, tradition, or the doctrine of Fathers and Councils, with the decrees of Popes. And as soon after she determined in the Council of Trent, 'that the Old and New Testament, and the traditions of the Church, ought to be received 'pari pietatis affectu ac reverential', (i.e. with equal piety and reverence) and that it suffices for laymen if they believe and practice what the Church believes and requires, whether they understand the ground of the doctrine or practice or not'.

4. How plain is it that this remedy was found out because they themselves observed that many doctrines, practices, and ceremonies of their Church, not only could not be proved by Scripture, but were flatly contradictory thereto.

5. As to the Fathers and Councils, we cannot but observe, that in a hundred instances they contradict one another: consequently, they can no more be a rule of faith to others, than the Papal decrees, which are not grounded on Scripture.[8]

CHAPTER FOURTEEN

JOHN WESLEY AND CHURCH ORDER

Troeltsch in his *Social Teaching of the Christian Churches* notes what he calls the democratic tendency in primitive Calvinism whilst acknowledging that Calvin's personal point of view was as undemocratic and authoritarian as possible.[1] Nevertheless the practical teaching of Calvinism brought about a stronger impulse in the direction of democracy. That this same principle came down through Puritanism into Methodism is what we are considering here. It is sometimes maintained that Wesley was throughout his life a High Churchman, rigid in his adherence to the forms and principles of Anglicanism. This view can easily be challenged by considering Wesley's own words on the subject of Episcopacy. He wrote:

> As to my own judgments, I still believe the Episcopal form of Church government to be scriptural and apostolical. I mean, well agreeing with the practice and writings of the apostles. But that it is prescribed in Scripture, I do not believe this opinion which I once zealously espoused. I have been heartily ashamed ever since I read Bishop Stillingfleet's *Irenicon*. I think he has unanswerably proved that 'neither Christ nor his apostles prescribed any particular form of Church government; and that the folly of divine right for diocesan episcopacy was never heard of in the Primitive Church'.[2]

In 1746, whilst he was riding from London to Bristol, he records that he read Peter King's book of 1691, *An Account of the Primitive Church*. King was a Puritan who ultimately became Lord Chancellor of England. He set out to demonstrate that in the New Testament, bishops and presbyters constitute the same order; and that consequently presbyters as well as bishops have the right to ordain; and that during the first 300 years of the Christian era presbyters did from time to time ordain.

Lord King's *Account of the Primitive Church* convinced me many years ago that bishops and presbyters are the same order, and consequently have the same right to ordain.[3]

Wesley clearly believed that Apostolic Succession was a figment and he described it in terms of being a broken chain:

I deny that the Romish bishops came down by one uninterrupted succession from the apostles. I never could see it proved; and, am persuaded, I never shall—and neither is a doctrine of your Church. That the intention of the administrator is essential to the validity of the sacraments which are administered by him—if you pass for a priest, are you assured of the intention of the bishop that ordained you? If not, you may happen to be no priest, and so all your ministry is nothing worth; nay, by the same rule, he may happen to be no bishop. And who can tell how often this has been the case; but if there has been only one such incident in a thousand years, what becomes of your uninterrupted succession? [4]

In the other letter, written only a few years before his death, he reiterated the same point in the clearest possible terms.

I firmly believe I am a scriptural *episkopos* (or bishop) as much as any man in England or in Europe. (For the uninterrupted succession I am not able to prove, which no man ever did or can prove.) [5]

As to the Rubrics and Rituals of the Church of England, he was led step by step further away from them, until significant departures were made from its traditions. Such practices as open-air preaching, and lay preaching, especially called forth the wrath of contemporary Anglican church leaders. Archbishop Secker bitterly attacked Wesley, and declared such practices to be:

Oppositions to the most fundamental principles and essentially constituent parts of our Establishment.[6]

In a letter dated 10th April 1761 Wesley dealt with these criticisms, and his reply shows how far he had travelled since the days of the Georgia mission:

'The most fundamental principles!'—No more than the tiles are the most fundamental principles of a house. Useful, doubtless they are, yet you must take them off if you would repair the rotten timber beneath. 'Essentially constituent parts of our Establishment.'—Well, we will not quarrel for a word. Perhaps the doors may be essentially constituent parts of the building we call a church. Yet if it were on fire we might innocently break them open, or even throw them for a time off the hinges. Now this is really the case. The timber is rotten, yea, the main beams of the house; and they want to replace that firm beam, salvation by faith, in the room of that rotten beam, salvation by works. A fire is kindled in the Church, the house of the living God; a fire of love of the world, ambition, covetousness, envy, anger, malice, bitterness, in a word, of ungodliness and unrighteousness. Oh! Who will come and help to quench it under disadvantages and discouragements of every kind, a little handful of men have made the beginning, and I trust they will not leave off till the building is saved, or they sink in the ruins of it.[7]

One of Wesley's great mottos became, *'Church or no Church, we must attend to the work of saving souls.'*[8]

We can also point out that even more remarkable than what Wesley said, was what he did, in our seeking to understand the nature of his church principles:

1. He disregarded all parochial limitations

Wesley took the message of the Gospel straight to the people. He was impatient with those who sought to put ecclesiastical barriers in his way. As W. B. Fitzgerald points out:

The vast majority of the early Methodists were never in the Church. The masses of the people were utterly neglected, and Wesley felt that their need was his opportunity. Within a little more than a year after the great spiritual crisis of his life, Wesley settled this point very definitely; in a letter to a friend he declared his intentions as follows...

'Suffer me now to tell you my principles in this matter. I look upon all the world as my parish; thus far I mean, that, in whatever part of it I am, I judge it meet, right, and my bounden duty to declare unto all that are willing to hear; the glad tidings of salvation.'[9]

2. Wesley built chapels all over the land

Not one of these chapels was consecrated. He never asked for consecration. Though it was at first that they were intended to supplement, and not to supplant the services of the Church, yet their building was a challenge to and a transgression of parochial rules.

Even more significant, than absence of consecration, was the fact that some of Wesley's chapels were actually licensed as dissenting places of worship. The New Room at Bristol was licensed in 1748. Other Methodists were deliberately described in the document as 'Protestant subjects dissenting from the Church of England'. That Wesley did this with his eyes wide open is evident from the vehement protest of his brother Charles when the proposal was endorsed.

3. Wesley allowed unordained laymen to preach

Wesley wrestled long and hard within himself before he took this step. He said, 'To touch this point was to touch the apple of mine eye.' However, convinced that it was right and necessary, he went ahead.

4. He revised and edited the Thirty-Nine Articles

He deliberately shortened and modified the Articles, reducing them to twenty five. Article 34 he altered as follows: 'Every particular Church may ordain changes, or abolish rights and ceremonies, so that all things be done to edification.'

5. He himself ordained men as bishops and presbyters

It was the need of appointing men to serve in America that at first led him to take this step. At the time of the American Revolution, the Church of England establishment was abolished, and the religious institutions of the country were in chaos. Methodism had already been established, but it needed care and help. There were 15,000 members, and 83 itinerant preachers, but as yet there was very little by way of organisation. On two occasions Wesley tried to persuade Lowth, the Bishop of London, to ordain at least one of the preachers, so that the ordinances might be administered to the people, but Lowth refused. After a long delay Wesley decided to resolve the difficulty himself.

In September 1784, Wesley met Coke at Bristol, and ordained him as the first Bishop of the Methodist Church in America; and, at the same time, he ordained two other preachers as presbyters. On crossing the Atlantic, their first action was to ordain Bishop Francis Astbury as the first indigenous American Bishop of the Methodist Church.

Having crossed this Rubicon, Wesley ordained three preachers in 1785 to administer the ordinances in Scotland. During the next year he did the same in regard to preachers in Ireland and the West Indies.

In 1787, at the Manchester Conference, Mather, Rankin, and Moore were ordained with authority to administer the sacraments in any part of England. Mather received Bishop's Orders, though Wesley preferred to use the term 'Superintendent'. Every Superintendent was a New Testament Bishop in Wesley's estimation.

6. Wesley framed the deed of declaration

This prepared the way for the existence of Methodism as a distinct Church. Wesley saw the inevitability of separation from the Church of England. Only three years before his death he wrote:

A kind of separation has already taken place, and will inevitably spread, though by slow degrees.[10]

Their enemies provoked them to it, the clergy in particular, most of whom, far from thanking them for continuing in the Church, used all the means in their power, fair and unfair, to drive them out of it.[11]

Horton Davies says that the Wesleyan societies

...were an amalgam of the great Puritan concepts, namely, of the gathered church and the priesthood of all believers.[12]

The same writer in his *The English Free Churches* comments:

Close as the affinities of Methodism appear to be with Anglicanism, its evangelical passion and experimental religion were a revival of Puritan religion, without the latter's austerities and asperities. Its deepest affinities lie with the older Nonconformist Churches, for all are united in claiming that the Church is the servant of the Gospel not the Gospel the servant of the Church. 'Puritanism,' says J. R. Green, 'won its spiritual victory in the Wesleyan Movement, after the failure in the previous century of its military and political struggles.'[13]

CHAPTER FIFTEEN

JOHN WESLEY—EVANGELIST AND INNOVATOR

In approaching this subject we might in passing observe a similarity in character and aim between John Calvin and John Wesley. A. Mitchell Hunter gives us the following description of Calvin's character:

> It may seem a perverse thing to say, but Calvin, accounted among the princes of systematic theology, was not primarily a theologian, one whose nature found its chief and deepest satisfaction in constructing an edifice of theological doctrine. He was not of the race of the dry as dust schoolmen. What was distinctive about him was that he was first and foremost a profoundly religious man. Piety was the keynote of his character. He was a God-possessed soul. Theology was of no concern to him as a study in itself; he devoted himself to it as providing a framework for the support of all that religion meant to him.
>
> To him his lifelong aim and business was to re-wed religion and morality and establish them in indissoluble union as directors of human activity in all its spheres religion to Calvin was not a matter of pious emotion, consequent on the assurance of being in a state of grace. It was the acceptance of the rule of God over one's whole life. It included dependence upon the will of God and obedience to the will of God not more the one than the other. A man's conduct in all his relationships must be governed by regard to God's will along with the ever-active sense of direct responsibility to him. In the provinces of whole life, social life, business life, political life, religion must be energetically operating to procure the dominance of truth, justice, purity, integrity.
>
> It is this fundamental and ultimate aim of Calvinism to moralise life by religion which interprets and explains the character of all Calvin's activities... It is a notable thing to

195

observe how closely Calvin keeps to life in his Commentaries. The application was the main thing to him. That is largely the reason why these expositions still retain their value.[1]

The same spirit was clearly in John Wesley. For him religion was nothing if it did not change the life for good, if it did not make the sinner holy. Wesley was absolutely committed to the teaching of Holy Scripture. What he wrote in 1745 in regard to Scripture as being the 'sole rule' of the faith he maintained to the end. In 1768 he wrote, 'I am, at this day, hardly sure of anything but what I learn from the Bible.'[2] 'Keep close to the Bible,' he exhorted a preacher, 'Enjoin nothing that the Bible does not clearly enjoin. Forbid nothing that it does not clearly forbid.'[3] Wesley's principle was that the Scriptures were to be the sole rule of faith, and the sole rule of life. It would be wrong to say that Wesley was not a theologian nor interested in doctrine, but his chief interest was that of the saving of souls and the spread of Scriptural holiness throughout the land.

> His purpose was not to formulate a new theology or a new theory of Church and State, but to touch dead bones with the breath of spiritual power, and to make them live; to release the winds of heaven, that they might blow upon the ashy embers of religion and kindle the purging, illuminating fire of righteousness and truth. He would substitute for the bondage of sin, the liberty, individual and social, of men newborn after the similitude of Christ. (Wesley sometimes emphasised these views to the point of misunderstanding.)
>
> 'I find more profit in sermons on either good tempers, or good works,' he protests, 'than in what are vulgarly called 'Gospel Sermons', the term has now become a mere cant word, I wish none of our society would use it. It has no determinate meaning. Let but a pert self-sufficient animal, that has neither sense nor grace, bawl-out something about Christ, or his blood, or justification by faith, and his hearers cry out, 'What a fine Gospel sermon!' We know no Gospel without salvation from sin.'[4]

This was Wesley's aim, as we have seen already, and in order to carry this out he would not be daunted by any opposition or any

CHAPTER FIFTEEN   197

man-made ecclesiastical rules or conventions. While standing firmly
on the Scriptures he would follow the dictates of the Spirit to do
whatever was necessary to fulfil the purpose of God. This is well
summed up in the hymn:

> Shall I, for fear of feeble man,
> The Spirit's course in me restrain?
> Or, undismayed, in deed and word
> Be a true witness for my Lord?
>
> Awed by a mortal's frown, shall I
> Conceal the Word of God most high?
> How then before Thee shall I dare
> To stand, or how Thine anger bear?
>
> Shall I, to sooth the unholy throng,
> Soften Thy truth and smooth my tongue,
> To gain earth's gilded toys, or flee
> The cross, endured, my God, by Thee? [5]

It was this same determination to bring the Gospel with all its
saving and sanctifying power to the multitudes, which caused him,
when the churches were closed against him, to go out into the streets
and fields and, wherever he could, gain a hearing. In fulfilling this
great end and purpose to make men vitally conscious of God, he would
use his God-given creative and organisational genius. This was that
same Puritan, practical genius that so characterised Cromwell,
Milton, Bunyan, Baxter and others. We can remind ourselves that it
was Oliver Cromwell who in his day favoured and sought to forward
the evangelisation of England by the placing of Gospel preachers in
every parish church; by his founding of *The Society for the
Propagation of the Gospel* (afterwards taken over and reconstituted
by the Church of England); and that it was he who also favoured the
work of evangelising the heathen and the Jew and the restoration of
the latter to Palestine. We can also remind ourselves of the methods
that Richard Baxter used in taking the Gospel to the everyday people
of Kidderminster. Wesley was clearly in this tradition.

Wesley also saw the need for organisation, if the effects of his
work were to continue. He was not averse to applying the rules of

commonsense to the situations which faced him on a practical level. Further, he was clearly aware of the needs of the hour, the outrageous claims of Deist philosophy, the decay of morality in society at large, the lack of Gospel preaching in the churches, the clogged up ecclesiastical machinery of the Anglican Church, together with the spiritual deadness of many of the Dissenting causes.

There is no real evidence of him having a master plan to meet this enormous need, except for his utter reliance upon the Word of God, and his belief that the Holy Spirit would guide him in his great work.

> By Thine unerring Spirit led,
> We shall not in the desert stray;
> We shall not full direction need,
> Nor miss our providential way;
> As far from danger as from fear
> While Love, Almighty love, is near.[6]

Telford, in his life of John Wesley describes his practical methods as follows:

> Lord Macaulay's judgment, that Wesley possessed as great a genius for government as Richelieu, is repeated on every hand. In a confidential letter to his sister, Mrs Hall, dated November 17th, 1742, Wesley acknowledges with gratitude the gift he possessed for the management of his Societies. 'I know this is the peculiar talent which God has given me,' are his words. No great statesman ever watched the course of public opinion more carefully than Wesley watched the progress of events in Methodism.
>
> He did not think out a system and force it on his people. There is no special evidence of inventive power in Wesley's administration. He himself speaks of his want of any plan for financial matters. (Works, VIII: 248, XIII: 148) His rule over the United Societies owed its success to the fact that he was always availing himself of the fresh light which experience gave.
>
> Methodist organisation was a gradual growth. Local experiments which approved themselves in practice were introduced into all the Societies. Leaders, stewards, and lay preachers, the main instruments in spreading and conserving the results of the Evangelical Revival, were all the fruit of this growth.

Wesley did not set his heart on such means, but when circumstances suggested, he saw their vast advantages, and soon incorporated them into his system. This method Wesley pursued from the beginning of the Revival to the last day of his life. It is the most marked feature of his work.

One might almost say that he never looked a day before him. His field preaching, his chapel building, his calling out preachers, and his Deed of Declaration all supply illustrations of this spirit. Methodist polity and Methodist Finance were all built up step by step. No man had a more candid mind than Wesley. He learned from everyone, and was learning until the last day of his life. Such a spirit in the leader gave confidence to preachers and people.

Charles Wesley would have forced Methodism into his own groove, and have shattered it to pieces in the attempt. His brother was willing to leave his cause in the hands of God and to wait for the unfolding of events which should mark his will. No cause was ever more happy in its head; no people ever loved their chief as the early Methodists loved John Wesley.[7]

CHAPTER SIXTEEN

JOHN WESLEY—LITURGY AND WORSHIP

In seeking to ascertain what Methodism owed to Puritanism in the area of liturgy and worship, mention can be made of the debt to Puritanism embodied in:

1. Wesley's use of extempore prayer

In *The Lives of the Early Methodist Preachers* by Thomas Jackson, he records George Shadford's account of an early Methodist Preaching Service that he attended at Gainsborough, Lincolnshire.

> When we came there, we found the persons we wanted; but I soon forgot them after the preacher began public worship. I was much struck with his manner. He took out the hymn book, and the people sang a hymn. After this he began to pray extempore, in such a manner as I had never heard or been used to before. I thought it to be a most excellent prayer. After this he took out his little Bible from his pocket, read over his text ......[1]

2. Wesley's emphasis on preaching

Wesley first preached out of doors in a brick field in the city of Bristol, on the text, *'The Spirit of the Lord is upon me to preach good news to the poor.'* This text might well be a summary of Wesley's life's work. He preached in fields and on commons, in barns, on hillsides, at market crosses, in town and city streets, in houses and cottages, at pit heads and even in graveyards, wherever he could get a hearing. He travelled some 300,000 miles on horseback in the course of his preaching activities. It is estimated that he preached on 45,000 different occasions, not always different sermons, though it is estimated that he preached about 1,000 new sermons each year. Eighty per cent of the sermons were preached out of doors. He travelled on average 30 miles per day and preached on average twice everyday whatever the weather.

He published more than 100 sermons, some make this as high as 153. His published sermons are generally theological, heavy and learned. Wesley had two collections of sermons. Beside his hundred printed sermons he had a collection of sermons used when preaching out of doors. These sermons were those listed in his *Sermon Register*. The register recorded the dates of the sermon preached, the location and the Scripture text used. Out of the many texts cited, his most often repeated were sermons on Matthew 16:26, (this sermon was used literally hundreds of times); Mark 1:15; Mark 12:34, Romans 8:33; and II Corinthians 5:18. Possibly the most frequently used sermon was that on Revelation 22:17.

John Nelson, a stonemason who heard Wesley preach on Kennington Common, London, left this report:

> As soon as he got up upon the stand he stroked back his hair and turned his face toward where I stood. His countenance struck such an awful dread upon me that my heart did beat like a clock. I felt his whole discourse was aimed at me. When he had done I said, 'This man can tell the secrets of my heart but he has not left me there, for he had to show me the remedy, even the blood of Jesus.'

Nelson was converted at this gathering. Another, Alexander Mather wrote:

> Wesley preached in West Street and under the sermon my heart was set at liberty.

Thomas Tennant wrote:

> When I heard him preach I thought he appeared as with a sword in his hand with which he cut me asunder.

Silas Todd wrote:

> I had never heard these doctrines preached in the church.[2]

Wesley's last open air sermon was preached on the 6th October 1790 at Winchelsea, Sussex, on the text, 'The kingdom of heaven is at hand; repent and believe the Gospel.'

The Methodist chapel until well into the 20th century was built according to the Reformed and Puritan pattern with a central pulpit, emphasising the central importance of the Word of God and its preaching taken to be the climax of all worship. Hugh Trevor-Roper, in his book, *Catholics Anglicans and Puritans*, comments:

> To the Arminian, as to the Catholic, the pulpit was a utilitarian feature, secondary to the altar, which was invested with an aura of mystery. To the Calvinist, the order was reversed, the function of the Church was preaching, the altar (we would say, communion table) was the utilitarian feature—often a mere table, brought into the body of the church for the occasion.[3]

Burdon gives the following outline of a typical 18th Century preaching service:

- Hymn
- Prayer
- Text
- Sermon
- Hymn
- Prayer

Joseph Nightingale, describing Methodist worship at the beginning of the 19th century, tells us that Methodist worship was the most regular and simple, being defective only in not having the Scripture read to the congregation, in all other respects being impressive and engaging.

> Here is no pomp; no idle parade; no vain show of unmeaning ceremonies, no vain show of tedious liturgies; all is simple and intelligible, agreeable to the easy decorum and decent order of a Christian temple, and a spiritual worship. It is not the least of its recommendations that musical instruments are not generally permitted in a Methodist chapel to divert the attention from the inward contemplation of divine and spiritual zeal, and animate the spirits, of numerous worshippers. Hence it is, in a great degree, that the meeting houses of the Methodists are always so well attended by hearers. Thousands, I make no doubt repaired to the meeting, as well as to the Church, not for the music, but the music there.[4]

The following is a description of the way Rev. Joseph Fowler, Wesleyan minister, conducted Public Worship in Kirkgate Chapel, Bradford, in 1811:

> His love of order and decorum and solemnity and seemliness in public worship show itself in his invincible dislike of late coming, slovenliness and irreverence in any form. To him a clattering and distracting mode of entering a place of worship, or a slovenly, indecorous joining in the conducting of the service, was offensive to the last degree. 'Keep thy foot when thou comest into the House of God,' was graven on the entablature of the sanctuary. One of his most frequent characteristic petitions was: 'Look upon Zion, the city of our solemnities: may our eyes behold Jerusalem a quiet habitation, a tabernacle that shall not be taken down.'[5]

The order of Methodist worship at the time of Methodist Union 1933, was as follows:

- Hymn
- Prayer
- New Testament Reading
- Lord's Prayer
- Hymn or Psalm
- Old Testament Reading
- Prayers
- Notices
- Collection
- Sermon
- Hymn
- Benediction

Horton Davies comments on the similarities and differences between Puritan and Methodist worship:

> Like the worship of the Puritans, Wesley's theory of worship emphasises the notes of simplicity, obedience, and edification. Ceremonial for its own sake is a distraction; the Christian attendance of worship may be a privilege, but it is certainly a duty and a homage to the Divine King; and its benefit is that the worshippers may be built up in the faith and into holiness and

love. The distinguishing note, which is reminiscent of Lutheranism, is that of the sheer joy of the believers who have been justified by their faith in Christ. As in Puritanism the worshippers are *'miseri e abiecti'*, but in Methodism they are *'laeti triumphantes'*. The element of adoration and union with Christ in his triumph over sin and suffering, death, and the devil is provided in the praise. For this purpose Charles Wesley's hymns were superbly fitted. A religion of the heart could want no better media for its expression than, 'O for a thousand tongues to sing my great Redeemer's praise,' or, 'Hark! The herald angels sing, Glory to our Lord and King.' In the 18th century they must have seemed to have recaptured the lost radiance of the New Testament faith itself.[6]

3. Wesley's use of hymnody

Thirdly, reference can be made to the use of hymn singing in Methodism, largely through the influence of Isaac Watts and the inclusion of a large number of Watts's hymns in the traditional hymn books of Methodism.

4. Wesley's introduction of the Covenant Service

Fourthly, the traditional Methodist Covenant Service was derived from the writings of Joseph and Richard Alleine as noted above:

> The Covenant was central to Puritan theology, and basic to any understanding of the Church as the elect people of God. In Puritan piety, however, to renew one's Covenant was primarily an act of individual devotion. Wesley, while retaining a searchingly personal reference in his service, transformed the renewal of the Covenant into a corporate act of the worshipping community. The service focused the societary nature of Methodism, and its concern for Christian fellowship and its earnest seeking after holiness.[7]

5. Wesley's adaptation of the Prayer Book

Fifthly, and finally, mention can be made of Wesley's adaptation of the Book of Common Prayer for the use of American Methodists. His revision was suggested by the points put forward by the Presbyterians at the Savoy Conference in 1661.[8]

CHAPTER SEVENTEEN

METHODISM AFTER WESLEY'S DEATH—
ITS SEPARATIONS AND DIVISIONS

In 1784 Wesley took two decisive steps in order to address matters that had been on his mind for some time. The first concerned the future of the work in England after his death, and the second, the work in America.

Wesley at this time was 81 years old. The one he had wanted to designate as his successor, Fletcher of Madeley, was himself in a poor state of health and in fact died the following year. Wesley could see that there was no prospect at all of the authorities of the Church of England taking up his work and continuing it, indeed he was sadly aware that many of them hoped that the work would die with him. At that time it was difficult to see any among his followers that stood out as a natural successor. He therefore, by a legal 'Deed of Declaration' lodged in the Court of Chancery, appointed a Conference of 100 specified men (The Legal Hundred), to be his successor, with power to fill up its ranks as death diminished them. In the 19th Century Joseph Rigg was wont to call the Conference 'The Living Wesley'.

Regarding his second concern, events transpired as follows. In 1784 the American War of Independence was over, and the Colony was free of British control. The Anglican clergymen who were working in the country when the war broke out, naturally enough, supported the British cause. When the war was over they were not welcome amongst the Americans and they returned to England. American Methodism was now without ordained clergy resulting in the situation in which it became almost impossible for Methodists to receive Holy Communion. In order to remedy this situation Wesley asked the Bishop of London, in whose diocese America technically was, to ordain a Methodist preacher as Bishop. The Bishop of London refused.

At the same time, one Samuel Seabury, an American, had been elected Bishop by his fellow preachers in Connecticut and had come over to England to seek ordination. The Archbishop of York (there being a vacancy at Canterbury at the time), also refused to ordain him. Realising the urgency of the situation Wesley took matters in hand and without consulting his Conference, ordained Richard Whatcoat and Thomas Vasey as deacons. On the following day he ordained them presbyters, and on the same occasion consecrated the Rev. Thomas Coke, who was episcopally ordained, as superintendent.

As we have previously noticed having crossed this Rubicon, Wesley ordained presbyters for Scotland and for the mission field in 1785 and 1786. Also in 1788 and 1789 he ordained a few men for working in parts of England where Methodists could not obtain the ordinance, and also consecrated one man as a superintendent. In 1786 the Methodist Conference allowed chapel services to be held at the same time as Church services in parishes where the minister was notoriously wicked or heretical, where there were not enough churches to contain half the population, or where there was no church within two miles. In doing these things Wesley clearly saw that separation from the Church of England was ultimately inevitable.

On 2nd March 1791 at 10 o'clock in the morning in his house in City Road London, John Wesley was called to his eternal and great reward.

On the 30th of that same month, twenty-eight days after Wesley's death a document known as *The Halifax Circular*, was drawn up under the leadership of William Thomson, an assistant minister of the Halifax circuit and proposed as a Constitution for Methodism on the basis of Mr Wesley's Deed of Declaration. W. H. Daniels comments:

> Its chief features were the filling of vacancies in the 'Legal Hundred' by seniority, and the appointment of different committees, on which all the circuit of the three kingdoms should be represented, to manage the affairs of their respective districts from one Annual Conference to another. Each of these committees was to choose its own president, who was to submit the action of his committee during the year to the review and judgment of the Conference at its next ensuing session.

ALEXANDER KILHAM (1762 – 1798)

HUGH BOURNE (1772 – 1852)

WILLIAM CLOWES (1780 – 1851)

MOW COP

FIRST CAMP MEETING ON MOW COP (MAY 31ST 1807)

PRIMITIVE METHODISTS.   *By W. H. Y. Titcomb.*

A NATION'S PICTURE

WILLIAM O'BRYAN (1778 – 1868)

ESCALLS BIBLE CHRISTIAN CHAPEL, IN THE PARISH OF SENNEN, AT LAND'S END, CORNWALL.

This proposition was a signal for battle, since it secured to the Conference the entire control of general Methodist affairs, to the exclusion of the boards of chapel trustees, among whom there was a strong combination for the avowed purpose of capturing and controlling the pulpits of the Connexion.

The English Methodists had become divided into two parties on the question of sacraments; one, called by their opponents 'The High-Church Party' demanding that the original status of Methodism as a society within, and subordinate to, the Established Church should be maintained; the other, significantly named 'Dissenters', claiming that Methodism had a life and mission of its own. The former desired to keep in the good graces of the Church by limiting the functions of the itinerant preachers to the work of lay evangelists; while the masses of the membership could not see why their ministers were not just as good as parish parsons, and entitled to celebrate the sacraments as well as to preach the Gospel.[1]

One party was seeking to establish Methodism in the pattern that was in the mind of their leader before the pressures of its increased evangelistic needs and opportunities forced him to run counter to the Established Church. The other party pointed out the direction in which Wesley was moving during the last years of his life and were determined to pursue that course towards liberty and independence. This fierce debate continued and in 1795 a compromise, known as the 'Plan of Pacification' was drawn up which was accepted by almost all. Telford comments:

After a day of fasting and prayer, a committee of nine preachers was appointed to draw up a Plan of Pacification. This was approved, both by the Conference and by the assembly of trustees, and was cordially received by the Societies. It brought to a happy close the four-year struggle as to the sacraments. In Ireland the 'Primitive Wesleyans' separated from the Wesleyan Methodists in 1816, when it was resolved to have the Sacraments in Methodist chapels, but in 1878 this little body rejoined the Wesleyans.

The Plan of Pacification decreed that the Lord's Supper, baptism, burial of the dead, and services in Church hours must not be permitted unless the majority of the trustees, stewards, and leaders of the chapel approved of such a step, and could assure the Conference, in writing, that no separation was likely to ensue. The consent of Conference had to be gained before any change was made. Where the Lord's Supper had already been peaceably administered, it was not to be interfered with. The Plan of Pacification also made certain regulations as to the trial of preachers, carefully guarding, however, the sole right of the Conference to appoint them to circuits.[2]

Though, as stated, this compromise was accepted by the majority, nevertheless Alexander Kilham, at the time superintendent of the Aberdeen Circuit, circulated another new constitution for Methodism intended to give the church members a very much larger share of power and office. Kilham's proposals reflect the Presbyterian polity as he conceived it to be working in Aberdeen where he was serving at the time. On the one hand it could be concluded that Wesley intended an Episcopal form of organisation to pertain in British Methodism as in American Methodism. This can be argued from his appointing 'superintendents' who, to all intents and purposes, served as bishops. However, Wesley's system of stewards, his annual Conference, his quarterly meetings of the ministers and laymen in every circuit, all follow very closely the Presbyterian system.

We have already noted that historically speaking the Presbyterian organisation of Methodism was due to Wesley's reading of Baron King's (of Ockham) *Inquiry*, and of Stillingfleet's *Irenicon*. It is at this point that we begin to see the tension that was in Wesley himself between the churchman and the dissenter emerging in his followers. George Eayrs writing in *A New History of Methodism* 1909, comments:

By birth and preference Wesley was an aristocrat, a ceremonialist, and a conservative. He was carried by conviction to become a democrat, he felt that, Church or no Church, he must attend to the work of saving souls, and became the most daring innovator of his age. The same conflict was experienced by his followers individually and among them collectively. Now mystic freedom, and a non-constituted authority, was in the ascendant. Wesley had freely violated authorised ecclesiastical canons and rubrics. Acting upon similar convictions, regnant in them as in him, many of his followers were led to claim electoral, administrative, and legislative rights in their church. They believed that all renewed souls were members of the royal priesthood. The constitutional history of Methodism is a record of the interplay of authority and freedom.[3]

Though by the Plan of Pacification of 1795, Methodism and the Established Church became separate bodies, and although all the preachers signed it, nevertheless Alexander Kilham, William Thom and four others refused to do so. The Conference had no option but to exclude them for their failure to conform to the will of the majority.

After exclusion those expelled founded what came to be known as *The Methodist New Connexion* which consisted in the beginning of about 5,000 members. Thus those various parts of Wesley's character began to be worked out in the divisions within Methodism throughout the years of the 19th century. It is to a brief survey of these various divisions within Methodism and the way that they reflect aspects of Wesley's character that we now turn.

Wesleyan Methodism

None of the divisions in Wesley's Methodism have been over doctrinal issues; all have been centred upon the issues of church government and church practice. The doctrines that we have highlighted so far in this study were those held essentially by all the early 19th century Methodists regardless of their various groupings.

The doctrinal downgrade from essential Methodism, which we see signs of in the later 19th century, and which were to come in like a flood in the 20th, also by and large affected all the groupings. In describing now the essential pattern of Wesleyan Methodism we are describing many features which would have been characteristic of all the various divisions. The differences we shall see later as we try and set out the general features of the various 19th century divisions within the Methodist body.

The Class Meeting System

The following outline of the system of Wesleyan Methodism is given by R. Spence Hardy in his *Memorials of Jonas Sugden*:

> No one is regarded as a member of the Methodist Church who does not meet in class. Each class consists of from 12 to 20 persons,

who are under the care of the Leader. They meet together every week to relate their spiritual experiences and exercises, and receive advice from the leader and one another. These meetings commence and conclude with singing and prayer and at the same time a small sum of money is collected towards the maintenance of the ministry. The leaders of each class meet together weekly, and there pay in the contributions received, to the society stewards.[4]

Gilbert Murray in his *The Methodist Class Meeting* sets out the following points as the chief advantages of meeting together in such a way:
1. The Class Meeting has repeatedly conserved the results of evangelism. Class leaders have gained a lasting and honourable distinction by urging converts to join the class; and there they have watched over their spiritual interests with an apostolic tenderness.
2. The Class Meeting has provided a means for spiritual growth. The members of the class know God and Jesus Christ, whom He has sent; they exchange views and relate experiences and *'help to build each other up'*.
3. The Class Meeting has played a great part in producing that brotherly feeling which is so evident amongst Methodists.

> Still let us own our common Lord,
> And bear Thine easy yoke.
> A band of love, a threefold cord,
> Which never can be broke.
>
> Make us into one Spirit drink,
> Baptize into Thy name;
> And let us always kindly think,
> And sweetly speak the same.'

4. The Class Meeting has been the place where the best workers in the church have invariably been discovered.
5. The Class Meeting has been instrumental in establishing a system of sound finance. Captain Foy's suggestion in 1742 seemed very innocent. The idea was only to meet a temporary requirement. But, in reality, it proved to be the first plank in a system of finance which was to become the wonder and the admiration of the world. The penny per week put the possibility

of rendering financial help within the reach of all but the poorest of the members. Moreover, it accustomed them to understand the duty of sharing in the financial responsibilities of the work and of the church and, perhaps best of all, it fostered from the beginning the idea of systematic support.[5]

The Quarterly Meeting

Another characteristic meeting of Wesleyan Methodism was the Quarterly Meeting of local preachers, leaders, stewards, and trustees of chapels, from all the societies in the circuit, when the society stewards handed over the contributions from the classes to the circuit stewards, from whom the ministers received their stipends. We first read of the Quarterly Meeting in 1750 when John Bennett, one of the preachers at that time, was asked to draw up a plan for conducting such a meeting. There have been modifications to it since then, but in classic Methodism it has remained essentially the same. Its purpose was eminently practical and intended to foster and promote a spirit of service. Every interest of the church was represented, and those present only entitled to attend by virtue of some duty assigned or in respect of some service in which they were actually involved. The following is taken from *The Roots of Methodism* by W. B. Fitzgerald, a Wesley Guild publication, circa 1900:

First of all there are the ministers appointed by Conference, the Superintendent at their head. He is a bishop in the New Testament sense of the word, for his official designation is simply another translation of the Greek 'episkopos', and signifies an 'overseer'. John Wesley had a genius for getting at the heart of things. He cared little for mitres and crosiers, but he cared a great deal for the loving conscientious oversight of the flock of Christ. Secondly, all fully accredited Local Preachers are entitled to be present.

Thirdly, there are the Stewards —Circuit, Society and Poor Stewards, responsible for the monies raised for the support of the ministry and the care of the poor.

Fourthly, the Trustees of all chapels and the Circuit.

Fifthly, Representatives of the Sunday Schools and the Young People's Societies, such as the Wesley Guild or Christian Endeavour.

Sixthly, Representatives elected by the Annual Society Meeting to the Leaders Meeting of each church.

From first to last it is a gathering of those who are aiming at the advancement of the Kingdom of God and who are willing to give their personal service for that end. The business is essentially practical. The Circuit Stewards present the quarterly budget, a careful and detailed statement of receipts and expenditure, open to consideration on the part of the meeting. The census of membership is submitted, and the spiritual, numerical and financial condition of the Churches in the Circuit, and of the working connection with the Sunday Schools, Christian Endeavour Societies, Temperance Societies etc. are reported on. Trust property must be annually reviewed. Candidates for the ministry are here nominated, invitations to ministers submitted, representatives elected to the District Synod.

The basis of 'work' was one of the unconscious ideas that shaped the whole organisation. That church is the healthiest which finds most work for its members, and most frankly admits its workers into council.[6]

The local preachers' quarterly meeting
The Local Preachers' Quarterly Meeting —This meeting dealt with all questions relating specifically to the work of local preachers and also with the examination and reception of new candidates for the Circuit.

The leaders' meeting
Within the local church itself there was the —Leaders' Meeting.

This meeting has the direct oversight over the whole of the spiritual work of the church. Its origin was exceedingly simple. Wesley divided up the members of the Methodist Society, as it was originally called, into little groups, each with its own leader to guide and help his fellow members. These leaders, meeting in consultation with the ministers and stewards, constituted what came to be known as the Leaders' Meeting.

Since those early days there been many developments, and all branches of Methodism found it helpful to add representatives of other interests of a directly spiritual character. But that which gives supreme importance to the Leader's Meeting is its oversight and control of the membership of the church.[7]

In Wesleyanism the leaders were regarded as sub-pastors and corresponded closely with the elders in the Presbyterian Church. The role of these leaders and their executive power within the Leaders' Meeting became one of the hotly disputed points between the notable Wesleyan leader Jabez Bunting, chairman of the Methodist Conference, in the conflicts and divisions which arose in the 1840s and 1850s.

The Band Meeting

In classic Wesleyanism, besides the Classes, there were also smaller meetings of four or five persons called 'Band Meetings'. These were first established by John Wesley in 1742. The purpose was to give opportunity to the members of the Society for more private and unrestrained confession to each other in accordance with the Apostolic exhortation, *'confessing your faults one to another.'*

The persons forming each Band, were to be all of the same condition, *i.e.* either married women or single women, married men or single men. The rules of the Bands were:

1. That nothing spoken in the Band should be spoken again. That is that there should be absolute discretion amongst all members.
2. That every member submit to his minister in all indifferent things.
3. That every member bring once a week, all he can spare to a common fund.

The four following questions were to be proposed to the members separately at every weekly meeting:

1. What known sins have you committed since our last meeting?
2. What temptations have you met with?
3. How were you delivered?
4. What have you thought, said, or done, of which you doubt whether it be a sin or not?

The preaching service

In regard to worship in classic Wesleyanism there was a measure of variety. In some places, especially the larger chapels of London and other major centres, the liturgy of the Church of England was in common and regular use. In other chapels the service was conducted wholly in an extemporary form. Where the Church of England liturgy was in use, it was in accordance with a revised form that Wesley had prepared.[8] The rite of confirmation was not practised in classic Wesleyanism, though in the early days some Wesleyan parents would take their children to be confirmed in the parish church.

The sacrament of the Lord's Supper
The Lord's Supper was usually administered in classic Wesleyanism according to the Book of Common Prayer.

The love feast and watchnight
Love Feasts were occasionally celebrated, and the Watchnight, or midnight service, at the close of each year was, and still is in some places, regularly observed. The practice of 'renewing of the covenant', at the beginning of each year when the members of the Society rededicated themselves to the Lord was, and still is, practised.

The quarterly fast
Originally each member of a Society was encouraged to take part in a Quarterly Fast.

Hymn books
The singing of hymns was a noted characteristic of Wesleyan Methodism and indeed of all branches of Methodism. The Wesleyans used the *Collection of Hymns for the Use of the People called Methodists,* originally published by John Wesley in 1780. To this was added a supplement compiled under the directions of a Committee appointed by the Conference in 1874.

As has already been hinted, the chief issue of dispute between Wesleyan Methodism and the other branches of Methodism was related to a difference of opinion in regard to the exclusive clerical composition of the Annual Methodist Conference. We might add that the nature of Wesleyan Methodism has always borne a more 'churchy' aspect than the other branches of Methodism. Many 19th century Wesleyan ministers wore gowns and bands whilst preaching and, as we shall see further, there was a tendency towards greater clerical authority within the churches. One might almost say that Wesleyan Methodism in its earliest form was characterised by a reluctance to separate from the Church of England.

The Methodist New Connexion

This body was sometimes referred to as the Kilhamites after its founder Alexander Kilham. Kilham was a native of Epworth in Lincolnshire, interestingly the birthplace of the Wesleys. He first became known when he began to press for the right of the Methodist people to meet for worship during Church hours and to receive the sacraments from their own ministers.

He published a pamphlet under the name of *The Progress of Liberty*, where he warmly advocated the necessity of the laity being admitted to a share of the government of the church. His opinions were not welcomed by the Conference, which in 1796 expelled him from the Connexion. However, a large number of Wesleyan Methodists (actually in the region of 5,000) sympathised with him, and his expulsion led, in 1797, to the formation of a separate body called the Methodist New Connexion. There was no doctrinal difference between the two bodies. Likewise the New Connexion continued with the same ecclesiastical arrangements, such as classes, circuits, districts, and an annual Conference. The fundamental difference between the two bodies lay in the degree of power allowed to the individual church members. In the Wesleyan body, authority was virtually vested in the preachers and ministers, who not only exclusively comprised the Conference, but also exercised the chief influence in the circuits and districts as well as in the chapels. The New Connexion, however, admitted on to all its committees and conferences representatives of the people, giving them a share along with the preachers in all matters of church government. Candidates for membership were to be admitted, not by the minister alone, but with the consent of the whole membership. Further, the practice was that the members could not be expelled, even on a charge of immorality, without the concurrence of the Leaders' Meeting. Officers of the New Connexion, whether leaders, ministers, or stewards, were elected by the church and ministers jointly, and both in District

Meetings and at the Annual Conference lay delegates to the same number as ministers were present, freely chosen by the members of the Societies. The Methodist New Connexion published its own magazine and also a magazine for the young, called *The Juvenile Instructor*. In the mid-Victorian period it produced a weekly newspaper called *The Methodist Pilot*. This body eventually combined with the United Methodist Free Church, and the Bible Christians to form the United Methodist Church in 1904.

The Primitive Methodists

During the early years of the 19th-century a revival broke out amongst the workmen of the potteries of Staffordshire. Amongst those moved by this revival was one, William Clowes. Touched by the revival in his 25th year, he was soundly converted and shortly afterwards his wife also was brought to faith. Their home soon became a centre of Christian activity. He wrote in his *Journal:*

> My soul feasted on the hidden manna, and drank the wine of the kingdom. My soul rose in spiritual greatness, and I felt withal such a burning sympathy for souls, and I saw their lost and perishing condition with such vividness, that I went into the streets among the licentious and profane, and addressed them in the name of the Lord. The rebels against God were struck with surprise and astonishment whilst I bore witness against them, and cleared my soul of their blood. Indeed, the fire of God's love became so hot in my soul, as frequently to constrain me to shout and praise aloud, as I went along the road. On one occasion I was praising my God aloud, as a happy inhabitant of the rock (it was near midnight), and a woman who had formed the dreadful resolution to drown herself, was actually approaching the waterside for that purpose, when hearing me shouting glory to God, she was instantly arrested in her purpose. She reflected upon the rash and awful deed she was about to perpetrate; and said to herself, 'Oh what a wicked wretch am I, and what a happy man is he that shouts and praises God yonder!' This poor creature was therefore mercifully diverted from her intention and returned home. My soul enjoyed such ecstasy, both night and day, but the time I spent in sleep was comparatively trifling, notwithstanding my daily labour and religious exercises were

very great; for, after the toil of the day I attended a meeting every evening, and usually laboured till my strength failed. My Sabbath labours were also unremitting. In the first place, there was the prayer meeting at six o'clock in the morning; another followed at nine; preaching at eleven; band meeting at one; preaching at two; visiting the sick at four; preaching again at six; afterwards a prayer meeting at my own house; besides reading the Scriptures, family and private prayer, and other occasional duties. In the midst of all this ponderous labour I felt strong, active, and unspeakably happy in God.

The prayer meetings in William Clowes' house started to be attended by great numbers of people, many of them under deep spiritual conviction. There were many conversions and the work of God made rapid progress among the working people at Tunstall, Harriseahead and the region of Mow Cop on the Cheshire-Staffordshire border. Two others joined William Clowes in this work, Daniel Shubotham and Hugh Bourne. These all agreed that greater efforts should be made to bring the Gospel to those in need.

In addition to the prayer meetings a local preachers' meeting was established for the mutual improvement of the preachers in spiritual things and the discussion of theological subjects. This meeting proved to be very profitable, and served as a school in which many preachers were trained and equipped for further usefulness. The effect of their work was seen in many conversions and the general moral improvement of the whole area of the Staffordshire Potteries. An association was formed with the object of putting a check upon Sunday trading and other violations of the Christian Sabbath.

A tract distributing society was organised in the town of Burslem. This society sent out men, two by two, around the district distributing Bibles, Testaments and tracts to all who would receive them and afterwards to call again to exchange the tracts for fresh ones. Hugh Bourne became very influential amongst this group. He was the owner of a farmstead near Stoke-on-Trent and a carpenter by trade, who by his own efforts acquired an extensive education, including the knowledge of Greek, Hebrew, Latin, and French. The religious perplexities of his younger days were partly resolved by reading some Quaker literature, and this may account for a trace of mysticism that can be found in some of the early Primitive Methodists (*e.g.* The Magic Methodists of Delamere Forest). Later, a copy of John Fletcher's writings came into Hugh Bourne's hands and he was so helped and influenced by these that he became a Methodist.

He built a chapel at Harriseahead in 1800. He had no authority or permission to do such a thing for he was not at that time officially accredited as a 'local preacher', but the value of this work was recognised, and his chapel was eventually included in the Tunstall Circuit by the Wesleyan Conference. However, Bourne was not content to act on the conventional lines of the Methodist preachers. He heard of religious gatherings called 'Camp Meetings' that were being held in America, and planned to imitate them. These were large open-air meetings often held in out-of-the-way places. They were literally improvised camps, where the people engaged themselves in prayer meetings interspersed with Gospel preaching for a day, a night, and a day, and sometimes longer with short intervals for sleeping and eating. Rupert E. Davies comments:

> Reports of these meetings reached England in various forms, many of them, no doubt, garbled. Bourne was much impressed, and when Lorenzo Dow, one of the organisers of this kind of 'revival', started preaching in England, he immediately invited his assistance. As a result the first English 'Camp Meeting' took place on Mow Cop on the 31st of May 1807.
>
> Now this was just the sort of thing that Conference was afraid of. In the first place, many of the reports of American Camp Meetings had told of violent emotionalism, not unmixed with sexual licence; and in the second place, large gatherings of people (something between 2000-4000 people were said to have been present) in secluded spots were bound to be suspected of sedition. Bourne was, of course, quite innocent of any attempt at subversion and would have dealt severely with any licence. But the Conference—without making any very careful investigation— forthwith forbade 'Camp Meetings'. Bourne was compelled by his conscience to go on with them, and in 1808 was expelled from membership of the Tunstall Circuit on the curious but convenient charge of absenting himself from the Class Meeting. Soon afterwards, not very far away in Burslem, Clowes who had been a speaker at the first Camp Meeting, and had since then be

organising his own, was expelled from membership for flouting the rules of the Conference. Bourne and Clowes joined forces, and in 1810 formed the Society of Primitive Methodists.[9]

The title 'Primitive Methodist Connexion' was given, quoting the words of Hugh Bourne's *Journal*, 13th February 1812 —*'because we wish to walk as closely as we can in the steps of John Wesley'.* The influence of Primitive Methodism began to spread throughout the country, with the county of Derbyshire being one of the first areas to be affected. At Belper several prayer meetings had been conducted with great success. Hugh Bourne tells us that *'when these very powerful meetings were closed, the praying people in returning home were accustomed to sing through the streets of Belper.'* This circumstance procured them the name of 'Ranters'. The name 'Ranter', which first arose on this occasion (in connection with Methodism), afterwards spread very extensively.

The doctrines of the Primitive Methodists are set out in their 'Deed Poll' to be those set out in the first four volumes of *Wesley's Sermons*, and certain notes by him on the New Testament. The characteristic doctrine of the Primitive Methodists was that of *'a full, free and present salvation'.* They also emphasised their belief in the doctrine of instantaneous conversion.

Other emphases included, an unfavourable attitude to all national establishments of religion; the practice of infant baptism (but making a clear rejection of the dogma of baptismal regeneration); the encouragement of Temperance Societies; the rule that none of the preachers should be allowed to make speeches at parliamentary elections or at political meetings.

The conditions under which members were admitted into the Societies were simply that the applicant be animated by 'a desire to flee from the wrath to come'. Three months probation was required before full admission into fellowship was granted. The Connexion was composed of classes, one member of which was called the Leader, and usually another called the Assistant. The members of each class had their names entered into the class book; and each member held a Society ticket which was renewed quarterly. The lay officers of the body consisted of the Leader, corresponding to the Elder of the New Testament, and the Society Steward, corresponding to the Deacon. It was regarded as an indispensable qualification of a preacher among the Primitive Methodists that he gave satisfactory evidence of a Scriptural conversion to God and of the Divine call. In the induction of preachers to the ministerial office, there was no ceremony or laying on of hands as in the case of ordination in other churches. From the period of a preacher being called out, he entered upon a probation of four years, after which, if successful, he was admitted into full connexion. The salary allowed to a preacher of the Gospel was 'proverbially small,' so that there could be no temptation to anyone undertaking the ministerial office from mere worldly motives. The object of Primitive Methodism was to extend the Kingdom of Christ throughout the world by preaching the Gospel in the open-air, private houses, at public edifices, and by holding various religious services throughout its societies, congregations, circuits, branches, and missions.

From its beginnings Primitive Methodism allowed and accepted female preachers or 'exhorters'. This was argued on the grounds that it was not specifically condemned in Scripture. At that time they were the only religious body except the Society of Friends which allowed such a practice. One 19th century writer on the denomination commented that he felt the practice would die out.[10]

Primitive Methodism was clearly influenced by the underlying tensions within the larger body of Methodism at that time in regard to lay involvement in the running of the chapels and circuits and the whole issue of local freedom of action. As noted above, there was clearly some influence of Quaker mysticism as there was also the influence of early American Revivalism. Interestingly, the North West of England witnessed several clashes with the main Wesleyan body over the issue of authority in the period 1796 to 1806. Several town-based 'Free Gospel' groups, often having little or no knowledge of each other, sprang up. These went under different local names: 'Manchester Band-Room Methodists,' 'Stockport Christian Revivalists,' 'Macclesfield Christian Revivalists,' 'Preston Free Gospellers,' 'Oldham Independent Methodists,' 'Warrington Independent, and Quaker Methodists', and the 'Delamere Forest Magic Methodists' under their leader James Crawfoot. In some of these movements one cannot help but see the struggle of Wesley with mysticism, and his final emergence from it, being re-enacted within elements of the body he founded.

The Bible Christians

The same crisis in Methodism which produced the Primitive Methodist separation was repeated in Cornwall in a slightly different form in 1815. Here again a fervent preacher William O'Bryan (1778-1868) could not keep the rules of official Methodism. William O'Bryan was a Cornishman of Irish descent, his father was a wealthy farmer, and consequently he received a very adequate education. After his conversion he became an enthusiastic local preacher in the neighbourhood of Newquay, but his zeal did not allow him to be local enough in his activities to satisfy Circuit and Conference regulations. The Methodist historian Rupert E. Davies gives us the following concise outline of the Bible Christian Movement:

> Expelled from Methodist membership in 1810, O'Bryan worked as a freelance evangelist, and formed Societies in several areas which the Methodists preachers had not so far visited. In 1814 he was readmitted to the Methodist ranks, and his Societies were incorporated in the Methodist Connexion. But he was soon restive again, and a repetition of his zealous indiscipline led to a second expulsion. Once again on his own, he accepted the invitation of James Thorne, not a Methodist but an Anglican profoundly dissatisfied with the ministrations of his Church, to work in the village of Shebbear in North Devon. Here, in 1815 the Bible Christian Society was founded, and organised on Methodist lines, with O'Bryan as the first President of its Conference and James Thorne the first Secretary.
>
> This was not, strictly, a Methodist schism, because, apart from O' Bryan himself, the first Bible Christians were not Methodists at all in the accepted sense. In the first years of the movement they operated in rural areas untouched by the Wesleyan Methodists, and were careful not to compete with them in any way; though they spread eastwards as far as Bristol and the Isle of Wight, there was never any deliberate opposition. Yet if O'Bryan had been more amenable and the Wesleyan Conference more flexible, it would have been natural for the Bible Christian

Societies to have become part of ordinary Methodism, to the great advantage of all. O'Bryan himself was no doubt a firebrand and an individualist: the Bible Christian Conference resisted his claims to be a perpetual President and decide all matters by his single vote, and he set off to found a new sect in America and Canada. But James Thorne was a balanced and catholic-spirited man, and under his guidance the New Connexion advanced steadily in the West Country. Its most notable, or notorious, achievements were the full authorisation of women itinerant preachers (whom the men preachers were advised to marry), and the evangelistic exploits of Billy Bray (1794-1868) a converted drunkard, whose name is still to be conjured with in Cornish Nonconformity.[11]

The Bible Christians united with the Methodist New Connexion and the United Methodist Free Churches, to form the United Methodist Church on the 17th November 1907.

The Protestant Methodists

In 1827 controversy arose over the installation of an organ in the Brunswick Wesleyan Chapel, Leeds. The dispute centred upon the prerogatives of the superintendent minister, the District Meeting, and of the Wesleyan Conference itself. It was once widely known within Methodism that the Brunswick organ cost over £1,000 to install, and also cost the Leeds Wesleyans 1000 members. The dispute was largely a further surfacing of the Congregational principle within Methodism, over against the clerical supremacy of the Conference. I quote the following accounts of the dispute as given by Joseph Kersop, a champion of the Protestant Methodists, in his now rare book *Historic Sketches of Free Methodism,* in which we sense at first hand a feeling of the tensions within the movement at that time.

> Organs were not permitted in Methodist chapels during John Wesley's day. 'A bass viol when required by the singers,' was at the extent of indulgence accorded by him to instruments of music. After his death a rule was made permitting organs under certain circumstances. As it was thought organs might be wanted in large chapels, the Conference determined that, on the recommendation of district meetings, consent might be given. If the district meeting thought that in any case consent ought not to be given, its decision

JABEZ BUNTING

MR. JAMES SIGSTON, PROTESTANT METHODISTS, 1828.

REV. R. ECKETT REV. J. EVERETT REV. S. DUNN
1797 – 1862   1784 – 1872   1797 – 1882

THREE PROTAGONISTS OF METHODIST REFORM

AN EXTERIOR VIEW OF BRUNSWICK CHAPEL, LEEDS

**THE INTERIOR OF BRUNSWICK CHAPEL,
SHOWING THE CELEBRATED ORGAN**

SAMUEL WARREN LL.D.
President of the
Wesleyan Association Assembly,

HALTON ROAD WESLEYAN CHAPEL, RUNCORN
The size and grandeur illustrating the dominance of Methodism
in the northern industrial towns during the 19th century

BALLIE STREET CHAPEL, ROCHDALE
Where the first UMFC Conference was held in 1857

BALLIE STREET CHAPEL, ROCHDALE
Interior

was final. On the erection of Brunswick Chapel, Leeds, some of the trustees and seat holders wished for an organ to be placed in it. On the matter being mentioned in the leaders' meeting, the executive of the church, the superintendent minister and his colleague assured the leaders that it could not be done without their consent. A memorial on the subject was presented to the leaders by those who favoured the organ, and it was determined, by 60 votes to 1, that it was not desirable that an organ should be put in the chapel. The trustees, however, by a majority determined to apply to the district meeting. When this meeting, which is the court next in importance to the Conference, assembled exception was taken to the consideration of the application, as it did not emanate from the leaders' meeting, which alone, and not the trustees, had a 'locus standi' in the matter.

The objection, however, was waived and on the subject being considered on its merits, the district meeting determined, by a great majority, that no organ should be erected. By the law binding on the connexion, the matter ought to have rested here. The Conference itself had made the district meetings supreme judges in such cases. No appeal lay from their decision. That this is the obvious interpretation of the rule I do not see how anyone can dispute. I quote it that my readers may judge for themselves. 'We think that in some of the larger chapels where some instrumental music may be deemed expedient, in order to guide the congregational singing, organs may be allowed by special consent of the Conference; but every application for such consent shall be first made at the district meeting; and if it obtain their sanction, shall be then referred to a committee at the Conference, who shall report their opinion as to the propriety of acceding to the request.' The words 'and if it obtains their sanction', show that the Conference had only to be consulted when the district meeting had given its consent.

The Conference itself, by its action, showed that the consent of the district meeting was necessary ere an organ could be erected. Yet the majority of the trustees, actuated by some motive which I shall not characterise, determined to apply to Conference. No doubt they knew they had a powerful friend in court whose influence was paramount. The Rev. Jabez Bunting for many years was the dominant authority in Conference Methodism. He wielded the power of a dictator. The eulogists of Dr Bunting contend that he cherished and developed lay influence in connexional affairs. No doubt there is a truth in this, but it must be remembered that in all his movements he was careful to retain and extend ministerial supremacy. An Augustus or a Louis Napoleon does not object to a senate, if its powers are only shadowy. Ecclesiastical absolutists reign all the more securely if their power seems to rest on a broad foundation. Dr Bunting did not believe in popular rights. It was in connection with the Leeds organ case that he uttered his famous saying: 'Methodism knows nothing of democracy; Methodism hates democracy as it hates sin.' A straw may show which way the way the wind blows.[12]

The Conference upheld the decision of the trustees to erect the organ in spite of the decision of the district meeting. They appointed the superintendent minister of the Leeds East Circuit the Rev. E Grindrod to implement the decision. The district meeting appealed to do nothing for a year in order for the next Conference to have opportunity of reviewing the whole affair. This however Grindrod ignored and suspended for three months the secretary of the local preachers for the 'offence' of calling them together to discuss the matter. Needless to say there was widespread dissatisfaction with the action taken and many of the leading preachers of the area resigned in protest. A Connexion of churches with several thousand members was formed having its own ministers and an Annual Assembly. They went under the designation 'Protestant Methodist', and founded churches throughout West Yorkshire, notably in Leeds, Sheffield, Barnsley and Keighley. The local nature of the dispute at first prevented the secession from being large or general, although as we shall see, further divisions on the same general principle were soon to follow.

These agitations within Methodism at that time are often attributed to the general unrest within society and the pressing for more universal political rights that resulted in the passing of the Reform Bill of 1832. There is no doubt that in spite of Methodism's official prohibition of political involvement by its preachers and leaders, many of them were involved in political reform. One only has to remember the Tolpuddle Martyrs and the fact that the Wesleyan Chapel in Rochdale at that time was in Toad Lane, the birthplace of the Co-operative Movement. Trade Unions became legal in 1824 and the Methodist Conference did not forbid its members to join them. It is well-known that because of long training in Class Meetings, the Methodist were often the most articulate members of their social group and soon rose up to positions of prominence within the Trade Union movement and other kindred movements of the time. This democratic spirit within Methodism may be traced back much further, to that within Protestantism itself. Georgia Harkness speaks of 'the leaven of democracy inherent in Calvinism'.[13] Ernst Troeltsch in his *The Social Teaching of the Christian Churches* speaks of the democratic tendency of Calvinism as follows:

> The first sign of this influence can be traced in a certain democratic constitutional tendency which the Geneva experiment produced. It is, of course possible to point out that Calvin's personal point of view was as undemocratic and authoritarian as possible; that, further, in spite of the fact that the whole community shared in the life of the church, Calvin's Church Constitution, with its basis in the Divine Church order and with its special connection with the aristocratic constitution of the city, was still in no sense a congregational democracy, and, finally, that the Geneva Constitution itself, under the influence of Calvin, and in line with the spirit of the period, developed more in the direction of an oligarchy than a democracy. That is all quite true. Nevertheless, in the last resort, the final effect of this interpretation of the City Republic with the National Church was a strong impulse in the direction of democracy, toward the principle of the sovereignty of the people. The reason for that is that the whole aim of the Government was to secure the reasonable welfare of the individual which is required by the law of nature, and in this sense the State was to be conformable to reason. A far greater influence on the direction of democracy was, however, exercised by the fact that the final and decisive method of influencing the political authority in this sense was the appeal to public opinion, and to the electors through the sermon.[14]

The same democratic spirit was evident in Puritanism:

> It can safely be said that wherever we see true democracy, the principle that the will of the people must prevail in the prominence

of the lay element in the church, there you have Puritanism under whatever new or old name it may be pleased to designate itself.[15]

Further, we can observe here the surfacing of the Nonconformist spirit of Wesley himself. These years were characterised by the outbreak of independent evangelistic outreach in various areas of Methodism (though it is true that as in the case of Primitive Methodism these movements were sometimes influenced by American revivalism). Certainly the Band Room Methodist of Manchester, incidentally founded by John Broadhurst of the famous textile firm, were of this character and resented the restrictions placed upon their activities by (we could say) the more sober-minded and respectable Wesleyan ministers in Conference.

Another similar group at this time were the Tent Methodists who again broke free from the more formal structures of Wesleyanism. This group had penetrated the working-class area of Ancoats, but in the same way its leaders, John Pyer and Peter Arrive, were expelled.

The fundamental principle of religious liberty lay at the heart of many of these controversies. At the height of the Leeds organ controversy the respected Wesleyan theologian Richard Watson stated that the people had no right to meddle with the question of religious worship. Though we can readily understand this principle and see that within the life of an individual church, the minister, called by the church, has the responsibility to see that worship is carried out decently and in order, a wider principle was at stake, *i.e.* that the local churches be allowed to worship according to the dictates of their conscience in regard to their interpretation of Scripture.

This was one of the great issues of the 17th century raising itself again at the beginning of the 19th century. As we shall see shortly these various groups of Free Methodists traced their lineal descent through John Wycliffe and the Puritans and saw the Conference's interference in these matters as akin to the Roman Church's persecution of Protestants in the 16th century, and later the Established Church's persecution of Nonconformists in the 17th century. Wesley, though conservative and wishing to remain within the Established Church, struggled with a contrary impulse. His inherent Puritanism and his desire to reach out with the Gospel

CHAPTER SEVENTEEN 229

caused him to defy restrictive authority and to follow the leadings of the Spirit of God. This trait within Wesley was well-expressed in his brother's hymn, as previously quoted, *Shall I for fear of feeble man the Spirit's course in me impede.*

There was yet another issue which contributed to this unrest that was evident in many of the large urban areas: i.e. a desire to build impressive and architecturally grand chapel buildings. For example, in Liverpool the Brunswick Chapel had an ionic porch and a semicircular interior of acknowledged elegance. In the same city Stanhope Street Chapel was so constructed that it had a 'semi-religious light' falling through an oval window of stained-glass designed to cast a certain glow upon the communion table. Many Wesleyan chapels at this time had paid choirs, doorkeepers and pew-openers. Many of these larger, prosperous chapels introduced fully liturgical services. The same Brunswick Chapel Liverpool set the pattern with a clerk in attendance to read the versicles.

Many resented these innovations as contrary to the spirit of Methodism. Moreover the new chapels of the period were strengthened in their influence by the fact that Conference seemed to adopt a policy of sending the more able ministers to them and the less talented to the older and plainer chapels. These issues lay behind the Methodist tensions and divisions of the first half of the 19th century. The fact that these tensions existed, and that they had to do with the tension between Anglican and Puritan, Established Churchman and Nonconformist that existed within Wesley himself, is the contention of this book.

The Wesleyan Methodist Association

The Wesleyan Methodist Association also came about as a result of the issues described above, but in particular it arose out of the determination of the Wesleyan Conference to establish a theological institution for the training of junior ministers. Quoting again from Joseph Kirsop's *History of Free Methodism*:

> To many it seemed that the evils which must attend the opening of the Wesleyan Theological Institution would far outweigh any possible advantages, and they did, therefore, conscientiously set their face against the proposal. The dismal apprehensions which

the objectors cherished are shown in a letter that the Rev. James Everett wrote to Dr Warren, dated December 4, 1834:

'All is dark; Methodism is ruined. I see in vision a fine natural orator lost, and instead of a bold, hale, original, and powerful ministry, there is the refined sentimentality of some other denominations—all form, all system; a shadow of the past; the ghost of a Primitive Methodist preacher—the moon in her frosty brightness; instead of the sun going forth in his might.'

Mr Everett sums up his objections to the proposal in a manner which would probably have been agreeable to nearly all who took part against it. His objections were fivefold. The people had not been consulted; the scheme was forced on by packed committees; the scheme was costly and extensive; it was suspected that one grand design of the scheme was to aid centralisation by keeping Dr Bunting in London; and it was likely to foster exclusive ideas of ministerial supremacy.[16]

The substance of Dr Warren's argument against the Theological College was that it threatened to overthrow a system of proven efficiency and success, that it lacked the general support of the Methodist people, and that the general improvement in educational standards would automatically guarantee a supply of intelligent young candidates. The principal objection however, was that the enterprise concentrated power in the hands of a few individuals, and as such, endangered the liberty of the preachers and the unity of the Connexion. 'The possibilities are frightening in the extreme', Warren observed in his conclusion.

Does not everyone see that we are all supposed to see the President of the Institution to be possessed of Episcopal propensities, and it follows, as a matter of course, that the Institution will soon become, neither more nor less, that neither better nor worse—if indeed worse can come of it—than a Dominant Episcopal Faction. From hence the Connexion must prepare itself to receive a liturgical Service, a splendid Ritual, and a legitimate Episcopal Ordination, a cassocked-race of Ecclesiastics, and whatever else may render this new—this improved edition of Methodism, imposing and magnificent in the eyes of the world.[17]

It is clear that the main opposition to the opening of a theological college was not that of opposition to a college as such, but to the fact that the scheme was pressed forward by the Conference without due consultation of the people. Indeed it was generally regarded that the Conference had broken the terms of the Leeds Concessions of 1797. These stated as follows:

> In order to prevent any degree of precipitation in making new rules, and to obtain information of the sentiments of our people on every such rule, we have agreed to the article mentioned under the seventh head, by which no regulations will be finally confirmed till after a year's consideration, and the knowledge of the sentiments of the Connexion at large, through the medium of all the public officers.

The Wesleyan Conference of 1834, it might be argued, broke the letter and the spirit of this rule. It is not my intention to go into every aspect of these now almost forgotten controversies, but the important point which they highlight is that there was a vital Free Church, with markedly Protestant and Puritan elements within Methodism at this time. These facts are important because they throw light upon an aspect of Methodism that is now almost entirely lost sight of, and also an aspect of John Wesley's character which the revisionists of the early 20ᵗʰ century have almost succeeded in obscuring.

To complete the history however, in 1837 the Wesleyan Association was formed out of an amalgamation of the Protestant Methodists, the Warrenites, the Scarborough Independents with their minister Matthew Baxter (who was later to write the *Memorials of the United Methodist Free Churches*) and the Arminian Methodists of Derby, sometimes called the 'Derby Faith Methodists'. The Arminian Methodists were, as their alternate name suggests, first established in Derby but also had circuits at Nottingham, Leicester, Redditch and elsewhere.

Their origin has been traced to the expulsion at Derby of four local preachers for continuing a Band Meeting longer than the usual period, on a Saturday evening. Regarding this as an arbitrary and unnecessary cause for discipline, six hundred sympathisers in Derby at once withdrew from the Wesleyan society. The Connexion was formed which took the name of 'The Arminian Methodists'. The title seems strange when we consider that those who formed the new body were leaving a Church avowedly Arminian. The Derby Methodists accused the Wesleyans of, in Wesley's own terms, leaning too much toward Calvinism, the inference of the term, however, was that the Wesleyan body were neglecting evangelism. We note that this body of Methodists still regarded Calvinism as synonymous with a neglect of evangelism. It is sometimes suggested that there was a slight divergence on the part of the Arminian Methodists from ordinary Methodistic belief. They held, it is said, that faith was entirely in man's own power, so they objected to waiting for or praying for faith, and held that faith was a mere intellectual assent, a kind of Sandemanianism.

That there were elements of this kind of teaching infiltrating Methodism slightly after this period, through the teaching of the American evangelist James Caughey, cannot be denied. However, this was never the official teaching of the Arminian Methodists. The Rev. Henry Breeden, their first Minister, declared, 'The doctrines held by the Arminians were the same as those held by the Wesleyans.'[18] It might also be added that the union of the Arminian Methodists with the Association also indicates that no doctrinal difficulties stood in the way.

The Wesleyan Reformers

This movement in effect came into being after the Wesleyan Conference of 1849 at which three ministers, James Everett, Samuel Dunn, and William Griffith were expelled. The reason for their expulsion was in consequence of their real or supposed connection with the publication of a series of pamphlets called *Fly Sheets* in which some of the procedures of the Conference, and notably the autocratic behaviour of the President of the Conference, the Rev. Dr Jabez Bunting, were criticised.

> What could, it may be asked at this point of time, for there have arisen a generation which knew not Jabez, what could have caused all this controversy? Turn to the titles of the *Fly Sheets*. The first dealt with 'Location, Centralisation, and Secularisation'—officials stayed too long in office, and were all, or nearly all, located too long in London; they were suspected of

cliquism and secret intrigues. The Connexional committees were the preserve of a select few. The second number dealt with the 'The Presidential Chair, the Platform, and the Connexional Committee'; the mode of electing the latter should be changed. The fourth dealt with the Stationing Committee, which it stigmatised as the 'slaughterhouse of ministerial character'.

On almost every page, Dr Bunting's name appears in an unfavourable light. The question that naturally strikes us is; Were these charges true? William Redfern, writing soberly in 1906 says, 'substantially, though perhaps not in every particular, the statements were true' —which no doubt is why they were never answered, and why, instead, attention was drawn to discovering if possible the anonymous author.[19]

The problem again was the fact that there was no lay representation within the Methodist Conference. It sat behind closed doors, and no public reports of it appeared, except against its will. It is generally regarded that the criticisms of the *Fly Sheets*, written and circulated anonymously, were justified on the grounds that all public criticism was stifled by the ruling party in Conference under Dr Bunting.

We need at this point to make some comment on the character of Jabez Bunting, who Dr John Kent, in his small biography, has described as *The Last Wesleyan*. He might also aptly be described as the greatest Methodist since John Wesley. Even his critics, such as Gregory, speak of him as possessing 'a surpassing genius for organisation and administration, and notes that he was a mighty theologian, a born orator, a born financier, a born debater, and a born pleader'.[20]

Even James Everett, who was accused of being the author of the *Fly Sheets*, was able to pay the following tribute to Dr Bunting:

All acquitted of selfishness; all unite in giving him credit for the purest motives; and when his proceedings are viewed in the aggregate, he will be found to be generally philanthropic in his views, dealings, and purposes. But we again inquire—How has he obtained such ascendancy in the body? Not by fraud, not by misconduct; but by lending his superior talents to promote the best interests of the Connexion.[21]

A further tribute comes from the testimony of Matthew Johnson, one of the men expelled in 1827 as a result of Bunting's intervention in the Leeds Organ Case:

> His knowledge of the human heart, its depravity, and the means for its recovery, was profound; his statement of divine truth was singularly clear and cogent; his reasoning is forcible and satisfactory; whilst his appeal to the judgment of conscience was such as I may, without hesitation, say, I never heard equalled by any other preacher of the Gospel.—But there was one other important qualification of a Minister of the Gospel in which Mr Bunting greatly excelled, and that was an extraordinary gift of prayer. Such earnest, heartfelt pleadings with the Almighty were seldom heard in the pulpit from the lips of any other man.

It is also a fact that Dr Bunting's famous sermon on *Justification by Faith Alone,* remains one of the spiritual crown jewels of Methodism.

Though all this is beyond doubt, it was also the case that Dr Bunting was, to use the description of his own deeply spiritual son, William McCardie Bunting, 'Masterful!' Dr Bunting could not brook opposition. Like a spoiled child, who could not get his own way, 'he would not play the game.' On one occasion when opposed, he threatened to leave the presidential chair and dissolve the Conference. On another, for a similar reason, he threatened to resign all his offices. On one occasion it is said that Charles Wesley threatened to leave the room when his mind was not carried, and his brother John replied: 'Reach my brother his hat.' It has been said that it would have been better if Conference had once or twice reached Dr Bunting his hat! Conference however seemed always to give in to Dr Bunting's threats, he always got his own way, and hence the *Fly Sheets* were written, resulting in the expulsion of Everett, Dunn, and Griffith. The main points for which the Wesleyan Reformers were contending were that they protested against arbitrary rule, urged temperance reform, and desired the cooperation of lay men with ministers in the legislation and government of Wesleyan Methodism.

George Eayrs in his *The Story of our Founders* comments:

> Few will now deny that in this struggle grievous mistakes were made on both sides. Principles were obscured by personalities.

Anonymity, mere bush fighting, is a strange method for Christian combatants, and should have been left, if used at all, to those who had no other protection. Was there as much anxiety to answer the accusations, or remove the grounds for them, as to find out the accusers? And did not the arbitrariness and harshness often shown to the Reform party amply illustrate their strictures and support its pleas; sometimes the story may be told as part of the history of Methodism and all its branches, and credit given to the Reformers, as well as the Conference for their share of suffering and services securing improvements since adopted, and as pioneers in temperance and social work, the champions of the freedom of the Press.

As the wars and fightings of Cromwell's days, and the sufferings of Bunyan and Baxter, secured the peaceful Revolution and settled liberty of 1688, so those of the Wesleyan Reformers found their sequel in the admission of lay men to the Wesleyan Conference in 1877, and other approaches towards scriptural liberty.[22]

Though this statement is fair-minded and aims to be conciliatory, one senses that Dr Eyres, who was in the Free Methodist tradition himself, greatly admired their cause and identifies it with the great Puritan struggles for religious liberty of the 17th century.

In 1850, a petition bearing 50,000 signatures was presented to the Wesleyan Conference seeking reform on the lines outlined above. This petition was rejected and many of those who signed it were also disfellowshiped from their churches. It is estimated that a total of more than 100,000 left Wesleyan Methodism over this period of disruption.

The United Methodist Free Churches

In 1857 there was an amalgamation of the Wesleyan Association and the greater part of the Wesleyan Reformers. The Foundation Deed of the Wesleyan Association was adopted as the deed of both bodies. The constitution endeavoured to combine connexionalism and circuit independence. In other words there was a bond of union between the churches but at the same time there was a large measure of independence given to each church and circuit. The local church and circuit were effectively self-governing while the Annual

Assembly composed of ministers and laymen, freely elected, exercised control on the ministry and all Connexional institutions. Its first President was the Rev. James Everett; and its second the Rev. Robert Eckett. Union was accomplished gradually. By 1859 the new body had a membership of 59,000.

A number of the Wesleyan Reformers did not enter into this union and they remain a separate denomination to this day.

The Free Methodists described above consistently advocated traditional patterns of Methodist life; there was a strong emphasis upon the class meetings, preaching and evangelism. The cry was often heard that the people were exchanging boxes of whistles (organs) for true praise, and forms of prayer for heart worship. They were particularly opposed to liturgical worship and complained of infrequent pastoral visitation. One noted Free Methodist, Henry Pooley, a once well known grate manufacturer, when expelled from his chapel, remarked dramatically: 'We are treading in the steps of Martin Luther.'[23]

Matthew Baxter, mentioned above, became one of the leaders of the movement and wrote its history. His book *Memorials of the United Methodist Free Churches* sets out to identify Methodism as being in the great tradition of Protestant Dissenters. His first chapter is entitled, 'The Obligations England owes to Protestant Dissenters'. He traces out the history of Protestant dissent in Britain through Wycliffe and the Lollards, stating of the Methodists:

> Our true ancestors were reformers before the Reformation. While hostile Popes in the latter part of the 14th century were offering rival masses in rival cities, and eagerly soliciting the suffrages of the various nations of Christendom, Wycliffe, notwithstanding that he had recently been accused by the Papacy of nineteen errors in doctrine, consecrated his energies with renewed zeal to the diffusion of evangelic truth over this country.

He goes on to describe the character of the Puritans of the 17th century and the noble character of the Nonconformists of that period. He sees Methodism and in particular the United Methodist Free Church as standing in the same tradition as the Nonconformists in 1662, opposing the Act of Uniformity.[24]

CHAPTER EIGHTEEN

CONCLUSIONS

1. That John Wesley followed broadly speaking in the tradition of the Protestant Reformers of the 16th century.

2. This work has sought to challenge certain common modern anti-Protestant misconceptions of John Wesley:
   a. That he epitomised a radical Arminian reaction against the influences of Genevan theology in English Christianity.
   b. That he was the historical successor and finisher of the work of Archbishop Laud.
   c. That he undertook to break the bond between the Reformation and English Christianity and to restore the Roman Catholic tradition.

3. I have also sought to challenge the well-known maxim, that 'Methodism is Arminianism on fire'.

I acknowledge that from the beginning of his ministry Wesley accepted an Arminian modification of extreme Calvinism. I further recognise that when he founded the *Arminian Magazine* in 1778, some 40 years after his conversion and the beginning of the revival, his stated aim in publishing it was that of checking the extravagances of ultra-Calvinism. Nevertheless I have sought to maintain that his doctrines were fundamentally those of the English Reformers and as he himself stated, 'within a hair's breadth of Calvinism.' I fully concur with the now almost forgotten sentiments of George Croft Cell writing in 1934, when he said:

> The fierce controversies that arose and raged around Wesley's staunch advocacy of the Arminian corrective of extreme Calvinism created and fixed the impression that Wesley's doctrine of Christian experience is fundamentally anti-

Calvinistic, so that the term Arminian has commonly been taken to describe the content of Wesley's preaching, at any rate a conspicuous, if not the most conspicuous element in it. But this thesis will not stand the test; it falls to the ground before an objective analysis of the content of Wesley's preaching. He himself said flatly that the corrective to extreme Calvinism was the special interest and burden of less than one in a hundred of his pulpit utterances (Letters IV, 297). The other ninety-nine were concerned solely with the fundamentals of Christian experience which he always claimed to share with Calvinism.

It may be then that the formula 'Methodism is Arminianism on fire', if intended as an objective description of the content of Wesley's preaching, of its regnant doctrinal ideas, is much more felicitous in the phrasing than accurate as to the facts. For Arminianism never has been, never was for John Wesley, Francis Asbury, and their colleagues, is not now and never will be the source of the fire. It admits of full proof that the religious energy of Wesley's message lay in its unity with the faith of the first Reformers and not in any deviation from them. There need be no doubt or uncertainty whatsoever that the principle of power and the supreme resource in the preaching alike of Whitfield and the Wesleys by which, all agree, a religious revolution was begun in England, was the Luther-Calvin idea of the sovereign saving significance of a God-given faith in Christ as a perfect revelation of God and the complete atonement for sin. It is often perhaps commonly supposed that the theological differences between Whitfield and the Wesleys were profound while their doctrinal agreements were superficial, at any rate far less important. But they certainly did not think so and Wesley roundly denounced that view as close to absurdity. Wesley is on record, not once but often and always, stating that the peculiar religious energy of the Wesleyan revival came out of the unity of the Protestant faith, the very heart of it, and not out of its divergences. 'It is the faith of our first Reformers which I by the grace of God preach.' (Letters II, 134).[1]

4. I have also sought to emphasise in the chapter on the Oxford Sermons and their being in effect the manifesto of the revival, that Wesley's great theme was salvation 'by grace alone', and

that 'It is God alone who worketh in us both to will and to do of his good pleasure'.

These manifesto sermons display not the slightest hint of an intention to correct Calvinistic theology but are rather a triumphant reaffirmation of the great principles of the Reformation.

It is true that in his sermon on Free Grace he called the doctrine of predestination, a doctrine full of 'horrible blasphemies,' also saying that 'No scripture can prove predestination.' However, it must also be acknowledged that such an extreme reaction against the doctrine did not represent him in the full maturity of his mind. He did some thirty years later retract the view that it was subversive of the very foundations of Christian experience.[2] It is true that he could never accept the doctrine of predestination in the full Calvinistic sense. However, we have tried to show that Wesley's difficulties in this area must not divert our attention from the fact that he thoroughly believed in the total depravity of man's nature, and man's utter inability to save himself, and that salvation was by faith altogether by the grace of God, all of which indeed are essentially Calvinistic teachings.

Arthur Cushman McGiffert in his *Protestant Thought before Kant,* observes that:

> Wesley's strong emphasis upon the Fall, and resulting depravity, was more akin to historic Calvinism than to a system which arose in opposition to it, by which in its inception felt, though ever so slightly, the influence of the modern interest in the ability and worth of man.

Pertinently Cell asks the question:

> How has the fact of Wesley's conscious and avowed concurrence with historic Calvinism in evangelical principles been obscured? How has his striking definition of his early theological position as a qualified or guarded Calvinism —'within a hair's breadth' —been ignored by his 'Arminian' interpreters? How has his theology been identified, at variance with the facts as well as with his own reiterated protests, by most of his latter interpreters, by some in part, by others outright, either with semi-Pelagianism or even Pelagianism, imputing to him a

doctrine of faith which he earnestly, indignantly repudiated; namely, that man is in moral matters by nature free, or that the feeling of freedom ever can be, for the Christian consciousness, a reality distinct from the grace of God? Wesley's whole relation to early Reformation principles has been clouded and forgotten under the influence of this serious misconception.[3]

It will also be noted that John Wesley did not develop a doctrine of free will but rather a doctrine of holiness in order, as he saw it, to be a correction to extreme Calvinism. In this again he follows in the steps of both Luther and Calvin in his insistence that man's power to co-operate with the Divine will both at the beginning of the Christian life and in the continuance of the Christian life, is only by the sheer undeserved grace of God.

'I have constantly declared and continually testified in private and in public these five and twenty years that we are sanctified as well as justified by faith, that exactly as we are justified by faith, so we are sanctified by faith.' Verily this is, as to the meaning of faith, once more the voice of Luther: 'Faith is, has and does all in the whole realm of Christian experience.' And there is never room in the Christian consciousness for any self-righteousness, a trust in man and taint of pride or self-will. The more advanced we are in Christian experience, the more it is true that we are after justification 'more ashamed of our best duties than formerly of our worst sins'.(Sermons 50) It is true not only of the entire work of God, but above all of Christian experience from first to last that it is permeated by 'A conviction of our helplessness, of our utter inability to think one good thought or perform one good action, but through God's free, almighty grace, first preventing us and then accompanying us every moment.' For Wesley then, all the true values of religion, be it natural religion or revealed religion, or under any other name, are forever wrapped up in the feeling of total dependence on God.[4]

It can also be noted that in the 19th century it was recognised that there was a marked difference between the Wesleys' Arminianism and that which was commonly known as Arminianism both in the 17th century and in modern times. R.W. Dale of Birmingham, the noted Congregationalist, writing of the theology of John Wesley commented:

The obligation which, under God, the older nonconformist Churches of England owe to Methodism cannot be measured. When John Wesley began his work their strength had been seriously diminished. There were complaints that congregations were wasting away; and that the sons and the daughters of the wealthier Nonconformists were passing over to the Episcopal Church. It was said that between the accession of George I in 1714, and the year 1731, more than 50 Dissenting ministers took orders in the Establishment. Those who contested the accuracy of these strong statements concerning the decay of the Dissenting interest, and who insisted that in some parts of the country Dissenting churches were declining, while in others their strength was growing, acknowledged that the Dissenters were discouraged; that they were suffering from a want of buoyancy and energy in their religious life; that the stricter manners and severer morals of an earlier generation were disappearing; and other movements of theological opinion among them gave occasion for great anxiety. To you (that is the Methodists) our fathers did not look for deliverance. Wesley's Arminianism filled them with alarm. Nor was their alarm without reason. There had been a great drifting among the Nonconformist churches during the first 30 or 40 years of the 18th century from the central articles of the Christian faith, and this was one of the principal causes of their weakness. The Divinity of our Lord had been denied, and the atonement which he had achieved for men by his death; and these grave and ruinous errors had almost always begun with a surrender of the characteristic doctrines of Calvinism. Even where Arminianism had not come to these disastrous issues, it had paralysed the strength of Christian faith and quenched the fire of spiritual earnestness. But creeds which coincide in some of the principal articles may cover wholly different systems of religious thought, and wholly different conditions of the spiritual life. The Arminianism of many of the Nonconformists at the beginning of the 18th century appears to have been the result, in part of that cold and powerless conception of God which is given by Deism, a conception which removes him to an infinite distance from all his creatures, and leaves man to work out his own destiny in an environment of unchanging mechanical laws. It was the result of the decaying sense of the energy and freedom of the life of the Eternal and of God's immanent presence and activity in the material universe and in man. It affirmed that man was free partly because it conceived of God as remote. Wesley's Arminianism had a wholly different root. For him the universe was not a wonderful mechanism which had been projected into being by a succession of creative acts, and then left to work according to the laws of its structure; for him God did not live apart from his creation, reigning on heights of inaccessible majesty. He believed that in God 'we live and move, and have our being'.[5]

Likewise the Methodist leader George Jackson in his *The Old Methodism and The New*, observes:

> Nearly all the fire and depth of religious life that remained among the Dissenters was found among those who held fast to Calvinism. It was, therefore natural that when Wesley began his vehement attack upon predestination the really devoted and earnest men among the Nonconformists regarded him with distrust and hostility. They had not then discovered that, as Dr Dorner has pointed out (*History of Protestant Theology* Vol II p92), the Arminianism of Wesley was really, as far as saving doctrines were concerned nearer to the old Reformed system to which they clung than to the Arminianism which not without reason they both feared and hated.[6]

In a fascinating article in the American-based *Methodist Review* of 1886, the editor, Daniel Curry, discusses the theological departures of the Calvinistic Churches in Europe and America, with a special emphasis upon the New Orthodoxy School of Andover College. The writer detects within this movement the dangerous trend towards making 'the operation of faith effectual by personal obedience'. The writer goes on to state:

> It is quite safe to declare that 'yielding the heart' is not identical with a faith that saves the soul, though it is very nearly related to it; and were it so, to yield the heart is a work that calls for much more than the natural willpower of the individual; and therefore we should hesitate without a very careful definition of terms to subscribe to his statement, 'It is a doing that must save you,' for the faith that saves is only in its last and least manifestations a doing at all.And then the purposed interposition of repentance and holiness as prominent conditions essential to salvation, is not quite

in harmony with Paul's doctrine of justification 'without the deeds of the law', or our Lord's unqualified declaration that 'He that believeth on the Son hath (not shall have) eternal life.' There is one thing, and only one, for the awakened sinner to do, and that is to pray, as 'the Spirit giveth utterance', and chiefly for one thing, the increase of faith. We are not forgiven because we repent; we are not rewarded with eternal life because we consent to trust Christ. Our reading and hearing of the utterances of many that are esteemed the most decidedly evangelical of the religious teachers of these times have made us very jealous for the simple truths of the Gospel, and for the honour of Christ, who saves only and absolutely graciously, giving salvation without price or condition to those who will receive it; and yet how slow are even Christians to believe this! We sing, 'In my hands no price I bring,' but still would like to bring with us the beginnings of penitence and the germs of inwrought holiness. We pray, 'Just as I am,' but still would like to have a little better preparation of heart in which to come before God.

In another place we have written something about saving faith, a few sentences of which we will here reproduce, as pertinent to the subject indicated above. 'In its last analysis, faith appears to be less an active than a quiescent state of the soul —its subjective spiritual estate. As in our sensations and perceptions we are acted upon rather than ourselves act, so in the processes of faith we are illuminated, taught, led, by something not of our own personality. The great things ascribed to faith are not of its own efficiency, but rather of that to which the soul willingly submits itself. And while continued unbelief is always the result of a vicious resistance of the truth, entailing personal guilt, the only possible merit of faith is the negative one of submitting to be saved. High as is the office assigned to faith in the soul's salvation, it nowhere rises above the character of a willing receptivity and earnest acceptance of proffered mercy. When it is said that we are justified by faith, it is not intended to ascribe to faith anything really meritorious, for it neither purchases any thing nor performs any active service in its acceptance.'[7]

The writer also detects within the New Orthodoxy the notion that conviction of sin is to be defined as 'an intelligent spiritual realisation' of guilt before God. The writer agrees with the statement as far as it goes, but clearly sees it as an inadequate statement of this element in the conversion experience. He comments:

> A man may have a clear, and intelligent, and scriptural theory of the way of salvation through Christ, and a painful sense of his need of salvation, and yet find himself unable to so take hold upon these things that through them he shall find peace for his soul and escape from the fear of wrath. The kind of believing which is the one indispensable condition of salvation is only in its lowest and least experienced form a predicate of the understanding. 'With the heart man believeth unto righteousness;' and the exercises of the heart are not directly subject to the volitions. The awakened conscience may realise guilt, but it cannot break the power of sin; it may cause the cry for deliverance, but the effectual help must come from Christ himself, for which man can only pray. The power to see how that help may come to the sinner is the gift of the Spirit, who also gives effect to the soul's struggles for its realisation.

The writer of the article however concurs with one writer of the New Divinity School, a certain Mr Cook in that he remains orthodox in his statement:

> God does not force the door, nor compel the choice, but he persuades the heart, and gives the needed power to make its choice effectual. Mr Cook seems to concede, and indeed to assert, all these things, and in so doing places himself precisely upon the grounds of Wesleyan Arminianism which, however, is not the same with the Arminianism of the later Remonstrants, and of the Church of England in the 18th century, in whose sight Arminius himself was essentially a Calvinist.

However, the writer warns of the general trend of this new movement in that it tends towards giving concessions to man's personal ability and man's own natural strength. He continues:

> No doubt 'to knock is an act of man's free will' —not, however, of a will unnaturally free, but a divinely emancipated will. Nor do the long spiritual impressions made by the invitations to repentance and salvation of the divine Word and Providence inspire the gracious

desires that bring the man to Christ; but, instead, it is the inward working of divine power in the soul. All this is stated alike clearly and beautifully in one of our hymns; for in these it may be said one may find an unequalled system of evangelical theology:

> Long my imprisoned spirit lay,
> Fast bound in sin and nature's night;
> Thine eye diffused a quickening ray,
> I woke, the dungeon flamed with light:
> My chains fell off, my heart was free,
> I rose, went forth, and followed thee.

The writer concludes with the warning that,

> There is a perilous possibility that the New Theology will make too much of natural ability, and good works, and free will and detract from Christ's sufficiency in salvation and the fact that the soul is 'completed in him' and needs no supplementary grace; and, being in Christ, the man will abound in all goodness.[8]

Few voices in modern Methodism have recognised these truths; France Hildebrandt in his *Christianity According to the Wesleys*, being the Harris Franklin Croll Lectures for 1954, delivered at the Garret Biblical Institute, Evanston, Illinois, was one exception. He opposed the modern concept that Methodism is an eclectic mix of Mysticism, High Churchism and Moravianism and calls his hearers back to Wesley's own statement of what Methodism is:

> Methodism, so-called, it is the old religion, the religion of the Bible, the religion of the primitive Church, the religion of the Church of England.[9]

We may note that when Wesley uses the term, 'the religion of the Church of England,' he means the religion of the Reformation. Indeed Hildebrandt said, 'Methodism is the revival of the Reformation.'[10]

Another modern writer Colin W. Williams in his *John Wesley's Theology Today* also very helpfully defends Wesley's Protestant position. He is particularly clear in explaining the often misinterpreted 1770 Minutes of Conference. These minutes have been seized upon by such as Father Burridge of the Catholic Truth Society, who sees them as a rejection of the solafidean character of

Protestantism. He says that the Catholic tendencies in Wesley come to the fore in these minutes and that the leaven of frankly Papist doctrine steadily purged out the antinomianism of Wesley's societies.

Yet another writer, Lee, in his *John Wesley and Modern Religion*[11] claims that Wesley gradually repudiated the Reformers, 'by faith alone,' in favour of, 'by faith with conditions.' Williams points out that this is a misunderstanding. Williams's notes on the 1770 minutes are too extensive to quote here but he does very helpfully remind us of the statement of Conference made the following year, where it was made absolutely clear that the 1770 Minutes had no intention of teaching justification by works.

> Whereas the doctrinal points in the Minutes of a Conference, held in London, August 7, 1770, are being understood to favour Justification by Works: now the Rev. John Wesley, and others assembled in Conference, do declare, that we have had no such meaning; and that we abhor the doctrine of Justification by Works as a most perilous and abominable doctrine; and as the said Minutes are not sufficiently guarded in the way they are expressed, we hereby solemnly declare, in the sight of God, that we have no trust or confidence except in the alone merits of our Lord and Saviour Jesus Christ, for justification or salvation either in life, death or the day of judgment; and though no-one is a real Christian believer, (and consequently cannot be saved) who does not good works, where there is time and opportunity, yet our works have no part in meriting nor purchasing our salvation from first to last, either in whole or in part.[12]

We might also quote the opinion of the highly regarded evangelical leader, E. J. Poole-Connor in his *Evangelicalism in England* where he says:

> Wesley and Whitfield were far more of one mind on certain points commonly regarded as Calvinistic than is generally known.[13]

5. That the Puritan and Nonconformist element in Wesley's character has been largely lost sight of and neglected by modern Methodists

Again it has been my purpose to point out that which cannot be denied *i.e.* the fact that John Wesley knew and loved the great

Puritans and included a very large selection from their works in his *Christian Library*. It is also true that he used them in his own sermon preparation and indeed based a course of sermons on Robert Bolton's *Directions for a Comfortable Walk with God*.[14] The theology of the Puritans formed part of what Bernard Lord Manning once called 'the massive foundation of his instructed faith'.[15]

It is also true that the early great leaders of Methodism such as Adam Clarke the Bible commentator, and Thomas Jackson, the preacher and leader drew largely on the great Puritan tradition. John A. Newton, already quoted, has written on Susanna Wesley and the Puritan tradition in Methodism. And Gordon S. Wakefield has highlighted the influence of Puritan devotional works on the piety of traditional Methodism. A.Skevington-Wood, in his *The Burning Heart* has very helpfully set out for us John Wesley's lineal descent through an impressive Puritan line. Iain Murray, in his *Wesley and the Men who Followed,* recognises Wesley's indebtedness to Puritan writers as follows:

> Certainly when he began his first extensive reading of the Puritans after the mid 1740s, it led him to a very considerable revision of his earlier estimates. In 1747 a clerical opponent likened the Methodist's work to the irregularities practised by Thomas Cartwright and the Puritans. Wesley responded:
> 'I look upon him and the body of the Puritans in that age (to whom the German Anabaptists bore small resemblance) to have been the most learned and most pious men that were then in the English nation. Nor did they separate from the Church, but were driven out, whether they would or no.'
> Just how much Wesley had been reading the Puritans was to become apparent in 1749 when he launched his *Christian Library*. From that date to 1755, he was to publish 50 small (duodecimo) volumes that would contain the 'choicest pieces of practical divinity'. 'My purpose,' he wrote to a friend, 'was to select whatever I had seen most valuable in the English language, and either abridge or take the whole tract, with only a little corrected or explained, as occasion should require.' So many Puritans appeared in the *Christian Library* that one Church of England critic put it down as an 'odd collection of mutilated writings of dissenters of all sorts'.[16]

Iain Murray in his work on Wesley also seeks to show that Wesley's conversion experience has many similarities to that of Christian in Bunyan's *Pilgrim's Progress.*

In reading John Bunyan's masterpiece, *The Pilgrim's Progress,* Wesley may have come to recognise in Christian something similar to his own experience. Christian, writes Bunyan, left the City of Destruction for Mount Zion with a burden on his back. Immediately he is in the company of Mr Worldly Wiseman who tells him to go to a town called Morality where a certain man named Legality, the son of the Bondwoman, was a great remover of burdens. Instead of deliverance the Pilgrim finds himself in the Slough of Despond about which Bunyan says, this Slough has 'swallowed up at least 20,000 cartloads; yea, millions of wholesome instructions —but it is this Slough of Despond still; and so will be when they have done what they can.

The picture is very like that of Wesley in the 1720s and 1730s, leaving the world, but entangled with authors who could provide him with no sure remedy. Thus Wesley endured long conviction of sin, an experience not uncommon among men whom God prepares to be eminent evangelists. Bunyan has been criticised for the way he describes the next stage in Christian's experience —go on and pass through the Strait Gate (regeneration), onto the narrow way, (where he ran with difficulty and with no deliverance from his burden) 'til he came to a place somewhat ascending, and upon that place stood a Cross and a little below, in the bottom, a Sepulchre. I saw in my dream, that just as Christian came up with the Cross, his Burden loosed from off his shoulders, and fell off his back, and began to tumble, and so continued to do so until it came to the mouth of the Sepulchre, where it fell in and I saw it no more —Then he stood still a while to look and wonder, for it was very surprising to him, that the sight of the Cross should thus ease him of his Burden —And then Christian gave three leaps for joy, and went on singing.For Bunyan's Christian there was a clear interval between passing through the Strait Gate (regeneration) and having such assurance as comes from a clear sight of Christ crucified. What Christian experienced at the cross, Wesley found on 24th May 1738 in Aldersgate Street. But when then, was the 18th century pilgrim regenerated? We do not know and nor did he himself; it is enough to say that there were signs in the 1730s that he was on the narrow way, before he and his brother Charles could sing,

No condemnation now I dread
Jesus, and all in him, is mine.[17]

This is an interesting link with Bunyan though personally I am of the opinion that Wesley was converted at Aldersgate Street.

We have also sought to prove through the reading of popular 19th century and indeed some early 20th century Methodist literature that it was then clearly assumed that Methodism was in the Reformation and Puritan tradition. Take for example a short book prepared for the United Methodist Young People's and Temperance Committee in 1908, entitled, *The Reformation—the Faith that Helped to Make the Modern World*. As we have seen the United Free Methodists clearly saw themselves in the succession of John Wycliffe, the Lollards, the Reformers, and the Puritans. The book before me concludes with the following paragraph, rejoicing in the principles of the Reformation and Nonconformity, the tradition in which the United Methodist Church at that time saw themselves as continuing.

It is in England after all however, that, characteristically from the practical side, the most serious experiments in Reformed Churchmanship have been made. The doctrine of Luther, with some of the discipline of Calvin, has found new expression in the Nonconforming type of Church, both Democratic and Independent, and expressing 'the priesthood of all believers.' It has survived a long struggle from tyranny to toleration, and will surely be maintained until its witness has permeated the universal Church of Christ.'[18]

We may also compare Wesley's whole action in regard to the authority of the Established Church with that of arguably the first Puritan, William Tyndale. Puritanism, we are told by Dr Martyn Lloyd-Jones is 'a type of mind', it is an attitude, it is a spirit and these characteristics begin to show themselves in the life of William Tyndale as far back as the 1520s. He had a burning desire that the common people should be able to read and know the Scriptures. However there were great obstacles in his way; and it was in the way, says Dr Lloyd-Jones that these obstacles were met and overcome that show that Tyndale was a Puritan. He issued a translation of the Bible, and this is the point, without the endorsement or sanction of the bishops.

> That was the first shot fired by Puritanism. It was unthinkable that such a thing should be done without the consent and endorsement of the bishops. But Tyndale did so. Another action on his part which was again most characteristic of the Puritans that is, he left this country without the Royal assent. That again was a most unusual act and highly reprehensible in the eyes of the authorities. But in his anxiety to translate and to print the Scriptures, Tyndale left the country without the king's assent, went to Germany, and there, helped by Luther and others, he completed his great work. Those two actions were typical of what continued to be the Puritan attitude towards authority. It means the putting of truth before questions of tradition and authority, and an insistence upon liberty to serve God in the way which you believe is the true way.[19]

In this attitude to authority again we see the Puritan spirit of John Wesley. In spite of all his conservatism, his regard for the past and his love of order, he would nevertheless allow nothing to come in the way of his making the Gospel known and the work of Christ's Church moving forward.

6. That there was a man-centred adjustment made in Methodist theology, beginning in the middle of the 19th century and increasing towards the end

I have included a summary statement of Methodist doctrine as included in the *Methodist Magazine* of 1815, as one of the appendices to this study. This statement is a useful summary of Methodist orthodoxy and its continuance of the teaching of John Wesley as the new century began. Richard Watson (1781–1833), was the great Methodist theologian amongst Wesley's immediate heirs. It was sometimes said at that period Methodists '*measured all things in heaven and earth by Watson's Institutes*'. Essentially Watson followed Wesley in his theological thinking, though it has also been said of him, 'that he tended to be more preoccupied with the evidences of faith than faith itself; he typifies the scholastic inclination of second generation Methodist theology.'[20]

It is in the theological writings of John Miley however (1813-1895) that we begin to see a distinctive departure from Wesley's original teachings. In 1879 Miley published his *Atonement in Christ* in which he embraced and advocated the Governmental Theory of the Atonement. R E Chiles sums up Miley's last departure from Wesleyan orthodoxy as follows:

> In Wesleyan fashion he interprets justification as pardon or forgiveness of sins. It removes man's amenability to punishment on the ground that Christ suffered provisionally in his stead, thereby upholding the interests of God's moral government and making forgiveness possible on the condition of faith in him. But justification cares solely for the guilt of man's own sins; its bearing on the guilt of Adam's sin is explicitly denied. Thus, rooted only in the need for governmental justice, and applied only to actual sins, forgiveness in Christ becomes more mechanical and less exacting than it was in Wesley.

Here we might include an important footnote of Chiles, quoting from Shipley's *Theology of American Methodism.*

> 'Miley's moralistic revisionism of the doctrine of salvation and the analysis of the human predicament is far too shallow and psychologically inadequate—if not contradictory —to retain a place as a creative contribution to theology.' It led 'to the necessity of revising the Methodist emphases in the doctrine of the atonement toward a morally rationalistic construct (in which) the meaning of the Incarnation and the saving work of Christ has to do primarily with enhancing the good motives amenable to unimpaired human free will, and thus actualising divine moral government essentially through man's rationalistic choice of the good'.

Chiles continues:

> The understanding of faith is also subject to revision. Faith for Miley required a 'mental apprehension' whose 'truth must have a ground in evidence'. Contrary to the Wesleyan stress on the necessity for gracious restoration of spiritual senses, divine truth

here commends itself to man's natural reason. God's objective truth includes the promise of needed help and an assurance that this promise is trustworthy. Thus, on the basis of evidence centred in Christ, man believes.

Faith also presupposes a 'true state of repentance—Because only in such a mental state can proper faith be exercised'. Repentance is one of the 'requirements of our own agency', though it requires divine assistance. Though faith is claimed to be one condition of justification, yet repentance is 'always presupposed'. Thus, to repentance Miley imputes a necessity which Wesley refused. Further, Miley specifically denies 'the view that faith is itself the gift of God'; rather its interpretation 'must accord with the nature of faith as a free personal act'. Usually he remembers to add that this personal agency rests on gracious influences, but, both in repentance and in faith, he stresses man's contributing capacity.[21]

It is this view of Methodism which is generally regarded by many as Methodist orthodoxy, and often, without any grounds whatsoever, attributed to Wesley himself, which largely prevails today. This view has in turn had the effect of steadily reducing the distance between God and man. Wesley's satisfaction view of the atonement in common with all essentially Biblical and Reformed understanding, emphasised the distance between God and sinful man and an irreconcilable contradiction, apart from God's costly act of grace in Christ.

The Grotian governmental theory, which gained in popularity until its conquest was completed in Miley, assumed far less antagonism between God's holiness and man's sin. In it the atonement promotes the general moral welfare of mankind; it is not intrinsic to man's release from guilt and bondage. The atonement, understood as moral influence, presupposes no chasm between God and man; in it man is free to respond to the ennobling example set forth in Christ. Thus the changes in the doctrine of the atonement tend to promote a simpler, less costly fashion for the reuniting of God and man.[22]

These shifts in doctrine are the key to understanding the whole nature, outlook, atmosphere, and aims of modern Methodism. They have undermined all Gospel urgency, brought about the situation whereby conversion in the Biblical understanding of the term is

almost completely lost sight of, and in the every day life of the local
church, regarded as unnecessary. An intellectual acquiescence in
the broad truths of Christianity and a concern for moral living, an
interest in the social well-being of mankind *etc.* seems to be the
sum total of the ordinary church member's understanding of what
it is to be a Christian. The situation in many of the churches of
Methodism today is nearly the same as that which Wesley
contended against at the beginning of the 18th century, and is
described in the earlier pages of this work.

7. To these deviations can also be added the disastrous surrender of belief in an inerrant Bible.

It needs to be said that the Methodists clung to their belief in an
inerrant Bible longer than many of the other large Protestant
denominations. We have already noted C. H. Spurgeon's recognition
of this and of his willingness to allow the Primitive Methodists to use
the facilities of the Metropolitan Tabernacle for their annual
gatherings. However, in the early part of the 20th century, particularly
under the influence of A. S. Peake a brilliant scholar, and principal of
the Hartley Primitive Methodist College Manchester, there came about
a guarded acceptance of higher critical views of Scripture. Some of
these opinions were popularised in Peake's classic, *Christianity, its
Nature and its Truth* (1908), and also in his famous commentary. The
former provides a popular apology for the Christian faith. However,
woven within its pages are such statements as—'the popular doctrine
of the Fall is not to be found in the story of Eden'; 'Paul's doctrine of
Adam is essentially independent of the historicity of Genesis'; 'Paul's
interest in Adam was not historical'; 'The theory of man's animal
descent greatly relieves the difficulty'—*i.e.* accounting for the
transmission of Adam's sin. Though Peake can be read with profit
there can be no doubt that he opened the door which led Methodism
in the 20th century far away from its Biblical foundations.

8. That there has come about a re-interpretation of Wesley's life and teaching in order to fit him into the modern ecumenical mould.

A monumental work on the history of Methodism was published
by Hodder and Stoughton of London in 1909, under the editorship

of W. J. Townsend, H. B. Workman and George Eayrs. Undoubtedly this two-volume work is both scholarly and valuable as a history of Methodism. However, its title indicates the general drift and purpose of the work *i.e. A New History of Methodism.* In the introductory essay, the place of Methodism in the life and thought of the Church, H. B. Workman rightly identifies Methodism's connection with the Reformation and the Puritan Movement, but he also labours hard to identify parallels between Methodism and some of the spiritual movements prior to the Reformation. He quotes from Bishop Lavington's *Enthusiasm of Methodist and Romanist Compared* and agrees with Lavington, that mysticism and Methodism build upon the foundation of conscious spiritual experience. He seeks also to draw comparisons between John Wesley and Ignatius Loyola. He says that Methodism and Jesuitism are one, up to a certain point. He compares Wesley's preachers to the friars sent out by St Francis. He compares Wesley's *Twelve Rules of a Helper* with the rules set out in St Francis's *Little Flowers*. He seeks to draw parallels between Methodism and monasticism and compares John Wesley with St Benedict. Workman seems to set the trend of seeking to reinterpret Wesley, toning down his Protestantism, drawing on the High Church connections of Wesley in his pre-conversion days, and seeing Wesley as a connecting link between Archbishop Laud in the 17th century and the Oxford Movement of the 19th century. I have sought in this book to demonstrate and to prove that this re-interpretation of the life of Wesley does not bear up to close historical scrutiny.

The latter part of the 1930s saw the birth of the Methodist Sacramental Fellowship. This development was welcomed in the Jesuit periodical *The Month*, with the comment, 'There is much we can welcome in this movement.'[23]*The Churchman's Magazine* the organ of The Protestant Truth Society[24] for that month also commented on the new movement within Methodism as follows:

> There has been undeniably a very noticeable trend in modern Methodism, especially the section that used to be known as Wesleyan, to squeeze out the lay ministry and substitute the officially ordained. An esteemed Methodist of many years standing as a local preacher sends us some further information from

Bournemouth, written in appreciation of our exposure, and telling of his determination to fight against the invasion of Sacerdotalism in his own circuit. He says that the Rev. Frederick Luke Kinnings, in charge of Victoria Park Methodist Church, Winton, baptised three infants on Sunday morning, December 20th using the words —'I baptise thee... with the Sign of the Cross.' This is deliberately contrary to the Methodist Prayer Book. Further that there is now a large brass cross on the communion table there. On the last Sunday in the year, the Rev. T. O. Beswick preached, wearing an ornamented stole in addition to a black gown.

The June edition of the same magazine reports on the second Annual Conference of this same Fellowship held in Birmingham from the 9th to the 12th of April, 1937.

The Saturday sessions started with 'Holy Communion' in the room fitted up to serve as a chapel. There was erected a small altar, backed by a blue curtain—it could not be described at all as a table, with a shelf at the back on which stood a cross between two vases filled with large lilies. There were no candles this time. The sacerdotal Eastward position however was taken every time the chapel was used, both at the 'Communion' and when they said what they entitled 'The Morning or Evening Office'. The Rev. S. H. Bosward knelt in front of me, his habit was to cross himself after the Roman Catholic manner as he said his prayers.

The Rev. Dr H. B. Workman addressed the conference on 'the History of the Eucharist and its Interpretation Throughout the Ages'. Later in the day the Rev. Edward Leach, Vicar of St. Oswald's, Small Heath, Birmingham, an extreme Anglo-Roman Churchman addressed the conference on the subject, 'The Christian Doctrine of the Incarnation.'[25]

9. That Methodism needs to recover its lost identity if it is to survive.

Throughout the 19th century Methodism exerted a tremendous influence upon the populations of the large manufacturing towns of the North and Midlands and other great centres of influence, such as Bristol, and, of course, London. In the country districts especially Cornwall in the West Country, her influence was extensive. The preaching of justification by faith alone in England as the 19th moved into the 20th century, it has been said, was as common a part of chapel on Sunday as a football match on a Saturday afternoon. The theological downgrade of this great body has played a significant part in the secularization of this country. Allied to this was the closure of many chapels at the time of Methodist Reunion in 1933, that led to the loss of many adherents and the consequently contact with literally thousands of families. Further, this union seemed to favour the more liberal side of the denomination, and on a practical level the more plainly built chapels of the former Methodist New Connexion, Free, and Primitive groups, seem to have been targeted for disposal. The leaven of these groups was hence quickly lost.

In one sense it is true that the distinctive teachings of traditional Methodism are, generally speaking as far as the fundamentals are concerned, no different from that of any other truly evangelical church. A book on Methodist teaching for the young summed up the Methodist Church's teaching as being: that she preaches, salvation by faith alone in Christ, that a believer can have full assurance of faith, that every Christian should strive after holiness in the Lord and is to follow after sanctification, that all Christians need the fellowship of other believers and that we cannot reach maturity in the Christian life on our own.

Methodism's great strength, however, lay not only in its authoritative teachings as such, but in its spirit and its zeal. This is well captured by Iain Murray in a chapter in his *Wesley and the Men who Followed*. Writing of a 19th century Wesleyan minister, Thomas Collins, he speaks of some of the characteristics of Collins's life as follows:

> Of the lessons that may be drawn from the life of Collins, one of the foremost would be the evidence it gives of the supernatural power bound up with the Gospel. Nothing else can explain the glorious changes he so often saw. None proved to be too guilty or too depraved for his message, and the fresh and artless language of those converted under his ministry witnessed to the reality of the new life.[26]

Collins attributed usefulness in the ministry to the following source:
Marvellous results come not of nothing. God giveth the increase.[27]

> The secret anointing of the Holy Spirit was the explanation and
> source of all real effectiveness in the ministry.

Another prominent characteristic of Collins's ministry was that
of unity amongst the people of God. To see the church united in a
brotherly spirit was his first priority in every field where he
laboured.

> Sacred sociality is the spirit, life, and leaven of genuine
> Methodism.

> > All praise to our redeeming Lord,
> > Who joins us by his grace,
> > And bids us each to each restored,
> > Together seek his face.

> > He bids us build each other up;
> > And, gathered into one,
> > To our high calling's glorious hope
> > We hand in hand go on.

> Colleagueship in the ministry, and class meetings for the
> members, are its result. They are our strength: but the strength
> of them is love. Let love decline, and such a system must at once
> be found to be a bondage and a fret.[28]

Another great strength of traditional Methodism was its method
of selecting candidates for the ministry. It had no formal
denominational selection committee or, in the beginning, theological
colleges to train them. However it did have very clear guidelines.
It followed the apostolic rule, *'let them first be proved.'*(I Tim. 3:10.)
If a man gave evidence of decided piety and talents for public
usefulness, he was put on trial as a local preacher and subject to
the inquiry of the Quarterly Local Preachers Meeting. After this
the superintendent minister could recommend the individual to the
Quarterly Meeting and, if his name was approved by that meeting,
to the District Meeting of the circuit where there was further
examination with such questions as the following:

Do they know God as a pardoning God? Are they holy in all manner of conversation? Have they a clear sound understanding? Have they a just conception of salvation by faith? Has God given them an acceptable way of speaking? Have they had any fruit of their labour? Have any been truly convinced of sin, and converted to God, by the preaching?

Murray also draws our attention to another ingredient in the training of these early Methodist preachers, that is, a model of a Gospel minister and ministers was set before them. For successive generations Methodism would have a common ideal. The day when the message and methods of the fathers would be seen as antiquated was not yet come, but rather —'the young felt that they were connected with bygone times, and associated with the fathers of Methodism, to catch their mantle, and a double portion of their spirit.'

Their vision was that the lessons that had been passed down to them should be kept alive. The history of their forefathers in the faith was an encouragement to them.

Iain Murray also sets out the following maxims of Collins. These maxims also very clearly indicate something of the spirit of early Methodism.

The old power can be obtained by three things: experimental consistency with our own teaching of truth; freedom from the manners, maxims, and spirit of the world; and passion for souls.

Be always tenderly yearning for sinners. This is a happy unhappiness. A man full of Christ-like tears is a noble creature. Such concern melts men, and tells with God.

In selecting the sermon to be preached consider the people, not yourself... Choose your hymns carefully. Give them out heartily, and with much inward devotion. In your first prayer plead until the people move; wait until the baptism of power falls. You must not preach without power.

Never doubt God's presence, God's word, God's pity, or God's power.

Wesleyan Theological Tutors have all been pastors. May it never be otherwise! Theory, unsobered by necessity of practical application, is a great source of German scepticism. Who would trust the therapeutics of one who never healed? Medical professors reach their chairs through hospital wards. According to Wesleyan usage our 'Masters in Israel' have to do the same.[29]

It is in the spirit of these maxims, and the maintaining of these principles that the great strength of Methodism lay. Her present-day adherents have an urgent need to return to them. And those who boast of their Reformed orthodoxy need to look again at Wesley and traditional Methodism, and consider whether or not they have misjudged it by being misinformed. It may be that they will still find elements in Methodism with which they will remain at variance. Nevertheless it is my hope in setting out this reappraisal of the issues, that many, by an informed reconsideration, will go on to derive much more from Wesley's ministry, which will prove to them a benefit and a blessing, and at the same time catch something of that holy fire and spiritual invigoration which he knew, and that we so urgently need today.

> O Thou who camest from above
> The pure celestial fire to impart,
> Kindle a flame of sacred love
> On the mean altar of my heart!
>
> There let it for Thy glory burn
> With inextinguishable blaze;
> And trembling to its source return,
> In humble prayer and fervent praise.

APPENDIX ONE

LUTHER'S PREFACE TO THE EPISTLE TO THE ROMANS
—A TRANSLATION BY DEREK JOHNSON[1]

'In the evening I went very unwillingly to a society in Aldersgate Street, where one was reading Luther's preface to the Epistle to the Romans. About a quarter before nine, while he was describing the change which God works in the heart through faith in Christ, I felt my heart strangely warmed. I felt I did trust in Christ, Christ alone, for salvation; and an assurance was given me that he had taken away my sins, even mine, and saved me from the law of sin and death.'

These are, perhaps, the best-known words in Wesley's Journal. But what of *Luther's Preface*? For English-speaking Methodists it seems to have disappeared almost without trace. This is a pity, for it has more than a merely academic interest, furnishing the Wesleyologist with some insight into the contents of Wesley's consciousness at the moment of his conversion, or setting him the puzzle of identifying the exact words being read when Wesley's heart's temperature began to rise. Though it does do these things, it also sets out fairly concisely, and quite graphically, Luther's own understanding of certain key words in Scripture and is a piece of devotional reading valuable in its own right.

The Epistle to the Romans is the foremost piece of writing in the New Testament, and it would be well worth a Christian's while to learn it, word for word, by heart. More than that, it is worth spending time over it every day as daily bread for the soul. For it can never be read or pondered upon too much, and the more it is drawn upon the more it improves in value and flavour. I therefore intend to make it my duty to prepare an introduction to it by means

261

of this Preface, as God has granted me, whereby its meaning may become that much clearer. For up to now it has been badly obscured by 'interpretations' plus all kinds of rigmarole, though in itself it is a bright enough light to floodlight the whole of scripture.

First of all we must acquaint ourselves with the language, and understand what Paul means by the words *law, sin, grace, faith, righteousness, flesh, spirit* and the like, or all our reading is to no avail.

Law: In Romans you must not understand this little word in a merely human way, as though it meant a set of instructions regarding things to be done or things to be avoided, as is the case with the laws of men (where you can satisfy the law with mere deeds even though your heart is not in it). God sets his sights upon the very centre of our being, 'the bottom of the heart' as you might say. Therefore his law also demands 'the bottom of the heart' and will not allow itself to be fobbed off with mere deeds. On the contrary, those deeds not done from the bottom of the heart it punishes as hypocrisy and lies. Hence all men are called liars (Ps. 116:11) because no one does keep or can keep God's law from the bottom of his heart; for everyone finds within himself some aversion to goodness and some attraction to evil. Now, where untramelled attraction to goodness is absent, the bottom of the heart is absent too. What certainly is present is sin; and all that is earned before God is wrath, despite the outward polish of an honourable life and many good deeds.

Hence Paul comes to the conclusion (2:9) that the Jews are all sinners, and he pronounces (2:13) that only doers of the law are righteous before God. What he intends to say with this is that no one is by mere deeds a doer of the law. Rather, he tells them (2:22), *You teach that one should not commit adultery—and you commit adultery!* Similarly (2:1), *In what you teach someone else you damn yourself, because you do the very thing you condemn.* As if to say: outwardly you live nicely in the mere deeds of the law, and condemn those who do not live as you do, and can set yourself up as everyman's teacher. You notice the speck of dust in someone else's eye, but are unaware of the plank in your own (Matt. 7:3). For, even though outwardly and with mere deeds you keep the law (from fear of punishment or love of reward) you nevertheless do it all without untramelled attraction and love for it, but rather with aversion and under compulsion. If there were no law, you would more likely do the opposite. It follows that from the bottom of your heart you are at loggerheads with the law. So what is the good of teaching others not to steal, while you yourself are a thief at heart (and would be one outwardly if you dared —though in the case of such hypocrites even the outward deed doesn't lag behind in the long run)? So, if you teach others but not yourself, if you do not even know for yourself what you teach, then you have not yet properly understood the law. In that case, in fact, the law even multiplies sin (which is what Paul says in 5:20) and the way it does so is that a man merely gets more and more at loggerheads with it the more it requires him to do things he finds impossible.

He declares therefore, in 7:14, *The law is spiritual*. What does that mean? If the law were material it would be satisfied with mere deeds; but since it is spiritual in fact you cannot satisfy it, whoever you are, unless everything you do proceeds from the bottom of your heart. But for everything to be done from a free heart, rather than from fear and under compulsion, the heart itself must be such as feels affection for the law. And that kind of heart is given by none other than the Spirit of God, bringing a man into a real affinity with the law. So the law is spiritual, since it desires to be loved and fulfilled with a heart spiritual in the way just described, and requires the same kind of Spirit. Where that is absent from the heart, there remain sin, aversion, enmity against the law, which itself, however, is good, righteous and holy.

So get used to the proposition that doing the mere deed of the law is a vastly different thing from fulfilling the law. *The mere deed of the law* is all that which, of his own free will and under his own steam, a man does in accordance with the law. But because such mere deeds are still kept close company in the heart by aversion and compulsion to the law, they are lost and are to no avail. That is what Paul means in 3:20 when he declares, *No man is righteous before God by means of the mere deed of the law*. Hence you see now the seductiveness of logic-chopping theologians and quibblers when they teach that one should, with mere deeds, prepare oneself for grace. How can anyone prepare himself for goodness with mere deeds, if he never does a good deed without some aversion and reluctance in his heart? How shall the deeds which proceed from a reluctant and unwilling heart please God?

Fulfilling the law, however, means doing its deeds because you like them and want to do them. It means living a good and godly life freely, without the compulsion of the law, as though neither law nor punishment existed. But such a desire to do them because you like them is put into your heart by the Holy Spirit, as he declares in 5:5, and the Spirit is given only in, with and by means of faith in Jesus Christ (as he says in the preamble) and in no other way. Similarly, faith does not come except through God's word, the Gospel which Christianity preaches, that he is God's Son and that he is man, who has died and risen from the dead for our sakes (as he says in 3:4 and 10).

Consequently, only faith makes a person righteous, and fulfils the law, for out of what Christ has earned, faith makes a free gift of the Spirit. And the Spirit makes a free heart, full of the desire the law demands. Thus good works proceed from faith itself. That is what he means in chapter 3, after he has repudiated the mere deeds of the law so that it sounds as though he would through faith abolish the law. No, he then declares, through faith we support the law, that is we fulfil it through faith.

Sin: In the Scriptures this does not mean just the outward deed of the body, but everything whose stirring and moving together within us results in such outward deed: in other words, the bottom of the heart, and every power we have. Thus to 'commit sin' (often treated as though it were a trivial phrase) should really be taken to mean that a man goes full tilt at sin and falls headlong into it. For no outward deed of sin occurs unless a man does go at it full tilt, body and soul. Moreover Scripture looks particularly into the heart and at the tap-root, the chief source of all sin, which is—unbelief (the opposite of faith) at the bottom of the heart. So just as only faith makes a person righteous, bringing the Spirit and the desire for deeds which are outwardly good, equally the only thing that sins is unbelief, exciting the flesh and bringing the desire for deeds which are outwardly evil—as happened to Adam and Eve in paradise (Genesis 3). Hence the only thing Christ names as sin is unbelief, when he declares (John 16:8-9) *The Spirit will judge the world of sin because they do not believe in me.* Therefore also before good or evil deeds occur (as good or bad fruit) there must be present in the heart beforehand either faith, or unbelief as root, sap and main strength of all sin. This is why Scripture calls unbelief *the head of the serpent* and *the head of the old dragon*, which the woman's seed (Christ) must trample, as was promised to Adam (Gen. 3:15).

Grace and *Gift* are not interchangeable. The difference between them is that grace is the favourable disposition of God towards us, whereas gifts are its result in us. This favourable disposition he himself sustains, and because of it he is disposed to pour into us Christ and the Spirit, with his gifts. All this becomes clear from 5:15, where he declares, *The grace of God, and the gift by grace, has much more abounded, etc.* Of course, the gifts and the Spirit need to grow in us daily. They are not yet complete, in that evil desires and sins are still left over in us, striving against the Spirit, as Paul says in 7:5 and in Galatians 5:16, and as is spoken in Genesis 3:15 regarding the dispute between the seed of the woman and seed of the serpent. Nevertheless grace achieves this much for us, that we are reckoned utterly and completely righteous before God. For his grace does not come piecemeal (as the gifts do) but raises us absolutely into favour— for the sake of Christ our advocate and mediator, and because the gifts themselves have made a start in us.

So now you can understand chapter 7, where Paul upbraids himself as a sinner and yet says (in 8:1): *there is no condemnation to those who are in Christ*—on account of the gifts (though imperfect) and on account of the Spirit. On account of the flesh as yet not put to death we are still sinners, but because we believe in Christ and have the onset of the Spirit in us God is so favourably and graciously disposed towards us that he has no wish to regard or judge such sin, but wants rather to deal with us according to our faith in Christ until our sin has been put to death.

Faith is not what many take it to be—a purely human thing, a fantasy, a dream. When they see that, despite all that may be said to them and by them about faith, the consequences are neither good deeds nor any improvement of life, they fall into error, declaring that faith is not enough—if one is to be truly devout and saved one must have *works* as well. The result is that when they hear the Gospel they trip over it. Using nothing but their own powers they make a thought in their heart, which says, *I believe*. Then they take this for a true faith. But being a mere creation of the human mind, affecting not at all the bottom of the heart, it achieves nothing. No improvement follows upon it. *Faith is,* instead, a divine work in us, that changes us and causes us to be born anew from God (John 1:13). It puts *the old Adam* to death and makes us—heart, mind, senses and all the powers we have—into quite different people, and brings the Holy Spirit with it. Oh! There is something about faith, lively, busy, active, mighty, that makes it impossible for it not to do good, and that without ceasing. It does not ask, 'Ought I to do good works?' Before the question can be put it has already done them, and keeps on doing them. But anyone who does not do such good works is a man without faith, peering about and groping after faith and good works, but having no idea what faith is, let alone good works; and yet about both he chatters away like an old washerwoman.

Faith is a living, daring confidence in the grace of God, so certain, that one would die a thousand times over for it. And such confidence and certainty makes one happy and steadfast, and full of delight towards God and all he has created—this the Holy Spirit does in faith. Hence, without compulsion, a man becomes willing—delighted even—to do anyone a good turn, and to put up with all kinds of things for love and praise to the God who has shown him such grace; and thus it is no more possible to separate good deeds from faith than heat and light from fire. So keep a sharp lookout both for your own wrongheaded notions and for useless drivellers who try to be clever at criticizing faith and good deeds—and are the biggest dunces. Ask God to work faith in you or you will remain without it for ever, even though you carry through all the schemes you like.

Righteousness is a faith like that. It is known as *the righteousness of God,* in other words the righteousness which really counts for something in the sight of God, because God gives it and reckons it as righteousness for the sake of Christ our mediator, as well as remodelling a man in such a way that he gives everyone his due. For through faith a man loses his sinfulness and gains a delight in the things God commands, whereby he not only gives honour to God and pays him what he owes him, but willingly serves men as he is able, and so gives everyone his due. This kind of righteousness cannot be brought about by the will nor by any of our natural powers, for just as no one can give himself faith, so no one can remove his own unbelief: how then can anyone take away a single one of the smallest of his own sins? Therefore, everything which takes place apart from faith or in unbelief is false, hypocrisy and sin (Rom. 14:23) varnish it how you like.

Flesh and *Spirit* are not to be understood here as though *flesh* referred only to unchastity, and *spirit* to an inward something in the heart. What Paul means by flesh is everything which takes its birth from the flesh, the total human being, body and soul, with its intellect and all its other faculties, since everything in it has a strong tendency towards the flesh. In this, Paul is in agreement with Christ (Jn. 3:6). So now when some graceless driveller teaches and writes about high spiritual things you can call him *fleshly* as you may indeed learn from a list of the *works of the flesh* (Gal. 5:19ff) where Paul even includes hatred and heresy. Further, in Rom. 8:3 he declares that the law is weakened by means of the flesh, by which he means not just unchastity, but every sin, and unbelief most of all, the most *spiritual* of all vices. On the other hand you should call spiritual anyone occupied with the most outward of deeds, such as Christ washing the disciples' feet or Peter putting the boat out and fishing. The meaning stands thus; *the flesh*—a person who inwardly and outwardly lives and works to profit the flesh and in this temporal life; but *spirit*—one who lives and works inwardly and outwardly for what serves the Spirit and the life to come.

Without such an insight into these terms you will never understand this epistle of Paul's, nor any other book of Holy Scripture. Be therefore on your guard against all those teachers who use these words in any other sense, whoever they may be—Origen, Ambrose, Augustine, Jerome, their equals or even their superiors.

APPENDIX TWO

METHODIST DOCTRINE 1818—BY G. MARSDEN[1]

The following is a summary of Methodist doctrine as it was set out in the *Methodist Magazine*, January 1818.

We recommend the following article, which has lately been put into our hands, to the very careful perusal of all those of our readers, who wish still to adhere to the genuine doctrines of Christianity, of the Reformation, of our National Church, and of Methodism.

I have lately been taking a view of the origin of Methodism; and of the manner in which it has pleased God so graciously to carry on that great work, which has proved a source of good to hundreds of thousands of precious souls; and which still continues so graciously to prevail.

When it pleased God to raise up the Rev. John Wesley, to be the founder of Methodism, he resolved, through Divine help, to make the Bible his only guide, in all the important doctrines which he embraced; and which he faithfully delivered to the people. His own language was, 'I designed plain truth for plain people; therefore, of set purpose, I abstain from all nice and philosophical speculations; from all perplexed and intricate reasonings; and, as far as possible, from even the show of learning, unless in sometimes citing the original Scriptures.'

The following sentiments are also truly worthy of that great man. 'I am a creature of a day, passing through life as an arrow through the air; I am a spirit come from God, and returning to God, just hovering over the great gulf; till a few moments hence I am no more seen! I drop into an unchangeable eternity! I want to know one thing, the way to heaven, how to land safe on that happy shore. God himself has condescended to teach the way; for this very end he came down from heaven. He hath written it down in a book. Oh give me that book! At any price give me the book of God! I have it, here is knowledge enough for me. Let me be *homo unius libri.* Here then I am, far from the busy ways of men. I sit down alone, only God is here. In his presence I open, I read his book; for this end, to find the way to heaven. Is there a doubt concerning the meaning of what I read? Does anything appeared dark and intricate? I lift up my heart to the Father of lights. Lord is it, not thy word, *'if any man lack wisdom, let him ask of God.' 'Thou giveth liberally, and upbraidest not.'* Thou hast said, *'If any be willing to do thy will, he shall know.'* I am willing to do, let me know thy will. I then search after, and consider parallel passages of Scripture; comparing spiritual things with spiritual. I meditate thereon with all the attention and earnestness of which my mind is capable. If any doubts still remain, I consult those who are experienced in the things of God; and then, the writings, whereby being dead, they yet speak, and what I thus learn, that I teach.'

It was in the same spirit that the first Methodist preachers examined into the doctrines of the book of God. When the first Conference was held, at which was present, the Rev. John Wesley, the Rev. Charles Wesley, the Rev John Hodges, Rector of Wenvo, and several others, it is evident that they entered on the subject of Christian doctrine, in that spirit which was likely to draw down the Divine blessing on their consultations. They resolved that all things should be considered as in the immediate presence of God; that every point which was proposed should be examined to the foundation; and that every question which might arise, should be thoroughly debated and settled.

Having entered on their work in that blessed spirit, and with a single eye to the glory of God, we may reasonably expect that they would be led into all truth. The truths which they thus learned, they faithfully preached. Divine power accompanied the word, thousands of persons were awakened to a sense of their guilt, and of their danger; and being directed to the Lord Jesus Christ, as their only, but all sufficient Saviour, they found redemption through his blood, the forgiveness of their sins; their lives became holy and happy, and many of the first Methodists are now safely landed on the heavenly shore. Through the peculiar providence of God, Mr Wesley was long spared as a father to the growing societies; and at various times, was led to write on almost every subject connected with Divinity. His *Notes on the New Testament*, though concise, are clear and full. His *Sermons* are probably unrivalled for a clear statement of Divine truth, and a practical and powerful application of that truth. His controversial pieces are on some of the most important truths of the Bible, which are defended in a masterly manner. In them truth is triumphant. His hymns, with those of his brother Charles, and a selection from some other authors, form a volume which, for real excellence, is probably the first in the English language. The whole of his works taken collectively, form a full statement of scriptural truths, properly explained, and practically applied. On the ground which was laid during his life, Methodism has continued to prosper in an extraordinary manner, and hitherto has suffered no decay. On the present system of sound doctrine and proper discipline, we have reason to expect that it will continue to prevail till the ends of the earth shall see the salvation of God. Yea, till suns shall rise and set no more.

As a member of the Methodist body, I feel anxious that we may ever preserve the purity, both of our doctrine, and our discipline; and the purport of my addressing you, especially at this time, is to state the peculiar necessity of our continuing to abide by our former truths, and of guarding the sacred deposit, which God has committed to our care.

There are two theories that have been advanced, which appeared to militate against our view of the important doctrine of regeneration, as stated in the writings of Mr Wesley, and more especially in the Book of God.

One of these theories is, that baptism, when properly administered, is regeneration. That the apostles were not of that opinion is evident, for when St Peter went to Samaria, he found Simon (generally termed Simon Magus) among the newly formed society of Christians who had been baptised. But so far was Peter from considering him as regenerated, that he said to him, *'thou hast neither part nor lot in this matter, for thy heart is not right in the sight of God. I perceive that thou art in the gall of bitterness, and in the bond of iniquity.'*

That our Reformers did not consider baptism as regeneration, is evident from the Catechism which they compiled, where they say, that 'Baptism is an outward visible sign, of an inward and spiritual grace'. And that Mr Wesley was not of that opinion is also evident from all his writings; but, especially from his Sermon on the New Birth, where he says, 'And, first, it follows that baptism is not the new birth; they are not one and the same thing.' Again, 'For what can be more plain, than that the one is an external, the other an internal work? That the one is a visible, the other an invisible thing and, therefore, that they are wholly different from each other; the one being an act of man, purifying the body; the other, a change wrought by God in the soul. So that the former is just as distinguishable from the latter, as the soul from the body, or water from the Holy Ghost.'

The other theory is, that all professing Christians are, in the same sense in which the New Testament writers use the expression, regenerate, born again, justified, and members of Christ's body. Strange as this doctrine may appear, it has its advocates. But if we examine the writings of the Reformers, of Mr Wesley, and also those who were inspired by the Holy Ghost, we shall find that this novel theory is without foundation.

Mr Wesley is remarkably clear on this subject. In his sermon on the marks of the New Birth, he says, 'But it is not a barely notional, or speculative faith which is here spoken of by the apostle. It is not a bare assent to the proposition, 'Jesus is the Christ,' nor indeed to all the propositions contained in our Creed, or in the Old and New Testament. It is not merely an assent to any, or all these credible things, as credible. To say this, were to say that the devils were born of God: for they have this faith. They, trembling, believe both that Jesus is the Christ, and that all Scripture having been given by inspiration of God, is true as God is true, etc. Yet, notwithstanding this faith, they are still 'reserved in chains of darkness, unto the judgment of the great day.' In his sermon 'On the Way to the Kingdom', his expressions are equally strong, and equally proper. 'A man may be orthodox in every point, he may not only espouse right opinions, but zealously defend them against all opposers; he may think justly concerning the incarnation of our Lord, concerning the ever blessed Trinity, and every other doctrine contained in the oracles of God; he may assent to all the three creeds, that are called the Apostles, the Nicene, and the Athanasian, and yet it be possible, he may have no religion at all, no more than a Jew, Turk, or Pagan. He may be almost as orthodox as the devil, and may all the while be as great a stranger as he to the religion of the heart.'

I might quote scores of passages, from his writings, equally clear and express on this subject, as also from the writings of the Reformers; but let us now turned to the sacred writers.

The Epistles are (in most cases) directed to the particular churches in those places, which bear the name of the Epistle; of course, the apostles would direct their letters to the people of each place collectively, who were united together in the Christian society. And, in addressing each society, they would address them as called, redeemed, regenerate, justified, and chosen. But when we inquire into the proper meaning of those expressions, as used by the apostles themselves in their letters, we find that they cannot, and never were meant, to apply in that lax manner which some persons have lately supposed.

When we examine into the meaning of the term justify, or justification, we find that its proper meaning is, to declare just, or righteous, *i.e.* to acquit, or absolve from past offences, and accept as just, the reward of righteousness. But this justification always was preceded by true genuine repentance—was always received by faith in Christ, and was uniformly accompanied by peace, love, and joy in the Holy Ghost. When they speak of regeneration, they always speak of it as a change which passes on the believer by the power of the Holy Ghost, whereby he is made a new creature in Christ Jesus. In the conversation which our Lord had with Nicodemus, he speaks of the New Birth, as being 'born from above,' and as clearly distinguished from every thing carnal, and fleshly. St John also, in the various passages in his first epistles where he enlarges so beautifully on the Christian privilege of our being the children of God, clearly states, that such persons have passed from death unto life; that they have fellowship with the Father, and with the Son, by the Spirit; and that, he that is born of God sinneth not. So far from those terms applying to all professing Christians, indiscriminately, they can only apply, in the scriptural sense, to those persons who were changed by the power of Divine grace, and are made new creatures in Christ Jesus.

Another doctrine which we are now especially called upon to support, is, the doctrine of the Trinity, as from the beginning believed, and maintained in the Christian church. On this important subject I would premise, but there is one grand error, into which, it appears to me, some persons have fallen; and that is, to attempt to bring everything to the bar of human reason; and if their reason cannot fathom the doctrine, they try to new model it, and so to form the system that it may come within their own comprehension. I allow that we are by reason to judge of the evidence in favour of the Bible as the Book of God, and also of the proper explanation of the terms used in that blessed book. But when it is proved to be a Divine revelation, we are bound to receive that revelation, though there may be mysteries in it which the human mind cannot fathom. Some years ago a celebrated Divine, who wished to comprehend the nature of our Lord, embraced the strange and unscriptural opinion, that the human soul of Christ was pre-existent; and he wrote a treatise to prove that it was the first, and most glorious part of the creation of God. Other persons have recently revived an entirely opposite scheme, but equally unscriptural, *viz.* the Lord Jesus Christ is termed the Son of God, only in reference to his human nature.

In speaking or writing respecting the deep things of God, we ought to do it with much caution. The human mind is limited with respect to its powers, and though it may comprehend much with respect to arts and sciences, and be continually advancing in knowledge and information on a variety of subjects; yet, with respect to the things of God, it becomes us to speak with a deep humility, but more especially when we attempt to define the nature of God, we must be careful not to make the reason of man the judge of that nature, for, 'Who by searching can find out the Almighty?' If the reason of man is to be the judge, and the definer of the nature of God, whose reason is to be the standard? The minds of men vary, and what one person may appear to prove to be the nature of the Divine Being, another may attempt to overthrow, and show to be totally incorrect. If man is to be our guide, and mere human reason to be our standard in judging of the Divine Being, we shall be left in a chaos of confusion.—In speaking thus of the reason of man, I do not mean to degrade it, or to suppose that we are not to use it even in spiritual concerns; but we should learn to know its province, and not apply it as the rule of our faith, where the revelation of God is our only guide.

I would also notice another source of false reasoning and error, which is, when we imagine that the terms made use of in the sacred writings, by which it has pleased God to reveal himself to man, are used in that gross sense, in which the same terms are used, as applicable to man. Thus no person can reasonably suppose that the Divine Being has arms or feet; that he walketh, or rideth upon the wings of the wind. Those expressions, and many others, it is well known, are used to convey to us the knowledge of the Divine power, goodness, justice, wrath, mercy, *etc.* So when the terms Father and Son are used, no person surely would apply them in the gross sense; but as it hath pleased God to make use of those expressions as the most suitable, we are to receive them as they are given in the Sacred Writings. The terms Father, Son and Holy Ghost, are there used to convey to us the doctrine of three Persons in one Godhead. That those words are the most proper, we cannot doubt, because, they are the terms used by the Holy Spirit, and used in reference to the Triune God; not merely in reference to the incarnation of our Lord, but to the Eternal Jehovah. If any person replies, 'but I cannot comprehend how those terms can apply to a spiritual and Divine Being,' we say, our reason is not to be the judge of the propriety of such expressions; but as it is the revelation of God, we receive it without attempting to fathom the mystery.

The primitive Christian church undoubtedly received that doctrine; and the compilers of our Liturgy have interwoven it throughout their excellent work. A few extracts from some of the ancient fathers, will be sufficient to show what the doctrine of the primitive church was, on that important subject.

Justin Martyr, in his *Apology for the Christians*, has the following expression; 'But now if we say, that the Logos of God, is properly the begotten of God, by a generation quite different from that of men, as I have already mentioned, yet even this, I say, is no more than what you might very well tolerate.'

Again, 'One article of our faith is, that Christ is the first begotten of God.' Again, 'For they who affirm the Son to be the Father, are guilty of not knowing the Father, and likewise of being ignorant that the Father of the universe has a Son, who being the Logos, and first begotten of God, is God.'

Tertullian, in his *Apology for the Christians*, reasons largely on the subject, and at the close of one train of arguments, has the following expression: 'Thus it is, that the Logos, which came forth from God, is both God, and the Son of God, and those two are one.'

Vincentius Lirinensis wrote his commentary in the year 434AD, and clearly states the doctrine of the primitive church to be, that 'there were two substances in Christ, one of which was Divine, the other human; the one begotten of the Father, the other born of his mother.' Again, 'Thus in one and the same Christ, there are two substances, but one Divine, the other human. One from God the Father, the other from the virgin mother. One co-eternal and equal to the Father, the other temporary and inferior to the Father. One of the same substance with the Father, the other of the same substance with the mother; yet these two different substances make but one and the same Christ.'

The errors which arose in the Christian Church, in the three first ages, were numerous, for one error generally opened the way for another. Sabellius began with denying Jesus to be the Son of God as to his Divine nature; but at the same time allowed him to be God. Dionysius, one of the Christian Bishops, in a letter which he wrote on that occasion, strongly reprobates the novel system of Sabellius, and speaks of Jesus as the 'the only begotten Son.'

When the Arian heresy more fully and openly appeared, a council of the chief Christian Bishops was held at Nice, at which the Emperor presided, and where the Creed, generally termed the Nicene Creed, was formed, and was signed by 318 Bishops. In that Council the following articles were inserted in the Creed, as expressive of our faith of the Christian Church, and also as a bulwark against any future attacks on that faith. 'And in one Lord Jesus Christ, the only begotten Son of God, Begotten of his Father before all worlds, God of God, Light of Light, Very God of very God, Begotten not made, being of one substance with the Father, by whom all things were made.'

Some time afterwards, the Creed which is generally termed the Creed of St Athanasius, was formed, still more effectively to explain and guard the important doctrine of the Trinity. The following parts of the Creed, fully prove what was then the catholic doctrine: 'The Son is of the Father alone; not made, nor created, but begotten.—For the right faith is, that we believe and confess: that our Lord Jesus Christ, the Son of God, is God and Man; God, of the Substance of the Father, begotten before the worlds: and Man, of the Substance of his Mother, born in the world; Perfect God and perfect Man: of a reasonable soul, and human flesh subsisting; Equal to the Father, as touching his Godhead: and inferior to the Father, as touching his Manhood.'

The same doctrine runs through every part of the Liturgy, and proves that the venerable Reformers stood firm on that important ground. In the Articles of Religion which were drawn up by them, they have particularly stated that sacred truth, 'The Son, which is the Word of the Father, begotten from everlasting of the Father, the very and eternal God, and of one substance with the Father.'

The venerable founder of Methodism, who appears to have been particularly directed of God, did not neglect to state that sacred truth.

> Thy co-eternal Son display,
> And call my darkness into day.
>
> Thou art the co-eternal Son,
> In substance with thy Father one;
> In person different we proclaim,
> In power and majesty the same!
>
> For all the plenitude Divine,
> Resides in his eternal Son.
>
> He spake the Word and it was done,
> The universe his word obeyed;
> His word is his eternal Son,
> And Christ the whole creation made.
>
> From Thee through an eternal now,
> The Son, Thine offspring flow'd;
> An everlasting Father Thou,
> As everlasting God.
>
> Thy wondrous love the Godhead show'd
> Contracting to a span:
> The co-eternal Son of God,
> The mortal son of man.

When we turn to the sacred writings, we find a variety of passages, which can bear no other construction than that, which has been uniformly given to them by the orthodox parts of the Christian Church. Our Lord is repeatedly spoken of as the only begotten of the Father, perfectly distinct from all created beings. In the conversation which our Lord had with the Jews, he said, *'My Father worketh hitherto and I work.'* The Jews immediately sought to kill him, because he said that 'God was his Father, making himself equal with God.' Our Lord says, *'I came forth from the Father, and am come into the world; again I leave the world, and go to the Father.'* Of the human nature of our Lord, it could not be said, *'I came forth from the Father,'* in the same sense in which it is immediately added, *'Again, I leave the world, and go to the Father.'*

Such, Sir, were the express testimonies of the ancient Fathers; of the venerable Reformers who were the compilers of the Liturgy; of the Rev. Mr John Wesley, the founder of Methodism; and above all, of the Sacred Writers.

Shall we leave those testimonies, and enter on the doubtful field of theory? Or leave the old way marks, and enter into the trackless desert? Certainly not; millions of Christians have followed the ancient guides, and have entered the gates of the heavenly Jerusalem; and I trust that, through the power of Divine grace, we shall walk in the same plain and beaten track, neither deviating to the right hand nor to the left. We must be careful not to anathematise those persons who do not think with us; to their own master they stand or fall; but we, as a body of people, whom the Lord has graciously raised up as out of the dust, and whom he has honoured with almost unexampled prosperity in the revival of his work, must be careful to 'walk by the same rule, and mind the same things'. Of Methodism, as to purity of doctrine, soundness of discipline, and true Christian experience, I would ever say, *'esto perpetua.'*

APPENDIX THREE

R L DABNEY'S DISCUSSION ON
THE MORAL EFFECTS OF FREE JUSTIFICATION[1]

The Articles of Religion adopted by the Episcopal Churches of Great Britain and America (the churches which love the parental relation to the great Wesleyan communion, if often step-parents), state the matter thus:

> Article XI.—Of the Justification of Man. We are accounted righteous before God, only for the merit of our Lord and Saviour Jesus Christ by faith, and not for our own works or deservings. Wherefore, that we are justified by faith only, is a most wholesome doctrine, and very full of comfort, as more largely is expressed in the homily of justification.
>
> Article XII.—Of Good Works. Albeit that good works, which are the fruits of faith, and follow after justification, cannot put away our sins, and endure the severity of God's judgment; yet are they pleasing and acceptable to God in Christ, and do spring out necessarily of a true and lively faith, insomuch that by them a lively faith may be as evidently known as a tree discerned by the fruit.

The Articles as held by our Methodist Episcopal Church are identical, save that in the former of them, the reference to the homily, and in the latter, the word 'necessarily' is omitted, and the idiom is a little modernised.

The Influence of the Moravian Church
A Reformed Church before the Reformation, whose character was illustrated by the labours and martyrdom of John Huss. This body, at the dawn of the Reformation, joyfully recognised the new Protestants as their brethren in the faith. The renewed discussions of the movement, begun by Luther and Zwinglius, caused the

Church of the Picards, as they were styled, to present their formal Confession to their prince, the Austrian king of the Romans, A.D.1535. At the end of the Article VI. they say:

> 'That men are justified before God by faith, or trust on Jesus Christ, alone, without any strivings, merits, and works of their own. As Paul teaches: 'But to him that worketh not, but believeth on him that justifieth the ungodly, his faith is counted for righteousness.' Again: 'But now the righteousness of God without the law is manifested, being witnessed by the law and the prophets.' And this righteousness is 'by the faith of Jesus Christ'. Elsewhere: 'Through him, whosoever believeth is justified.' And this sixth Article is among us held the most fundamental of all, as being the sum of all Christianity and piety. Accordingly, our people teach and discuss it with all diligence and zeal, and strive to inculcate it on all.'

Article VII.—To this they add: 'Let those who are justified by the sole grace of God, and faith on Christ, do the good works which God commands, and let each one walk worthily in them according to his vocation, in whatsoever grade of life, state and age he may be. For thus the Lord, with Matthew: 'Teach them,' saith he, 'to observe all things which I command you.' But, since many things are extant in Scripture touching this, we forbear to treat it farther....But they teach that good works must be done, that faith may be by them approved. For good works are the sure witnessings, seals, and indices of the living faith within, and fruits thereof, by which the tree is distinguished (Matthew 7) as good or evil.'

The point of present interest to us in this witness is, that the great founder of the Wesleyan communion was so largely indebted, under God, to the descendants of this Moravian communion for his final and joyful establishment in the peace of the Gospel. A shattered remnant of these Christians, fleeing out of fiery persecution in the 18th century, found refuge under Count Zinzendorf, at Herrnhut, in Prussian Lusatia, and spreading thence, planted themselves in several spots of Europe and America. It was during Wesley's voyage to Georgia that he first saw these humble Christians, and was struck with their possession of an assured spiritual peace which he then lacked, notwithstanding his ardent strivings. After his return he entered into more intimate relations with their ministers in England; and, finally, seeking the rest his soul craved, he visited their headquarters at Herrnhut. There he met Christian David, a Moravian minister, whose simple and sincere wisdom he learned to esteem above that of the others, and of Count Zinzendorf himself, from whose mouth he received this testimony:

> 'The word of reconciliation which the apostles preached, as the foundation of all they taught, was: That we are reconciled to God, not by our own works, nor by our righteousness, but wholly and solely by the blood of Christ.'
>
> 'The right foundation is not your contrition, not your righteousness, nothing of your own, nothing that is wrought in you by the Holy Ghost, but it is something without you, *viz.*, the righteousness and blood of Christ.'...'And when they have received this gift from God, then their hearts will melt for sorrow that they have offended him,' *etc.*

Wesley tells us, in his Journal (May 24, 1738), the issue of his doubts and fears.

> 'I was now thoroughly convinced, and by the grace of God I resolved to seek it (faith) unto the end.
> 1. By absolutely renouncing all dependence, in whole or in part, on my own works or righteousness, on which I had really grounded my hope of salvation, though I knew it not, from my youth up.
> 2. By adding to the constant use of all other means of grace continual praying for this very thing —justifying, saving faith, a full reliance on the blood of Christ shed for me, a trust in him as my Christ, as my sole justification, sanctification, and redemption.'

Thenceforward he was able, with a triumphant hand, to sweep his hallowed lyre, as he took up that strain which was silenced no more, and which today he is singing in glory.

> Jesus, thy blood and righteousness,
> My beauty are, my glorious dress;
> 'Midst flaming worlds in these arrayed,
> With joy shall I lift at my head.

We shall close our appeal to this 'great cloud of witnesses' with two emphatic sentences from those sermons of Wesley, which are recognised by Methodists as carrying almost the force of a doctrinal covenant among them. In Sermon V., 'On Justification,' he says: 'Faith, therefore, is the necessary condition of justification; yea, and the only necessary condition thereof. This is the second point carefully to be observed, that the very moment God giveth faith (for it is the gift of God) to the 'ungodly', that 'worketh not', that faith is counted to him for righteousness.'

APPENDIX FOUR

AN EXTRACT FROM THE 'RULES OF METHODIST SOCIETIES'[1]

There is only one condition previously required in those who desired admission into these Societies, *viz.* 'a desire to flee from the wrath to come, and to be saved from their sins'. But wherever this is really fixed in the soul it will be shown by its fruits. It is therefore expected of all who continue therein, that they should continue to evidence their desire of salvation,

FIRSTLY, by doing no harm, by avoiding evil in every kind, especially that which is most generally practised.

Such is
> The taking the name of God in vain;
> The profaning the day of the Lord, either by doing ordinary work thereon, or by buying or selling;
> Drunkenness; buying or selling spirituous liquors, or drinking them, unless in cases of extreme necessity;
> Fighting, quarrelling, brawling; brother going to law with brother; returning evil for evil, or railing for railing; the using many words in buying or selling;
> The buying or selling uncustomed goods;
> The giving or taking things on usury; i.e., unlawful interest;
> Uncharitable or unprofitable conversation, particularly speaking evil of Magistrates or of Ministers.
> Doing to others as we would not they should do unto us;
> Doing what we know is not for the glory of God as,—
> The putting on of gold or costly apparel.
> The taking such diversions as cannot be used in the name of the Lord Jesus.
> The singing of those songs, or reading those books which do not tend to the knowledge or love of God;

Softness, and needless self-indulgence;
Laying up treasures upon earth;
Borrowing without a probability of paying, or taking of goods
without a probability of paying for them.

It is expected that they should continue to evidence their desire of salvation.

SECONDLY, by doing good, by being in every kind merciful after their power; as they have opportunity, doing good of every possible sort, and as far as possible, to all men: —

To their bodies, of the ability that God giveth, by giving food to the hungry, by clothing the naked, by visiting or helping them that are sick or in prison;
To their souls, by instructing, reproving, or exhorting all they have any intercourse with; trampling underfoot that enthusiastic doctrine of devils, that 'we are not to do good, unless our heart be free to it'.—
By doing good especially to them that are of the household of faith, or groaning to be so; employing them preferably to others, buying one of another, helping each other in business; and so much the more, because the world will love its own, and them only.
By all possible diligence and frugality, that the Gospel be not blamed.
By running with patience the race that is set before them denying themselves, and taking up their cross daily; submitting to bear the reproach of Christ, to be as filth and off-scouring of the world; and looking that men should say all manner of evil of them falsely, for the Lord's sake.

It is expected that they should continue to evidence their desire of salvation.

THIRDLY, by attending all the ordinances of God; such are,

The public worship of God;
The ministry of the word, either read or expounded;

The Supper of the Lord;
Family and private prayer;
Searching the Scriptures; and
Fasting or abstinence.

These are the General Rules of our Societies: all which we are taught of God to observe, even in His written word, the only rule, and the sufficient rule, both of our faith and practice. And all these we know His Spirit writes on every truly awakened heart. If there be any among us who observe them not, who habitually break any of them, let it be made known unto them who watch over that soul, as that they must give an account. We will admonish him of the error of his ways: we will bear with him for a season. But then if he repent not, he hath no more place among us. We have delivered our own souls.

May 1st, 1743.

APPENDIX FIVE

METHODIST APOSTASY: FROM FREE GRACE TO FREE WILL

Summary of a Lecture given by Robert E Chiles, Autumn 1955, at the Indiana Wesley Society, Green Castle, Indiana, U.S.A.

On the basis of this review of the transition within American Methodism from free grace to free will, several summary statements can now be made. These statements presuppose the Wesleyan theology as normative as, indeed, this entire discussion has done. The measure of departure from this norm is the measure of the apostasy of Methodism in this critical area of theology.

(1) The context of the debate between free grace and free will is seen to shift gradually. The debate begins in Wesley with a strongly soteriological concern, marked by the conviction that freedom cannot be discussed apart from the gracious realities of the wider context of redemption. Midway in the nineteenth century, however, the discussion has shifted to an anthropological setting. Freedom is derived from psychological and philosophical analysis of man. The doctrine of freedom thus developed is latterly brought to the process of salvation and effort is made to fit it in. Wesley stresses man's need and helplessness and the discontinuity between the human and the divine. Knudson stresses man's capacity and power and the continuity between the human and divine.

(2) The basis of freedom comes to be viewed in quite a different way. Because he shares the consequences of the Adamic sin, man, in Wesley's view, is wholly depraved. His original freedom is lost and his will paralyzed so that he is unable to will salvation. But by prevenient grace a measure of freedom is restored and with it a responsible part in salvation. For Knudson, man's freedom is assigned to the order of creation, not redemption. By nature man is free to choose either good or evil, God or sin. For Wesley, grace

is the basis of man's freedom; for Knudson, freedom must necessarily be intrinsic to man's own nature.

(3) The limits of freedom are greatly expanded in later Methodist theology. In Wesley, even assisted by prevenient grace, man is not able to will God but only to still his sinful efforts to save himself. Man is free only to submit to the further grace of God by the inactivation of the will through despair. All that follows in salvation is dependent upon God's action. Knudson holds that man by nature is free to choose good and God. Man must concur with all additional ministrations of grace in the process of salvation. Salvation is made to depend upon the co-operation of intrinsic human freedom and divine grace.

(4) A significant change is evident in the understanding of responsibility. Wesley was not driven, by a need for logical consistency, to establish a neat correspondence between man's obligation and his ability. He was not frightened by the thought of guilt beyond accountability, of responsibility beyond freedom. Man for him is responsible, even though not free to be good; he is wholly without merit when, empowered by preventing grace, he submits to God. Watson is more concerned to equate responsibility and freedom. In Miley the systematic principle of Arminianism becomes free personal agency as the sole ground of guilt. The highly nominalistic character of his restricted doctrine of moral responsibility ignored the subtle complications intrinsic both to man's expression of freedom and to his awareness of guilt. In Knudson, responsibility requires essential freedom, the gracious context of which is explicitly denied. Thus a realistic and extensive understanding of responsibility becomes simple and superficial, and subversive of a proper understanding of freedom in grace.

(5) The critical and constructive principles which are successively employed through later Methodism also reflect the defection from the Wesleyan norm. For Wesley, free grace is the determinative category in the discussion of the divine and human factors in salvation. He is one with classical Protestant theology in his insistence that salvation is by grace alone. In Whedon and Miley, this principle has been exchanged for the Maxim of Responsibility or free personal agency, which was employed to gain consistency

and clarity in systematic theology. In Knudson, this principle receives formal explication as a doctrine of metaphysical freedom. It is central not only for the divine-human relationship but is critical also for all religion, philosophy and science. Through this declension revelation gives way to reason, and philosophy and logic increasingly limit the theological understanding and statement of the Christian realities.

APPENDIX SIX

THE NON-CONFORMIST SPIRIT—BY HENRY W. CLARK [1]

The Non-conformist spirit is, in succinct summary, the spirit which exalts life above organisation. More than that, it is the spirit which holds that life should make organisation, and that organisation is at least greatly reduced in value (sometimes even valueless, sometimes even harmful) unless it be the direct product of life. That all religious organisation finds its ultimate aim and object in the development of religious life is, of course, a doctrine common to all religious men; and in this sense life is exalted above organisation by all serious thinkers upon the theme. But it is when we strengthen the statement to the pitch of declaring that life should make organisation that we come upon the crucial dividing line. For with one school of thought— the Conformist, the more distinctly ecclesiastical—it is with organisation that thought about the matter begins: the organisation is looked upon as the power-house, the manufactory in which the forces which make the life reside and out of which they issue; so that the primary duty of the religious man is to conform himself to, become a member of, the organisation, in order that he may obtain the needed action upon life.

Life is the ultimate aim, certainly; but in the actual construction of things, organisation stands first; and the idea which the candidate for life must first of all impress upon his mind is the idea that in linking himself with the organisation life is secured. The causal connection between the given organisation and the desired life he must at the outset take for granted, or must believe in on the strength of argument presented to his mind. He moves into life indirectly: and, although intrinsically life is more important, yet the organisation is the immediately imminent matter and in this way is exalted above life. The conception in the forefront of

291

this reading of things is that organisation makes life. While the other school of thought—the Nonconformist—the starting point is different. The nonconformist spirit begins, not with the construction of an organisation which, on theoretical or argumentative considerations, is held to be the one necessary for the production of life, but further down and further back, whatever organisation comes into existence must be the already existing life weaving for itself an outward and visible dress: it must be the natural and automatic producing, by the existing life of a system which that existing life finds necessary and helpful for its own health, and which, precisely because it is thus produced by life, becomes, one must not say the producer, but the deepener and intensifier, of life in its turn: the whole process must be like that of a primary life-germ fashioning for itself its own members and its own physical frame which, once fashioned are to react upon and help in maintaining the life out of which they came.

So the primary duty of the religious man, on this view, is not to conform to whatever religious organisation he finds already occupying the field, but to secure for himself the presence and energizing power of a religious life, and thereafter to let that work itself out into an organisation which shall be at the same time the life's product and the life's new inspiration. He will find of course (for whatever theoretical objections might be taken on this score, in practice the thing does not work out to a mere individualism wherein all organisation and ecclesiasticism is lost)—he will find that as life works itself out into organisation in his own particular case, he ranges alongside of many others in whom life is doing the same. But it is in the idea of a life that he is immersed. He does not begin with organisation: he comes to it—comes to it inevitably, but still as to a thing second both in importance and in time.

This is the Nonconformist spirit—the spirit which does not begin by looking outward for something to which it may cling, but which flies at once to the innermost place, sets the spiritual process going there, and then lets the outward things determine themselves as they may. Organisation has no primary value in its eyes, but only a derived. The Nonconformist spirit stands, not as the too exclusively negative character of its title might be taken to imply, for a refusal to conform (though under the stress of faithfulness to its own principle it may be and has been driven to this), but for a refusal to make conformity the first care. If it sees no virtue in the mere attitude of conformity, it is not that it sees any more in the attitude of Nonconformity either. It is not its attitude, either of acceptance or rejection, to any organisation, that it troubles about most. It puts the whole question of organisation into an inferior place. Life is the all important, the initial and generative thing. The Nonconformist spirit exalts life above organisation, not only as being a matter of greater intrinsic importance (as to that all would be agreed), but as being the master of more immediate practical interest and concern, and declares that the second must be the automatically wrought product of the first.

APPENDIX SEVEN

A CHAPTER BY CHAPTER SUMMARY
OF THE ESSENTIAL ARGUMENT OF THIS BOOK

Chapter 1: Wesley's Puritan Ancestry

The opening chapter comments on Wesley's statement 'If I were to write the story of my life, I would begin it before I was born.' Wesley's ancestry on both his father and his mother's side was of a solid Puritan stock. One could describe them as moderate Calvinists and firmly committed to the great doctrines of the Reformation. His paternal grandfather, Bartholomew Westley was ejected from his living at Winterbourne-Whitchurch, Dorset, in 1662. It is fascinating to see how Wesley and he were so alike both in character and outlook. Nehemiah Curnock described him as 'A brave witty, scholarly, simple-minded itinerant Evangelist.' In his attitude to church authority, and his itinerant ministry after his exclusion from the regular ministry, he in many significant ways anticipated the ministry of his grandson.

I have endeavoured to explain why Wesley's parents, Samuel and Susanna, left Nonconformity for Anglicanism, arguing that Nonconformity at that point had in many respects become contentious, and inward looking. I have noted the significant fact that Wesley's father was taught by Richard Davies, the fiery hyper Calvinist of Rothwell, Northants. Samuel Wesley was clearly in reaction against this kind of teaching. The chapter concludes by stating that the Wesley family home, though Anglican, was of an essentially Puritan character but distinctly prejudiced against the hyper-Calvinism of the age.

Chapter 2: What is meant by the term 'Arminian'?

This chapter is an examination of the nature of Arminianism. Here I seek to show that the Church of England at the time of the

Reformation embraced a broad type of moderate Calvinism; and that the type of Arminianism which developed in England in the 17th century under such leaders as, Archbishop Laud and Bishop Jeremy Taylor, was not the only type of Arminianism to be found in England at that time. I point out that there was a strand of 'Arminianism', for want of a better word, which traced its origin back to the residual Lutheranism within the English church. This line can be traced through the Puritan 'Arminian' John Goodwin, and clearly had an influence on John Wesley. What is very clear is that the rational Arminianism of Laud and Taylor, which became the popular creed of many Anglicans at the time of John Wesley, was radically different from the 'Arminianism' of John Wesley. This is plain from the fact that Wesley found himself utterly at odds with the Arminian establishment of his day. It was this that excluded him from their pulpits and caused them to actually accuse him of being a Calvinist.

Rational Arminianism was semi-Pelagian in its teaching on justification, and was in effect, if not in intention legalistic, turning faith from a means of receiving from God into a work that merits before God. The Wesleys' 'Arminianism' emphasised salvation as a work of God's free grace alone. Without a work of grace there could be no salvation, man in and of his own strength can do nothing. To incorporate this into his theology Wesley adopted the principle of prevenient grace, that is grace given to every man, that cancels the bondage to sin brought about by the Fall. In this formulation Wesley affirmed the Protestant doctrine of original sin, with its insistence upon total dependence on the mercy of God, and sought to avoid the pitfall of a Pelagian inherent free will, while at the same time restoring a measure of responsibility to humanity. One is reminded how in Puritan Covenant theology, a tension is maintained between man's utter inability and his responsibility within the Covenant to respond to the Gospel. We see that Wesley comes close to Calvinism in saying that the true Gospel touches the very edges of Calvinism.

In this chapter we also see that Rational Arminianism denied the doctrine of Imputed Righteousness. We also challenge the oft repeated assertion that Wesley denied the doctrine of Imputed

Righteousness. I further observe that Rational Arminianism tended towards Socinianism and the denial of the doctrine of Christ's penal substitution, and show that without a shadow of doubt, Wesley taught the doctrine of Penal Substitution.

Chapter 3: Why did Wesley call himself an Arminian?

Here I have sought to answer this question under the following headings:

The influence of his mother;

A fear of limiting the free offer of the Gospel;

A fear of antinomianism;

A wrestling with the principles of particularity and universality.

I have also tried in this chapter to describe the type of Calvinism *i.e.* hyper-Calvinism, that Wesley was exposed to at this time.

Chapter 4: An examination of the influences which Wesley came under in his pre-conversion days at Oxford

Here are considered some of the chief influences of Wesley's reading at this time, appreciating that he read a vast number of books, in the region of 691 in these years, and by a wide range of authors. We know that though the doctrine of justification by faith was largely lost sight of in Anglicanism at the time Wesley must have been familiar with it, at least intellectually, through reading the works of the former Archbishop of Canterbury, William Wake. I note here also the influence of the mystics in his reading, principally Thomas à Kempis and William Law, from whom he learned that true religion was seated in the heart and that nothing godly can be alive in us but what derives its life from the Spirit of God. The chapter shows that Wesley was influenced by these men and derived benefit from them, but ultimately rejected the main teachings of mysticism.

I note also that Wesley was influenced by Jeremy Taylor, and the fact that Taylor, whilst a High Churchman and Rational Arminian was nevertheless a practical Puritan. The title of Taylor's work *Holy Living and Holy Dying* became one of the chief emphases of Wesley's understanding of the Christian life *i.e.* the pursuit of holiness.

Emphasis is also given to the fact that the designation 'High Church' in Wesley's day did not signify Anglo-Catholicism. Wesley was never a Sacerdotalist, and never a sympathiser with the teachings of the Church of Rome. Throughout this work, the notion that Wesley sought to bring about a synthesis between Protestantism and Roman Catholicism is rejected.

Chapter 5: Wesley's conversion and the influence of the Moravians

This chapter deals with Wesley's conversion and the part played by the Moravians. I briefly trace the history of the Moravian Church, noting that its origins were one of the first-fruits of the Reformation. It was through the ministry of the Moravian missionaries that Wesley was first convicted of sin and saw his need of faith in Christ. I also note that Wesley's moment of conversion came 'while one was reading *Luther's Preface to St Paul's Epistle to the Romans*'.

Chapter 6: A description of the doctrinal content of the four sermons preached before the University of Oxford, after Wesley's conversion, sometimes called the 'Manifesto of the Evangelical Revival'

In these sermons Wesley sets out his teaching on justification by faith and the need for true conversion through repentance and faith in Christ. Here we see the great evangelical principles of the Reformation reasserted. Wesley is nailing his colours to the mast and preaching the essence of the Thirty-Nine Articles of Religion.

Chapter 7: The Methodist Revival was a reaction against the humanising influences of Arminian Anglicanism

In this section I attempt to set out in greater detail, a challenge to the oft repeated assertion that John Wesley taught an updated version of Laudian-Anglicanism and was in fact attacking the last residue of Genevan Calvinism in the Church of England. I seek to prove that if this had been the case, Wesley would not have been opposed by the Anglican establishment in the way that he was.

Chapter 8: An examination of the nature of what have been designated 'the first, second and third Calvinistic controversies within Methodism'

Here we notice that within Methodism at this time there were Calvinistic elements, their chief spokesman of course being George Whitfield, and Arminian elements who looked to John Wesley. The nature of the movement meant that all gathered in Conference on an annual basis. Here doctrine and evangelism and all the business of the Societies were discussed. It is often out of the white heat of these excited debates that critics of Wesley have taken hold of statements and quoted them as examples of his settled beliefs. This is particularly true of the so-called third Calvinistic controversy of 1770. Clearly many things quoted from the minutes have been taken out of context, and have greatly distorted our understanding of Wesley's theology. Some have even taken elements from this debate to argue that Wesley did not believe in justification by faith alone, which when considered within the context of Wesley's whole life and teaching, is most preposterous. My aim in this chapter is to put these debates into their right context in order that we may correctly understand the statements that were made.

Chapter 9: A glimpse at the theology of Wesley's hymns

In this chapter I have drawn on comments made in a lecture given by C.H. Spurgeon, at the time of the opening of the Metropolitan Tabernacle in London. In the lecture Spurgeon makes the comment, 'Mr Wesley's hymn book which may be looked at as being the standard of his divinity, has in it upon some topics higher Calvinism than many books used by ourselves.'[1]

Chapter 10 and following

In these chapters I look at Wesley the Puritan. Amongst Wesley's contemporaries were such as Bishop Warburton, Samuel Johnson and Horace Walpole who all identified Methodism as a return of Puritanism. Here I have commented on the very high percentage of Puritan works included in Wesley's *Christian Library* and tried to highlight the similarities between his theology and practice with that of the Puritans.

The later chapters of the study deal with the various 19th century disruptions in Methodism, and the founding of the various strands of Methodism, such as the New Connexion, the Primitives and the United Methodist Free Churches. I seek to show that these separations from the main body were, by and large, paralleling Wesley's own personal spiritual development, and at the same time manifesting the Puritan side of Wesley's nature. In these movements we see the Puritan love of liberty surfacing in the controversy with Jabez Bunting, the President of the Conference. The Puritan reaction against ecclesiastical strait-jacketing in regard to the preaching of the Gospel, first manifested in Wesley's grandfather, Bartholomew Westley, clearly reappears in Primitive Methodism. Also the Puritan love of Scripture once again reappears in the Bible Christians.

Further, in this section I note something of the 19th century deviations from the essential doctrines of Methodism and the decline in emphasis on free grace to an emphasis on free will. The point is made that it is often this deviation that is mistaken for Wesley's own teaching.

Conclusion

My main objective in this study has been to show that John Wesley was essentially within the broad harbour of the Reformed and Puritan tradition and that he believed the truth to be, as he said, 'within a hair's breadth of Calvinism.'

It is important to hold to this belief because, in so doing, we maintain that Evangelicalism has but one root, as far as Church History is concerned, that is, the Protestant Reformation and essential Calvinism, not two roots i.e. Calvinism and Arminianism. Methodism was not, is not, and never will be 'Arminianism on fire'. I have endeavoured to show that Methodism is not a synchronism between Protestantism and Roman Catholicism, neither is Methodism the connecting link between Laudianism and the 19th century Oxford Movement.

I have also sought to identify those influences in 20th century Methodism which have tried to make these links. Positively I have tried to draw attention to the fact that modern Evangelicalism has a lot to learn from Wesley's emphasis on holiness of living, and thoroughgoing 'out and out' commitment to the things of God.

Finally, I have sought to demonstrate that Wesley teaches us how to preach, that is with a sense of the love of God for the lost upon our hearts, and that this outstanding individual is a challenge to our laziness, our narrow exclusiveness and our deadness. Wesley's spirit in preaching is well summed up in the lines of his brother's hymn:

> His arms of love still open are
> Returning sinners to receive.

END NOTES

Chapter 1

1. A. Skevington-Wood, *The Burning Heart*, p.19.
2. *Ibid.*, p.19.
3. Note the 't' in the surname was not dropped until John Wesley's father went up to Oxford.
4. Martin Schmidt, *John Wesley: A Theological Biography*, p.36.
5. Skevington-Wood, p.20.
6. Schmidt, p.36.
7. *Ibid.*, p.21.
8. John Wesley, *Journal*, Vol.5, pp.121-122. 25th May, 1765, quoted by Skevington-Wood, p.22.
9. Schmidt, Vol. I, p.38.
10. R. Southey, *Life of Wesley*, p.5.
11. See Peter Naylor, *Picking Up a Pin For the Lord*, pp. 69-70.
12. Schmidt, pp.40-41.
13. *Journal*, Vol. 5, p.2. quoted by Skevington-Wood, p.24.
14. Schmidt, p.42.
15. John Kirk, *The Mother of the Wesleys*, pp.13-15.
16. *Ibid.*, pp.16-17.
17. John Wesley, *A Christian Library*, quoted by J.A. Newton, *Susanna Wesley*, p.40.
18. See *Dictionary of National Biography*.
19. Skevington-Wood, p.25.
20. *Ibid.*, p.25.
21. Newton, p.57.
22. *Ibid.*, p.58.
23. See P.Toon, *Puritans and Calvinism*, p.87.
24. *The Reasonableness of Christianity*, p. 76. quoted by Toon, p. 93.
25. F. Baker, *Charles Wesley as Revealed by His Letters*, quoted by Newton, p.115. See also John Wesley's Sermon on the Education of Children. *Sermon XCV*, Vol.3. p. 92.
26. Newton, p.63.
27. *Ibid.*, p.63.
28. Iain Murray, Lecture at Banner of Truth Conference, 2003.
29. *Ibid.*
30. John A. Newton, *Susanna Wesley*, p. 27

31 J. A. Newton, *Methodism and the Puritans,* p.5.
32 Skevington-Wood, p.27.
33 *A New History of Methodism,* pp.168-169.

Chapter 2
1 Elizabeth and the English Reformation, Cambridge 1968. quoted by H. McGonigle, *Sufficient Saving Grace,* p. 43.
2 McGonigle, p.45.
3 International Calvinism, ed. Menna Prestwich, p.125.
4 A. W. Harrison, *Arminianism in England,* p.22.
5 *The Life of William Grotius,* London 1925, p.143.
6 Prestwich, p.218.
7 Quoted by Paul Zahl, *The Protestant Face of Anglicanism,* p. 32.
8 Harrison, p.122.
9 Mandell Creighton, *Historical Essays,* p.164.
10 F. Stamp, '*Studies In The Origin of English Arminianism*' Harvard University PhD. Thesis 1950, quoted by McGonigle, p.??.
11 J. Plaifere, *A collection of Tracts Concerning Predestination,* p. 29. quoted by McGonigle, p.60.
12 *Ibid.,* p.29. quoted by McGonigle, p.60.
13 *Ibid.*
14 J. I. Packer, *Honouring the People of God,* p.293.
15 George Croft Cell, *The Rediscovery of John Wesley,* pp.16-19.
16 Packer, p.285.
17 Jacob Harmenzoon latinized his name to Arminius, originally the name of a first Century German chief who resisted the Romans.
18 'The Arminians insist that their emphasis on conditional predestination and man's power to resist divine grace does not in any way weaken man's utter dependence upon divine grace to think or do anything good.' Cunliffe-Jones, *Christian Theology since 1600,* p.22.
19 *Creeds of Christendom,* quoted by Packer, p.287.
20 Packer, pp.287-288.
21 *Institutes* II XI.23, quoted by Packer, p. 290.
22 *Ibid.,* p.291.
23 *Ibid.,* p.296.
24 Schmidt, *John Wesley—a Theological Biography,* quoted by Packer, p.298.
25 Ed. Albert C. Outler, *John Wesley,* p.62.
26 J. Calvin, *Institutes* III.2.7, quoted by Packer, p.299.
27 Packer, p.299.
28 Harrison, p.191.

²⁹ *Ibid.*, p.199.

³⁰ *Ibid.*, p.200.

³¹ R. L. Dabney, p.73, See Appendix 3: *The Moral Effects of a Free Justification—Discussions Evangelical and Theological*, Vol. I. Banner of Truth.

³² R.C. Monk, *John Wesley and His Puritan Heritage*, p.75.

³³ *Ibid.*, p.77.

³⁴ See G. Carter, 'Robert Hawker,' *The Blackwell Dictionary of Evangelical Biography*, Vol. 1, Oxford 1995, quoted by David Bebbington, *Holiness in Nineteenth Century England*, Paternoster 2000, p.537.

³⁵ James Buchanan, *Justification*, Banner of Truth, Edinburgh, p.179.

³⁶ *Ibid.*, p.180.

³⁷ John Fletcher, *Works*, London 1814 II, pp.232-234, quoted by Packer, p. 283. See also Wesley's, 'The Doctrine of Original sin According to Scripture, Reason and Experience 1759', *Works* V, p.492ff.

³⁸ Packer, p.283.

³⁹ Franz Hildebrandt, *Christianity According to the Wesleys*, p.12.

⁴⁰ *Ibid.*, p.13.

Chapter 3

¹ Iain Murray, *Wesley and the Men who Followed,* p.60.

² John Calvin, *Sermons on Deuteronomy,* p. 167. quoted by Murray, p.60.

³ John Calvin, *Commentary on John 1:29.*

⁴ John Calvin, *Commentary on Rom 5:18.*

⁵ John Calvin, *Commentary on Gal. 5:12.*

⁶ See *Letters, Vol.3.* p.230.

⁷ Murray, p.62.

⁸ Hildebrandt, *From Luther to Wesley,* p.98.

Chapter 4

¹ V.H.H. Green, *Religion at Oxford and Cambridge,* p.179.

² *(for lists of editions of the Fathers produced by Oxford scholars, see ibid. page176)*

³ Green, p.167

⁴ Henry Bett, *The Spirit of Methodism,* p.65.

⁵ *Ibid.,* p.65.

⁶ See for example, O.A. Beckerlegge, *John Wesley and The Church of Rome.*

⁷ Bett, pp. 66-67.

⁸ Cell, p.359.

⁹ *From Luther to Wesley,* p.80.

¹⁰ J. Nockles, *The Oxford Movement in Context,* p. 25. See notes on

Archbishop Laud, The Protestant Dictionary, Harrison Trust.
11 p.96.
12 C.J.Abbey, *The English Church*, pp. 96-9.
13 William Wake, p.16.
14 *Works Vol. XI*, p. 336. quoted by Skevington-Wood, *The Burning Heart*, p. 44.
15 *Ibid.*p.45.
16 *Letter, 18th June 1725.*
17 Wood, p.45.
18 Cell, pp 401-2
19 William Leary, *Man of One Book,* p.9.
20 *Journal* Vol.1. p.464.
21 *Journal* Vol.1. p.222.
22 Leary, p.10.
23 Outler, p.vii.
24 Cell, p.117.
25 *John Wesley and William Law,* p.65. quoted by Leary, p. 11.
26 *The Roots of Methodism,* p.99.
27 George Every, *the High Church Party, 1688-1718,* pp.174-175.
28 See J.S.Simon, *John Wesley and the Religious Societies,* p.240.
29 *Ibid.,* p. 247.
30 Cell, *The Rediscovery of John Wesley,* pp.96-97.
31 See *Letters VI,* p. 292. and *Journal I,* p. 416.
32 Cell. p. 101.

Chapter 5
1 E R Hasse, *The Moravians,* p.12.
2 Hasse, pp.15-16.
3 *Ibid.,* p.20.
4 Edward Miller, *John Wesley, The Hero of the Second Reformation,* p.45.
5 Coke and Moore, *Life of the Rev. John Wesley,* J S Pratt, London, 1855, p.108.
6 Garth Lean, *John Wesley Anglican,* p.31.
7 *Ibid.,* p.32.
8 Hasse, p.32.
9 See Appendix 1

Chapter 6
1 Cell, p.39.
2 *Ibid.,* pp.219-220.
3 *Ibid.,* p.220.

4 *Ibid.,* p.198.
5 *Ibid.,* p.18.
6 *Ibid.,* p.58.
7 *Conference Minutes* quoted by Cell. p.39.
8 *Foundations Magazine* Autumn. 2004 p.12.

Chapter 7
1 *Ibid.,* pp.17-19.
2 Hilderbrandt, *Christianity According to the Wesleys,* p.14.
3 Skevington Wood, *The Burning Heart,* p.262.
4 Lindström, *Wesley and Sanctification,* pp.20-21.
5 p.153.
6 p.392.
7 See *Oxford Dictionary of the Christian Church* article on 'The Remonstrants'.

Chapter 8
1 J C Ryle, *George Whitfield and his Ministry,* 1958.
2 Albert Brown Lawson, *John Wesley and the Anglican Evangelicals of the 18th Century,* p.155.
3 *Ibid.,* pp.59-60.
4 *Ibid.,* p.163.
5 *Ibid.,* p 166, quoting *Whitfield's Journal,* p.565.
6 Quoted in W H Daniels, *A Short History of The People called Methodists,* p.78.
7 Daniels, p.84.
8 We may add however that it only seems to have been at times when there was a movement towards a greater emphasis upon Calvinism amongst Wesley's friends and followers that these reactions took place— my own observation.
9 Brown Lawson, p.179.
10 There is uncertainty as to who this author was. Dr H McGonigle, principal of the Nazarene College Manchester, believes it was extracted from a work entitled *The Order of Causes* by a Baptist named Henry Haggar, 1654. See H. McGonigle, *Sufficient Saving Grace,* Nazarene College Manchester, p.80.
11 *Ibid.,* p.180.
12 *Ibid.,* p.185.
13 *Ibid.,* p.188.
14 *Ibid.,* p.206 quoting Hervey's *Works* Vol 7 p.10 'Letter to Mr Ryland'.
15 *Ibid.,* pp.207-208. quoting Hervey's *Works* Vol 1 p.80.

[16] *Ibid.*, p.256. quoting Hervey's *Aspasio Vindicated*, 1771, p.112.
[17] *Ibid.*, p.240.
[18] See Luke Tyerman, *Life and Times of John Wesley*, Vol. II. London 1872, p.293.
[19] John Wesley, *Sermons*, Vol II p.506.
[20] Brown Lawson, p.262.
[21] John Wesley's *Letters*, Vol. 5. pp.258–260.
[22] Brown Lawson, p.308. quoting John Wesley, *Journal*, Vol. 5. p.427.
[23] Tyerman, Vol. 2. pp.510–511.

Chapter 9
[1] John Telford, *The Methodist Hymnbook Illustrated*, 1922 p.2.

Chapter 10
[1] Robert C Monk, John Wesley and His Puritan Heritage, p.1.
[2] *Ibid.*, p.27.
[3] Luke Tyerman, *The Life and Times of the Rev. Samuel Wesley*, p.150.
[4] Monk, p.18, quoting from John Wesley, *Works*, Vol. 26, p.323.
[5] *Ibid.*, p.20 quoting from *The Christian Library*, Vol. 4, p105.
[6] *Dr William's Library Lecture, 1964*, pp.8-9.
[7] Monk., p.42.

Chapter 11
[1] Horton Davies, *English Free Churches*, p.41.
[2] Monk, p.80. quoting Joseph Hall, *Works*, Meditations and Vows, Vol. 6, p.43.
[3] Monk, p.80. quoting Alleine's *Vindiciae Pietatis*, p.152.
[4] *Ibid.*, p.52.
[5] See Wesley's *Works* Vol.9. pp.327,345-397.
[6] Monk, p.54.
[7] David G Fountain, *Contending for the Faith*, p.154.
[8] See sermons on Justification by Faith, The Righteousness of Faith, and The Scriptural Way of Salvation. *Works* I: 182-216; II: 153-169.
[9] Monk, p54.
[10] *Ibid.*, p.54.
[11] *Ibid.*, p.55. quoting Wesley's *Works*, Vol.10. p.316.
[12] Wesley's *Works*, Vol.26. p182.
[13] Monk, p.63. quoting Wesley's *Letters*, Vol.3. p.159.
[14] *Ibid.*, p.64. quoting Wesley's *Works*, Vol.22. pp.163-171; *Letters*, Vol.2. pp.233-235; Vol.4. pp.376-381.
[15] *Ibid.*, p.65.

16 John Owen, *Works*, Vol.10. p.310.
17 *Ibid.*, p.70.
18 *Ibid.*, p.71.
19 John Preston, *New Covenant*, p.351.
20 *Ibid.*, p71.
21 Wesley, *Works* Vol. 3, p.30.
22 *Ibid.*, p.77.
23 Monk, p.73. quoting J.Preston, *The New Covenant*, p.317.
24 Wesley's *Works*, Vol.10. p.239.
25 John A Newton, *Methodism and the Puritans*, p.14.
26 Wesley's *Works*, Vol.13. p.337.
27 Monk, pp.91-92.
28 W. E. Sangster, *The Path to Perfection*, p.103.
29 Cell, p.362.
30 Monk, p.92.
31 Colin W. Williams, *John Wesley's Theology Today*, pp.174-175.
32 Gordon Rupp, *Principalities and Powers*, p.82.
33 Wesley's *Letters*, Vol.5 p6.
34 John Owen, *Works*, Vol.3. p.386.
35 Wesley's *Works*, Vol. 1. pp.403-404.
36 From 'A Further Appeal to Men of Reason and Religion', Wesley's *Works*, Vol. 22 p.108.
37 Gordon Wakefield, *Puritan Devotion*, p.137. quoting Richard Greenham, *Works*, p.34.
38 Wakefield, p.137.
39 *Ibid.*, p.139.
40 John Preston, *The New Covenant*, p.219.
41 W.R. Inge, *Protestantism*, p.58.
42 Bebbington, p.62.
43 *Banner of Truth Magazine*, Nov.1970. No.86. pp.32-33.
44 Richard Carwardine, *Transatlantic Revivalism*, p.127.
45 Murray, *Wesley and the Men who Followed*, p.183. quoting *Early Victorian Methodism: The Correspondence of Jabez Bunting 1830-58*, OUP. 1976.
46 Bebbington., p.65.
47 Bebbington., p.66. quoting James Caughey, *Ernest Christianity Illustrated*, p.152.
48 Martyn Lloyd-Jones, *God's Ultimate Purpose*, p.261.
49 *Ibid.*, p.275.
50 Benjamin Field, *A Handbook of Christian Theology*, pp.217-219.

Chapter 12

[1] E. Gordon Rupp, *Studies in the making of the English Protestant Tradition*, p.77.
[2] *A Collection of Hymns for the use of the People called Methodists* (1896) no.465.
[3] *Ibid.*, Hymn no.467 v. 1-4.
[4] Ernst Troeltsch, *The Social Teaching of the Christian Churches*, Vol. 2.p.681.
[5] See *The Rules of Methodist Societies*, (Appendix 4).
[6] See John A. Newton, *From Methodism and the Puritans*, p.17.
[7] Newton, *Susanna Wesley*, p.201.

Chapter 13

[1] Hildebrandt, *Christianity According to the Wesleys*, p.12.
[2] *Letters*, Vol. 3, p.117.
[3] Williams, p.26.
[4] Williams, p.26. quoting Wesley's *Works*. Vol. 7. p.198.
[5] *The Methodist Magazine*, 1818, Vol. XLI. P.13.
[6] Williams, p.33. quoting Tyerman, *The Life and Times of Rev. John Wesley*, Vol.3. p.519.
[7] Williams, pp.35-35.
[8] Oliver A. Beckerlegge, John Wesley's *Writings on Roman Catholicism*, p.72.

Chapter 14

[1] Vol. II. p.628.
[2] Wesley's *Works*, Vol. XIII. p.211.
[3] *Ibid.*, p.251.
[4] *Ibid.*, Vol. III. pp.44-45.
[5] *Ibid.*, Vol. XIII. p.253.
[6] W. B. Fitzgerald, *The Roots of Methodism*, p.159.
[7] *Works*, Vol. XIII. p.235.
[8] Watson's *Works*, Vol. 5. p.199. 'Letter to Charles Wesley', quoted by W. B. Fitzgerald, *The Roots of Methodism*, p.161.
[9] *Works*, Vol. I. p.201., quoted by Fitzgerald, p.161.
[10] *Works*, Vol. XIII. p.264.
[11] *Ibid.*, p.266.
[12] Horton-Davies, *Worship and Theology in England*, p.183.
[13] Horton-Davies, *The English Free Churches*, pp.141-142.

Chapter 15

1   A. Mitchell Hunter, *The Teaching of Calvin*, pp.296-297.
2   *Works*, Vol. VI. p.142.
3   *Letters*, Vol. VIII. p192, quoted by Iain H. Murray, *Wesley and the Men who Followed*, p.80.
4   J.Wesley Bready, *England Before and After Wesley*, p.202.
5   *A Collection of Hymns for the People called Methodists*, no.279.
6   *Ibid.*, no.326.
7   John Telford, *The Life of John Wesley*, p.363.

Chapter 16

1   Adrian Burdon, *The Preaching Service—The Glory of the Methodists*, p.18.
2   From *The Journal of Hester Ann Row*, John Ryland's Library, Manchester. Information supplied by Herbert McGonigle, Principal, Nazarene Theological College, Manchester.
3   p.94.
4   *A Portraiture of Methodism*, p.252. Quoted by Adrian Burdon, *The Preaching Service—The Glory of the Methodists*, p.30.
5   Benjamin Gregory, *Sidelights on the Conflicts of Methodism*, p.7.
6   Horton-Davies, *Worship and Theology in England, from Watts and Wesley to Maurice*, p.197.
7   Newton, *Methodism and the Puritans*, p.14.
8   See Horton-Davies, p.71.

Chapter 17

1   W.H.Daniels, *A Short History of the People Called Methodists*, pp.387-388.
2   John Telford, *The Life of John Wesley*, p.371.
3   Edited by W.J. Townsend, H.B. Workman, & George Eayrs, *A New History of Methodism*, p.486.
4   James Gardner, *The Faiths of the World*, p.439.
5   From Gilbert Murray, *The Methodist Class Meeting*, pp.32-41.
6   Summarised from Fitzgerald, pp.146-149.
7   *Ibid.*, p.151.
8   See section on Wesley's adaptation of the Prayer Book. (Chapter 16).
9   Rupert E. Davies, *Methodism*, p.136.
10 Rev. James Gardner M.A.
11 Davies, p.138.
12 Joseph Kirsop, Historic Sketches of Free Methodism, pp.20-21.
13 John Calvin—The Man and His Ethics, p.250.

14 Vol.II. p.628.
15 John Stephen Flynn, Puritanism, p.18.
16 Kirsop, p.27.
17 Samuel Warren, Remarks on the Wesleyan Theological Institution for
    the Education of Junior Preachers, p.23. quoted by D.A. Gawland,
    Methodist Secessions, p.36.
18 Kirsop, p.33.
19 Oliver A. Beckerlegge, The United Methodist Free Churches, p.34.
20 Beckerlegge, p.34. quoting Benjamin Gregory, Side Lights on the
    Conlicts of Methodism.
21 Ibid., p.35. quoting James Everett, Wesleyan Takings.
22 Pamphlet to be found in the John Rylands Library, Manchester.
23 D. A. Gowland, Methodist Secessions, p.101.
24 See Matthew Baxter, Memorials of the United Methodist Free Churches.

Chapter 18
1   Cell, pp.246-247.
2   *Letters*, Vol.IV. p.295.
3   Cell, p.250.
4   Cell, p.255.
5   R. W. Dale, *Fellowship with Christ*, pp.222-224.
6   George Jackson, *The New Methodism and the Old*, p.16.
7   Daniel Curry (ed.), *The Methodist Review*, Vol. LXVIII. 5th series Vol. 2
    pp.446-448.
8   *Ibid.*, p.445.
9   p.11.
10 Franz Hildebrandt, *From Luther to Wesley*, quoted by Robert E. Chiles,
    Theological Transition in American Methodism, p.31.
11 pp. 161-173.
12 Williams, p.63.
13 p.153.
14 Gordon S. Wakefield, *Puritan Devotion*, p.vii.
15 *Ibid.*
16 Murray, *Wesley and the Men who Followed*, p.54.
17 *Ibid.*, p.55.
18 *Ibid.*, p.53.
19 Martyn Lloyd-Jones, *The Puritans*, p.240.
20 R. E. Chiles, p.49.
21 *Ibid.*, p.174.
22 *Ibid.*, p.194.
23 January 1937.

[24] The magazine of the Protestant Truth Society.
[25] See *Churchman's Magazine*, June 1937. pp.34,163-164.
[26] Murray, p.211.
[27] *Ibid.*, p.211.
[28] *Ibid.*, p.212.
[29] *Ibid.*, pp.211-213.

Appendix 1
[1] From the *Epworth Review*, May 1982, pp.52-57.

Appendix 2
[1] *The Methodist Magazine*, Vol. XLI, 1818 pp.12-22.

Appendix 3
[1] R. L. Dabney, *Discussions*, Vol. I. pp.80-82.

Appendix 4
[1] John and Charles Wesley, *Rules of Methodist Societies*, quoted by Leslie F. Church, *The Early Methodist People*, pp.186-188.

Appendix 6
[1] From Henry W. Clark, *History of English Nonconformity* Vol. 1, p.2.

Appendix 7
[1] C.H.Spurgeon, *Metropolitan Tabernacle Pulpit 1861*, p.298.

BIBLIOGRAPHY

The Works of John Wesley, Baker Books (1998)
Wesley's Sermons   John Mason, (Finsbury, 1863)
The Journal of John Wesley, ed. Thomas Jackson, Wesleyan Conf. Office (1901)
Wesley's Hymns, Wesleyan Meth. Bookroom (1896)
The Methodist Hymn Book (1933), The Methodist Conf. Office
The Catechisms of the Wesleyan Methodists
A Plain Account of Christian Perfection, Epworth Press (1952)
The Arminian Magazine Vol. I, J. Fry & Co. (London 1778)
The Arminian Magazine Vol. III, J. Fry & Co. (London 1780)
Wesleyan Methodist Magazine Jan. 1818 Conference Office London
Wesleyan Methodist Assn. Minutes 1836-1856
Minutes of the Methodist Free Church 1857, John Rylands Library
        (Manchester)
Moravian Liturgy and Hymns, Moravian Publications Office 1914

Baker, Eric W., *A Herald of the Evangelical Revival,* Epworth Press (1948)
Banks, John S., *A Manual of Christian Doctrine,* Charles H. Kelly (London 1903)
Barber, B. Aquila, *A Methodist Pageant,* The Holborn Publishing House (1932)
Barclay, Thomas, *The Class Leader at Work,* Charles H. Kelly (London 1905)
Baxter, M., *Methodism - Memorials of the United,* Methodist Free Churches,
        W. Reed (London 1865)
Bebbington, David, *Holiness in 19th Century England,* Paternoster Press (2000)
Bebbington, David, *Evangelicalism in Modern Britain,* Routledge (2000)
Beckerlegge, Oliver A., *The United Methodist Free Churches,* Epworth Press (1957)
Beckerlegge, Oliver A. ed., *John Wesley's Writings on Roman Catholicism,*
        P.T.S. (London)
Beckerlegge, Oliver A., *The Three Expelled,* Foundary Press
Bett, Henry, *The Spirit of Methodism,* Epworth Press (1937)
Bett, Henry, *The Hymns of Methodism,* Epworth Press (1913)
Biggs, W. W., *John Goodwin,* Indep. Press Ltd. (1961)
Bishop, John, *Methodist Worship,* Epworth Press (1950)
Bready, J. Wesley, *England Before and After Wesley,* Hodder & Stoughton (1938)
Brown-Lawson, Albert, *John Wesley and the Evangelical Anglicans of the
        Eighteenth Century,* Pentland Press (1963)
Buchanan, James, *The Doctrine of Justification,* Banner of Truth (1991)

Burdon, Adrian, *The Preaching Service—The Glory of the Methodists*, Grove (1991)
Burton, Robert W. &

Chiles, Robert E. ed., *A Compendium of Wesley's Theology*, Abingdon Press
 (New York)
Cell, George Croft, *The Rediscovery of John Wesley*, Henry Holt & Co. (New
 York 1935)
Chew, Richard, & James Everett, Hodder & Stoughton (1875)
Chiles, Robert E, *Theological Transition in American Methodism*, Abingdon
 Press (New York 1965)
Church, Lesley F., *The Early Methodist People*, Epworth Press 1949
Clark, Henry W., *History of English Nonconformity* Vol. II, Chapman & Hall
 (1913)
Clifford, Alan C., *Cranmer's Doctrine of Justification*, Banner of Truth
 Magazine, (December 1989)
Coke and More, *Life of the Reverend J. Wesley*, J. S. Pratt (London 1855)
Cox, H. F. Lovell, *The Nonconformist Conscience*, Independent Press (1943)
Creighton, Mandell, *Historical Essays*, Longman, Green & Co. (1903)
Cunnliffe-Jones, *Christian Theology since 1600*, Duckworth & Co. (1970)
Curry, Daniel ed., *The Methodist Review*, Phillips & Hunt (New York 1886)

Dabney, R. C., *Discussions* Vol. I, Banner of Truth
Dale R. W., *Fellowship with Christ*, Hodder & Stoughton (1891)
Dale, R. W., *The Evangelical Revival*, Hodder & Stoughton (1880)
Daniels, W. H., *A Short History of the Methodists*, Hodder & Stoughton (1882)
Davies, Horton, *Worship and Theology in England*, Princeton Univ. Press
 (1961)
Davies, Rupert P., *Methodism*, Pelican (1961)

Edwards, David L., *Christian England* Vol. III, Collins (1984)
Edwards, Maldwyn, *Methodism and England*, Epworth Press (1944)
Erwin, E. C., *John Wesley—Christian Citizen*, Epworth press (1937)
Erwin, E. C., *The Significance of 1849*, Historical Soc. Lectures (1949)

Field, B., *Handbook of Christian Theology*, Hodder & Stoughton (1884)
Fisher, G. P., *History of Christian Doctrine*, T & T Clark (1949)
Fitchett, W.H., *Wesley and his Century*, Smith, Elder & Co. (London 1906)
Fitzgerald, W. B., *The Roots of Methodism*, Epworth Press
Fletcher, John, *Five Checks to Antinomianism*, Wesleyan Conf. Office (1876)
Flynn, John Stephen, *Influence of Puritanism*, John Murray (London 1920)
Fountain, D. G., *Contending for the Faith*, Wakeman Trust (2005)
Frost, Stanley B., *The Pattern of Methodism*, Methodist Youth Dept .(1952)

Gardner, J., *The Faiths of the World*, A. Fullerton & Co. (London & Edinburgh)
Geoffrey, David Lyle, *English Spirituality in the Age of Wesley*, W. B. Eerdmans
    (1994)
Gowland, D. A., *Methodist Secessions—The Origins of Free Methodism in Three
    Lancashire Towns,* Chetham Soc. (Manchester 1979)
Green, V. H. H., *The Young Mr Wesley*, Wyvern Books (1961)
Green, V. H. H., *Religion at Oxford and Cambridge*, S.C.M. Press (London 1964)
Gregory, Eleanor C., *Christian Mysticism*, H. R. Allinson (London)
Gregory, Benjamin, *Side Lights on the Conflicts of Methodism 1827-1852,*
    Cassell & Co. (1898)

Harrison, A. W., *Arminianism*, Duckworth 1937
Harrison, A. W., *The Evangelical Revival and Christian Reunion*, Epworth
    Press (1942)
Hasse, E. R., *The Moravians*, N.C.E.C. (London)

Hilderbrandt, Franz, *Christianity According to the Wesleys*, Epworth Press (1956)
Hobhouse, Christopher, *Oxford*, B. T. Batsford Ltd. (London 1942)
Hunter, J. Mitchell, *The Teaching of Calvin*, James Clark & Co. (1950)

Inge, Dean, *Protestantism*, Thos. Nelson London 1935

Jackson, George, *The Old Methodism and the New*, Hodder & Stoughton (1903)

Keeling, Annie E., *Susannah Wesley*, Charles H. Kelly (London 1897)
Kelly, Douglas F., *The Emergence of Liberty in the Modern World*, P & R (New
    Jersey 1952)
Kent, John, *Jabez Bunting—The Last Wesleyan*, Epworth Press (1955)
Kirk, John, *The Mother of the Wesleys*, Jarrold & Sons (London 1876)
Kirsop, Joseph, *Historic Sketches of Free Methodism*, Andrew Crombie (London
    1885)
Knockles, P., *The Oxford Movement*, Cambridge University Press 1994
Kuyper, A., *Calvinism*, Hoveker & Wormser (Amsterdam & Pretoria 1898)

Lawson, John, *Comprehensive Handbook of Christian Doctrine*, Prentice-Hall
    Inc. (1967)
Lindstrom, Harald, *Wesleyan Sanctification*, Epworth Press (1956)
Lloyd-Jones, D. Martin, *Letters*, Banner of Truth (1994)
Lloyd-Jones, D. Martin, *The Puritans—their Origins and Successors*, Banner
    of Truth (1987)
Lloyd-Jones D. Martin, *1662-1962- From Puritanism to Nonconformity*, Ev.
    Library (1962)

Loane, Marcus L., *Masters of the English Reformation*, The Church Bookroom
      Press(1956)

McGonnigle, H., *Sufficient Saving Grace*, Nazarine Col. Manchester
Miller, Edward, *John Wesley—The Hero of the Second Reformation*, The Sunday
      School Union
Monk, Robert C., *John Wesley and His Puritan Heritage*, Scarecrow Press
      (1999)
More, P. E. & Cross F. L. ed., *Anglicanism*, S.P.C.K. (London 1962)
Murray, Gilbert, *The Methodist Class Meeting*, Robert Culley (London)
Murray, Iain, *The Forgotten Spurgeon*, Banner of Truth (1973)
Murray, Iain, *Wesley and Men who Followed*, Banner of Truth (2003)

New, John F.H., *Anglican and Puritan*, A & C Black (London 1964)
Newton, John A., *Methodism and The Puritans*, Dr. Williams Trust (1964)
Newton, John A., *Susannah Wesley and the Puritan Tradition in Methodism*,
      Epworth Press (1968)

Outler, Albert C. ed., *John Wesley*, O.U.P. (New York 1964)
Outler, Albert C, *Evangelism in the Wesleyan Spirit*, Tidings (Nashville, Tenn.
      1971)
Overton, J. H., *The Evangelical Revival in the Eighteenth Century*, Longmans,
      Green & Co. (1886)
Owen, John, *Works* Vol. II & III, Banner of Truth

Packer, J.I., *Honouring the People of God*, Paternoster Press (1999)
Parry, Geraint, *John Locke*, George Allen & Unwin (1978)
Peake, A. S., *Christianity—it's Nature and its Truth*, Duckworth & Co. (London
      1908)
Piette, Maximin, *John Wesley and the Evolution of Protestantism*, Shed &
      Ward (London 1937)
Piper, J, *Counted Righteous in Christ*, I.V.P. (2002)
Portrey, Joseph, *Society Meetings in Wesleyan Methodism*, Wesleyan Conf.
      Office (1874)
Prestwich, M. ed., *English and International Calvinism*, (Article by Patrick
      Collinson)

Rack, Henry D., *Methodism and the Old Dissent*, Methodist Historical Soc.
Rack, Henry D., *The Magic Methodists of Delamere Forest*, Englesea Brook
      Lecture
Rack, Henry D., *A Reasonable Enthusiast*, Epworth Press
Rack, Henry D., *How Primitive was Primitive Methodism*, Englesea Brook
      Lecture 1996

Rattenbury, J., Ernest, *Wesley's Legacy to the World*, Epworth Press (1928)

Rigg, James H., *The Living Wesley*, Charles H. Kelly (London 1891)

Ritson, Joseph, *The Romance of Primitive Methodism*, P.M. Publishing House (1909)

Roper, Hugh Trevor, *Catholics, Anglicans and Puritans*, Fontana Press (1989)

Rose E. A., *Methodism in Cheshire, to 1800*, Richmond Press (Wilmslow, Ches.)

Rupp, E. Gordon, *Methodism in relation to Protestant Tradition*, Epworth Press (1954)

Rupp, E. Gordon, *Making of the English Protestant Tradition*, Cambridge University Press(1966)

Sangster, W. E., *The Path to Perfection*, Hodder & Stoughton (1943)

Schmidt, Martin, *John Wesley*, Epworth press (1962)

Scougal, Henry, *The Life of God in the Soul of Man*, I.V.P. (1961)

Selbey, W. B., *Nonconformity*, Williams & Norgate,, London

Sigston, James, *Memoir of William Bramwell*, William Nicholson (Halifax 1861)

Simn, J. S., *John Wesley and the Religious Societies*, Sharp (1921)

Skevington-Wood, A., *The Burning Heart*, Paternoster Press (1967)

Smith, David R., *John Fletcher*, Rushworth Lit. Enterprise (1972)

Smith, H; Swallow J. E. & Treffry W., *The Story of the United Methodist Church*, Henry Hooks (London 1932)

Southey, Robert, *John Wesley*, Hutchison & Co. (rep of 1820 edition)

Sparrow-Simpson, W. J., *John Wesley and the Church of England*, S.P.C.K (London 1934)

Spurgeon, C. H., *Expositions of the Doctrines of Grace*, C. H. S. Jewel

Stoughton, John, *History of Religion in England* Vol. V, Hodder & Stoughton (1901)

Taylor, E. R., *Methodism and Politics, 1791-1851*, Cambridge Univ. Press (1935)

Telford, John, *The Life of John Wesley*, Epworth Press (1929)

Telford John, *The Methodist Hymn Book Illustrated*, Epworth Press (1922)

Thompson, Edgar W., *The Methodist Doctrine of the Church*, Epworth Press (1939)

Towelson, Clifford W., *Moravian and Methodist*, Epworth Press (1957)

Townsend, W. J; Workman, HB; & Eayres George (eds.), *A New History of Methodism*, Hodder & Stoughton (1909)

Troelsch, Ernst, *The Social Teaching of the Christian Churches*, George Allen & Unwin Ltd.

Turner, John Munsey, *Conflict and Reconciliation*, Epworth Press (1985)

Vulliamy, C. E., *John Wesley*, Epworth Press (1954)

Wakefield, Gordon S., *Puritan Devotion*, Epworth Press (1957)
Wand, J. W. C., *Anglicanism in History and Today*, Readers Union (1964)
Watson R., *Life of Wesley*, Wesleyan Conf. Office (1831)
Watson R., *Sermons*, John Mason City Rd. 1855
Watts, Michael R., *The Dissenters*, Clarendon Press (Oxford 1978)
Wearmouth, Robert F., *Methodism and The Working Class Movements of England 1800-1850*, Epworth Press (1947)
Wilkinson, John T., *William Clowes*, Epworth press (1951)
Williams, Colin W., *John Wesley's Theology Today*, Epworth Press (1962)
Wycherley, R. Newman, *The Pageantry of Methodist Union*, Epworth Press (1936)

Zahl, Paul F. M., *The Protestant Face of Anglicanism*, Eerdmans (1998)

Anon, *The Reformation: The Faith that, Helped to make the Modern World*, United Meth. Pub. Dept
Anon, *Origin and History of the Wesleyan Reform Union*, Wesleyan Reform Bk. Room (1896)

One is Your Master—the Story of One Hundred Years of the Wesleyan Reform Union, W. R. U. Sheffield

Foundations Magazine Autumn 2004, Gary Williams, Where do Evangelicals Come From?

The Churchman's Magazine, Protestant Truth Society London (1937)

Epworth Review May 1982, Methodist Publishing House London

The American Pulpit of the Day R. D. Dickinson London 1875

Dictionary of National Biography Smith Elder and Co. London 1901

Also available from Tentmaker Publications

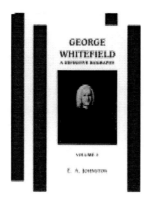

George Whitefield — A Definitive Biography (2 vols.)
by Dr E. A. Johnston
2 volumes, 572 + 600 pp, dark green cloth with d/w. £49.95
Foreword by J. I. Packer
Preface by Richard Owen Roberts

E. A. Johnston, Ph.D, D.B.S. is a fellow of the Stephen Olford Institute for Biblical Preaching and the author of several books, including A Heart Awake: The Authorized Biography of J. Sidlow Baxter (Baker Books, 2005).

"In this massive biography of George Whitefield, preacher par excellence of the Great Awakening who travelled thousands of miles to preach thousands of sermons to thousands of people, we find immense stimulation to rekindle the psalmist's prayer, 'It is time, Lord, for thee to work.' O that God would raise such men of godly zeal and endurance in our day!"
Dr. Joel Beeke, Puritan Reformed Theological Seminary, Grand Rapids, MI.

"Illuminating and informative, Dr. E. A. Johnston's new biography is an inspiring portrait of the great 18th Century evangelist. I heartily commend these well written volumes."
Dr. David S. Dockery, President, Union University, Jackson, TN

"The time is right for a new biography of George Whitefield, the powerful evangelist of the First Great Awakening. That book has arrived. Read it for your profit and inspiration. You will not be disappointed."
Dr. Daniel L. Akin, President, Southeastern Baptist Theological Seminary, Wake Forest, NC

BIOGRAPHICAL

England & Methodism

George Whitefield: A Definitive Biography (2 vols) - Dr E A Johnston £49.95
Lives of Early Methodist Preachers (3 vols.) - T Jackson (Editor) £47.95
Journal of Charles Wesley (2 vols.) - Charles Wesley £38.95
Life and Times of John Wesley (3 vols) - Tyerman £64.95
Life and Times of Samuel Wesley - Tyerman £18.95
Wesley's Designated Successor (John Fletcher) - Tyerman £18.95
The Oxford Methodists - Tyerman £17.95
Journals of William Clowes - William Clowes £13.95
Life & Labours of Hugh Bourne (2 vols.) - Hugh Bourne £36.95
Biographical Sketches of Primitive Methodism - G Herod £17.95
Bunhill Fields - Alfred W Light £19.95
The Bible Christians - F W Bourne £19.95

Wales & Calvinistic Methodism

Life of Griffith Jones of Llandowror - David Jones £6.95
Life of Howell Harris the Welsh Reformer - Hugh Hughes £16.95
Life of Selina, Countess of Huntington (2 vols.) - A Seymore £47.50
Some of the Great Preachers of Wales - Owen Jones £17.95
Sweet Singers of Wales - Elvett Lewis £2.95

Scotland

Life of John Kennedy - A Auld £13.95
Memoir of William Chalmers Burns - Rev Islay Burns £20.95

Ireland

Charles Graham - Apostle of Kerry - W G Campbell £11.95
Irish Worthies - Thomas Hamilton £12.50

United States

Life of Samuel Miller DD, LLD (2 vols.) - Samuel Miller £36.95
My Life and Times - John Bailey Adger £24.95

Missionary

Faith Working by Love (Life of Fidelia Fiske) - D T Fiske £13.95

CHURCH HISTORY

England

History of the Dissenters (3 vols.) - Bogue & Bennett £47.95

History of the Early & Later Puritans (2 vols.) - J B Marsden £37.90

History of the Puritans (3 vols.) - Daniel Neal £64.95

Guide to Bunhill Fields (2 vols. In 1) - Alfred W Light £19.95

The Origin & History of Primitive Methodism (2 vols.) - Kendall £49.95

The Mow Cop Revival 1807 - David Allen £3.95

The Two Thousand Confessors of 1662 - Thomas Coleman £11.95

Wales & Calvinistic Methodism

Echoes from the Welsh Hills - David Davies £15.95

John Vaughan and His Friends (or More Echoes) - David Davies £15.95

Favoured with Frequent Revivals (Wales 1762-1862) - D Geraint Jones * £3.99

Ireland

Days of Revival (Methodism in Ireland) (3 vols.) - Crookshank £48.95

History of the 1859 Ulster Revival (7 vols) £139.95

Progress of the Reformation in Ireland - Earl of Roden £10.95

Europe

Israel of the Alps (History of the Waldenses) - Alexis Muston £15.95

The Rise of the Huguenots of France (2 vols) - Baird £44.95

United States

A History of the Presbyterian Church in America
    - Richard Webster £23.95

Denominational

Baptist History * - J M Cramp £19.95

History of the Plymouth Brethren - William B Neatby £13.95

*Titles marked by * are published under another publisher's imprint.*
Prices correct for August 2008

For complete catalogue and means of ordering books go to
www.tentmaker.org.uk (UK£) or www.tentmakerpublications.com (US$)